GILDED
YOUTH

GILDED YOUTH

An Intimate History
of Growing Up in the Royal Family

TOM QUINN

Biteback Publishing

First published in Great Britain in 2023 by
Biteback Publishing Ltd, London
Copyright © Tom Quinn 2023

ISBN 978-1-78590-764-7

10 9 8 7 6 5 4 3 2 1

A CIP catalogue record for this book is available from the British Library.

Set in Adobe Caslon Pro

Printed and bound in Great Britain by
CPI Group (UK) Ltd, Croydon CR0 4YY

FSC
www.fsc.org
MIX
Paper | Supporting
responsible forestry
FSC® C171272

CONTENTS

INTRODUCTION

'Insanity is hereditary. You get it from your children.'

SAM LEVENSON

This book is not simply a survey of royal children down the ages. That has been done a number of times. Instead, I have looked at the patterns of childrearing in the British royal family and have discovered how they are remarkably unchanging throughout history. While most of us are fairly conservative in how we treat our children – one generation passing on the things they learned from their parents to the next generation – compared to the royal family we are far more open to new views and new ways of bringing up our children. As parents, we change in the light of new evidence and the discovery that what previous generations have done may be far from ideal; we accept that some childrearing practices may actually be very damaging and are therefore best discontinued.

The royal family, it seems to me, is not like this. They do change but very slowly, and in some important respects they don't change at all. Which means we have a family in our midst – a family whose very function has at times been to provide an exemplar for the rest of us – that in terms of childrearing has hardly changed in centuries. The result is that generation after generation of royal children have been forced to endure what might very reasonably be described as dysfunctional parenting; parenting that is obsessed with clinging to long outmoded traditions that centre on emotional coldness and detachment, toughness and duty. The result is that dysfunctional childhood experiences produce royal adults – especially male adults – who go on to damage their own children. So this book is, if you like, almost as much about royal parents as it is about royal children.

There is more interest today than ever before in the early lives of members of the British royal family. After all, one might ask, what sort of childhood and education could produce a character such as Prince Andrew? And how could an upbringing of immense privilege have also produced the nervous, over-sensitive Prince Charles, now Charles III, or the rebellious Harry or the alcoholic party girl Princess Margaret?

One anecdote, variously told about the Earl of Leicester, Edward VII and even George V, epitomises the lives of royal children and their parents. The king, wandering through his palace one day, comes across a maid pushing a baby in a pram. 'What on earth is that baby doing here?' asks the king. 'Whose baby is it?'

The maid replies, 'It's your baby, sir.'

Of course, the remarkable thing about royal childhood is that, despite its often damaging effects, it is also capable of producing the late Queen Elizabeth II, a woman with an almost inhuman devotion to duty.

There have been previous books about royal childhood, but they have almost always been straightforward historical accounts of a succession of royal childhood lives, or they are based on information given by senior royal officials to authors who could be trusted to paint a highly sympathetic picture. Authors of these books feel privileged that senior advisers and members of the family have given them a few quotes. Very few authors, it seems to me, have talked to the people who really know what goes on – by that I mean the servants, the below-stairs staff. As a journalist writing in the satirical magazine *Private Eye* noted, 'Any royal hack knows that [talking to] lower grade staff is the best way to get the real gossip.' The same writer goes on to say that books about the royals would be better if their authors spent more time 'below stairs'.

Much of this book is based on time spent below stairs. Since the 1980s I have interviewed many below-stairs royal staff, from maids to drivers, secretarial and kitchen staff, gardeners, gamekeepers and gillies. I've also spoken to friends of nannies and former nannies as well as, in a few cases, the nannies and nurses themselves. I've also talked to a number of senior staff over the years, and many of these are aristocrats whose jobs came to them through connections with the royal family going back generations. The aristocratic flunkeys respond to questions with extravagant praise for the royals and irritated looks when the question of bad behaviour is hinted at – perhaps this is perfectly understandable. If your family has been closely linked to the royal family for a century and more, you don't want a careless word to damage your children's chances of becoming, in turn, ladies-in-waiting or equerries.

But staff lower down the pecking order don't have these grand aspirations, and in the 1980s and 1990s when I began interviewing them, they were more than happy to talk. This of course was in the days before contracts were introduced that made it unlawful for staff to speak to anyone outside royal circles about their work. A number of staff were also able to talk about their parents' work for the royals, even in some cases their grandparents', and so their memories go back to the 1930s and beyond.

The world they describe is very different from the world described in most books about the royal family's children. Far more in touch with the day-to-day royal world than more aristocratic staff, they were able to give me a nuanced and credible account of how royal children have been treated over the past seventy years and more; an account that is sometimes shocking and extraordinary but also deeply sympathetic.

This book seeks to weave these memories with more guarded accounts from those who have worked for or looked after more recent royal arrivals – I mean the children of William and Kate and Meghan and Harry. I say guarded because recent employment contracts for those working for the royals include even more dire legal threats against anyone who breaks the code of silence. But through intermediaries I have found that a friendly approach and a promise of anonymity has produced some wonderful stories of what really happens inside the daily lives of the more recent generations of royal children.

I have woven personal accounts and memories and first-hand testimony with quotations from published accounts of royal children, such as, for example, Marion Crawford's famous book *The Little*

Princesses about Princess Elizabeth and Princess Margaret, whom she looked after devotedly as a nanny when they were children.

Crawford's book has always been referred to as a sweet, uncritical, deeply flattering portrait of the two princesses that says nothing untoward, but look a little closer and you see that Crawfie, as she was known to the children, was very astute in her ability to seem to say innocuous things while actually painting a critical portrait of her charges and the family for which she worked. The reaction to the book among the royals showed a side of 'the Firm' that Crawford would never have mentioned directly: the royal capacity to behave with absolute vindictive ruthlessness was revealed when, following publication of her book, Crawfie was never again spoken to by any member of the royal family; she was never allowed to visit the children who had once adored her. Even the young Princess Elizabeth's pleas to let Crawfie return were ignored. The royal family had been able to read between the lines as few others have done, and they did not like what they read. Elizabeth came across on this reading as almost suffering from obsessive compulsive disorder, while Margaret was a buffoon who expected everyone to laugh at her endless jibes and her often cruel practical jokes.

The Queen Mother had given Crawford permission to anonymously advise on articles written about the children, but a memoir under her own name had been definitively rejected. Following the publication of the book, the royal family, which never forgives or forgets a perceived slight (rather in the manner of the Italian mafia), cast their former nanny into outer darkness. Elizabeth and Margaret were never again allowed to mention their once adored nanny other than to say when someone had been disloyal that they had 'done a Crawfie'. Poor Crawfie lived on for decades after her disgrace, even attempting suicide. The royal reaction to her book proved its subtle message was true – the royal children, the royal parents, were not all sweetness and light as Crawfie had seemed to suggest. The family's reaction to the book proved they were ruthless, even stony hearted, where there was a perceived betrayal of confidence. Crawfie would never have accused them of that.

This cold-hearted, unforgiving streak has always been a key element in all members of the royal family and it springs from the bizarre, emotionally damaging way in which royal children have traditionally been brought up. It is only with the youngest generation – Prince George and his siblings and cousins – that centuries of varying degrees of child neglect and malpractice, combined with absurd luxury, have to some extent come to an end.

A clue to the strange yet largely hidden nature of royal childhood comes from one of Princess Margaret's former ladies-in-waiting, Anne, Lady Glenconner.

In her intriguing autobiography, *Lady in Waiting*, Lady Glenconner refers frequently to the deeply damaging nature of aristocratic childrearing practices that she herself both experienced as a child and inflicted on her own children. We know that what was considered appropriate for the children of the aristocracy was certainly also considered appropriate for royal children, so Lady Glenconner's insights are uniquely valuable. She explains how she assumed her mother knew, for example, that her nanny was tying the little girl to her bed every night – Lady Glenconner had so little intimate contact with her mother that she assumed she must have wanted her daughter to be treated like this. Her mother was entirely elsewhere, as she explains: 'I was brought up by nannies ... My mother didn't wash or dress me or my sister Carey; nor did she feed us or put us to bed ... It was a generation and a class who were not brought up to express emotions.'

Lady Glenconner brought her own children up in a similar way and although other factors were involved – most significantly the mental instability of her husband – there is no doubt that farming the children out to a series of paid staff contributed to her sons' later difficulties: two died young, one as a result of a long-term heroin addiction, another from AIDS. Neither boy seemed able to cope with adulthood. In Lady Glenconner's account of their lives it is clear that their early years – years in which they were looked after by sometimes uncaring staff – were a major contributory factor.

Many if not most of the problems of royal adults – from wife-killers such as Henry VIII through liars and philanderers such as Edward VII to disgraced Prince Andrew – stem, as this book will show, from their bizarre childhoods.

The royal family above all others proves the old adage: give me a child until he is seven and I will show you the man.

* * *

Many of those who write about the British royal family – authors rather than journalists – seem unaware of the difference between hagiography and biography. Even when the follies and occasional criminalities of members of the royal family are mentioned, they are somehow always discussed in a brief and understanding aside. Barely concealed deference is the watchword.

Yet the era of automatic deference to the royals ended, for society in general and for the newspapers and other media in particular, sometime in the mid-1960s, overlapping perhaps not entirely co-incidentally with the availability of the contraceptive pill. Before that, writers and commentators didn't automatically praise the royals because they felt it was their duty to do so – though that was part of what was going on – they simply responded unthinkingly to an institution that had not really been looked at with a more critical eye since the days when Gillray and Cruikshank lampooned the Prince Regent.

But if authors have remained fairly gentle in their treatment of the royals – with one or two exceptions – the same is not true of newspapers and magazines and the media in general.

From the 1960s onwards, newspapers, especially, began a tradition of building the reputation of a particular royal and then finding every reason to demolish it. In Fleet Street this was referred to as 'build them up and knock them down' or doing 'a reverse ferret'.

Authors of books about the royals have taken a very different approach; arguably most have stayed in the 1950s, writing either detached factual books or sympathetic portraits that emphasise the virtues of the royals and gloss over their vices.

Of course, there have always been refreshing exceptions. Lytton Strachey's works on Queen Victoria and the Victorians, though lacking the enormous number of 'facts' contained in more recent books about Victoria, are by far the most literate and entertaining books ever written about any member of the royal family, with the possible exception of Craig Brown's brilliant book *Ma'am Darling*. Strachey is not obviously attacking or directly critical, but his tone is delightfully acidic, ironic, sceptical; he paints a picture of an absurdly dysfunctional institution and the ridiculous (and very badly behaved) monarch it produced. The philosopher Bertrand Russell said in a radio broadcast in the 1950s that when he first read Strachey, he was in prison for criticising the government's stance on the First World War. He laughed so loudly that a prison officer came into his cell and told him that prison was a place of punishment and he should not be enjoying himself. I can't think of any other book on any royal that would similarly cheer up a prisoner in Wormwood Scrubs.

Strachey's tone is always slightly teasing. Here he is on Victoria the toddler: 'The child … was extremely fat and bore a remarkable resemblance to her grandfather. "C'est l'image du feu Roi!" exclaimed the Duchess [her mother]. "C'est le Roi Georges en jupons," echoed the surrounding ladies, as the little creature waddled with difficulty from one to another.'

The key problem for the royal family, and this is a problem picked up instinctively by Strachey, is that they feel obliged to live like eighteenth-century aristocrats in order to fulfil the fantasies of a large part of the public. But at the same time, as society evolves, they also need to seem less aloof and more part of ordinary humanity. It has been and is a tremendously difficult transition to make. Even by the time Strachey was writing, the eighteenth-century manners and customs to which the royal family still adhered were no longer supposed to suggest that the royal family was aloof or snobbish or that they despised the lower orders. Instead, living in the grand eighteenth-century manner was increasingly considered a physical embodiment of the royal family's role as symbols of continuity and tradition; the grand houses, the elaborate etiquette and wealth also fitted a long cherished ideal of a leisured elite to whom in fantasy we could all aspire.

Beyond the bowing and curtseying, the powdered wigs and grand palaces, monarchs after Edward VII sensed they needed to seem to combine the glitter of the leisured, aristocratic past with the common touch. It was almost as if Victoria's grandson George V looked around him and, seeing his relatives across Europe dethroned and sometimes murdered in the years after the end of the Great War, decided the road to survival lay not in being aloof and magnificent but in being – at least superficially – quiet, dutiful, unassuming and dull. Becoming more middle class was worth it if that meant survival. That the royal family was prepared to do almost anything to survive can be judged, for example, by the fact that George V personally intervened to prevent the British government offering asylum in England to his recently overthrown cousin the Tsar of Russia. The result was that the tsar and his whole family were murdered.

The royals have always been ruthless in cutting off anyone who threatened their reputation or their survival. Prince Philip repudiated his sisters who had all married into the German royal family, some of whose members were ardent Nazis. The House of Windsor famously changed its name from Battenberg to avoid the taint of German association after the end of the Great War. The Queen Mother refused to speak to Mrs Simpson for more than thirty years after Edward VIII abdicated. The list is almost endless.

Royal princes in the early medieval period were equally ruthless but they tended to use violence rather than social ostracism to achieve their ends. Often semi-literate, they were prized by their peers for their ability to intimidate and to fight to the death. It has been said with some justification that the average heavyweight boxer today would have made an ideal medieval monarch. But by the end of the seventeenth century, monarchs had largely lost their power either to fight or to govern and so began the long slide into political if not social irrelevance. But the British public's nostalgia for an earlier age, an age in which the royal family represented continuity and an elevated, leisured existence – an existence that we were all assumed to aspire to – kept them going and keeps them going still.

Whatever changes have occurred in the world of adult royals, much less had changed until very recently in the manner in which royal children were brought up.

The fighting princes and the philandering princes, the dutiful daughters and the tearaways, the mad, the bad and the sad, have always been subjected to a bizarre upbringing that in its determination to cling to old values has often been highly damaging.

Many of the oddities and occasional defects of adult royals from Edward VIII to Prince Andrew stem directly from an upbringing and an education that seems at times almost designed to produce madmen and mavericks; men (and sometimes, though less often, women) who believe that by virtue of birth alone they are both great in themselves and destined to do great things. In this respect and surrounded by teams of nannies, tutors and governesses, the early years of royal children have not changed that much, as this book hopes to show, in 500 years and more.

From the days when child princes and princesses were used as political pawns – frequently married or at least betrothed in their infancy – to the modern era when cosseted and praised, flattered and fawned over, yet with too much time on their hands, royal children sometimes become royal monsters.

The first part of this book looks at how the governesses and nannies, the 'rockers', wet nurses and footmen, the emotional and physical detachment of parents, the daily care of young children given to paid functionaries and the emphasis for royal males on military service would all have been immediately familiar in Anglo-Saxon England and on down the centuries after the Norman conquest into the Georgian, Victorian and modern eras.

Chapters on the twentieth century and down to the present day make up the second part of the book, largely because so much more information is available about them.

The history of royal childrearing is fascinating, as I hope readers will agree, but it is also, at times, surprisingly amusing and many of the anecdotes I have included in this book show that one of the reasons the monarchy has lasted so long is that the royal family is a wonderful source of eccentric and bizarre stories.

CHAPTER ONE

WHIPPING BOYS AND INFANT KINGS

'The age was tainted, degraded by its sycophancy.'

TACITUS

Until well into the eighteenth century, in Britain at least, the idea of childhood barely existed. Children were simply miniature adults. It was Romantic writers, especially Jean-Jacques Rousseau, who began to develop new ideas about the innocence of childhood. As the academic Kimberley Reynolds put it in an article written for the British Library in 2014:

From around the middle of the eighteenth century, many people in Britain began to think about childhood in new ways. Previously, the Puritan belief that humans are born sinful as a consequence of mankind's 'Fall' had led to the widespread notion that childhood was a perilous period. As a result, much of the earliest children's literature is concerned with saving children's souls through instruction and by providing role models for their behaviour. This religious way of thinking about childhood had become less influential by the mid-eighteenth century; in fact, childhood came to be associated with a set of positive meanings and attributes, notably innocence, freedom, creativity, emotion, spontaneity and, perhaps most importantly for those charged with raising and educating children, malleability.

These ideas would have seemed extraordinary in the early medieval period, when education, specifically the ability to read and write, was largely the preserve of the church. The vast bulk of the population was illiterate – in 1500 around 11 per cent of the English male population was literate and for women the figure was less than 1 per cent. If you were a shoemaker's or farm labourer's son, you had little need for reading and writing. You learned your trade from your father, and your sisters learned from your mother how to cook and clean and look after children.

For the royal family in this early period things were different but not that different. Anglo-Saxon kings may have been literate – the evidence is mixed – but their key role above all was to fight anyone who threatened their position and their sons had quickly to learn that this too was their role. Literacy was of secondary importance. There was a tradition among the Anglo-Saxons that when a king died his ealdormen – nobles who ranked just below the king – would choose the king's successor from among themselves. The leader chosen would be the most deserving, the most noble, the most obviously a leader, and that meant primarily a man who could win battles, not a man famed for his letter writing. The greatest of all Old English poems, *Beowulf*, neatly encapsulates the core value of Anglo-Saxon kings – bravery and prowess in battle in the face of the monster Grendel. Writing in 'The Uses of Literacy in Anglo-Saxon England and Its Neighbours', published in 1977, C. P. Wormald points out that even the Emperor Charlemagne could not write. According to Wormald, 'the ability to read and write was apparently confined to the clerical [i.e. religious] elite'.

Justin Pollard's biography of Alfred the Great sums the situation up perfectly:

> The kings of Wessex had to consult their witans over many great issues of state, not because they formed some sort of representative protodemocracy but because they were members of powerful families whose agreement was essential to maintain order in the kingdom. Whilst later kings such as James I of England claimed to rule by 'divine right', the kings of Wessex were elected by their witan from amongst their own members. This meant not only that the witan did not necessarily have to approve that king's heir, it also meant they could 'unelect' any king who did not continue to enjoy their approval during his reign ... The Wessex witan had unelected a king before, back in 757, when they had deposed King Sigeberht for his 'unjust acts'.

This kept monarchs and their children in check and the shift to ruling by right of birth undoubtedly increased the monarch's sense that whatever they did was right – divinely appointed, they could never be wrong. It became impossible for the nobles to 'unelect' a king and impossible for them to choose one. This sense of the monarch's absolute worth and power was inculcated in princes from the time of their birth. It came in the end to infect all royal children, whether heirs or spares, down into the modern era.

Although the common people still spoke Old English long after the Norman conquest, Latin and French succeeded as the language of government. Norman kings were as violent and warlike as their Saxon predecessors, but from this time literacy began to increase in importance because unlike Anglo-Saxon England, which had been a predominately oral culture, their new French masters had a largely written culture. Anglo-Saxon culture in England had relied on an oral tradition that meant little to the Norman invaders – stylistic devices in the many Anglo-Saxon poems reveal that they were meant to be heard not silently read. By the time many Anglo-Saxon poems were written down, sometimes just in time to save them from being entirely lost, they still frequently began with the single word *hwæt*, meaning listen. In an oral culture, there was always less need to be literate.

Norman French culture was very different, although the two cultures gradually melded – echoes of Old English and Norman French can still be read three centuries after the conquest in the works of Chaucer.

But if the English language and the qualities required of a ruler were changing, much less changed in the world of the royal nursery. A royal pregnancy was a matter of national interest and the queen's importance in this sense was reflected in the number and status of those who attended a royal birth.

Anglo-Saxon queens were surrounded by women as the time of birth approached, with the birth itself probably taking place on a birthing stool – a wooden chair or stool with a large part of the centre of the seat cut away to allow the baby to drop through into the hands of the attendants. This made sense simply because it meant gravity could be harnessed to help with the birth. The modern practice of lying on your back in bed – a practice greatly encouraged by Queen Victoria – actually makes giving birth far more difficult.

Fast forward a few centuries and, as we shall see in the next chapter, an obsession seems to have developed in royal circles that there was a risk that a baby would be switched at birth or a girl replaced by a non-royal boy if the queen was not sufficiently policed – she had to be surrounded by courtiers and officials at the moment of birth to ensure there were numerous witnesses.

So far as the royal family was concerned, childrearing practices were never tested or questioned. Like almost every aspect of life, childrearing was based entirely on precedent. If something had been done in the past, it was unquestioningly done in the present, which is why, when royal children were ill, a popular cure for almost any ailment was a recently killed pigeon split open and placed on the child's head.

All medieval princes and princesses were handed over after birth to a wet nurse – a less exalted woman who was already producing milk for her own children. The idea of a queen breastfeeding her own child would have seemed extraordinary, although it was universal among poorer classes, and employing a wet nurse, for royal and aristocratic women, lasted until late into the nineteenth century (and in some cases beyond) when, reluctantly, aristocratic and royal mothers either took over from the wet nurse themselves or resorted to bottled milk. Edward VII was the last British monarch to have been put out to a wet nurse, Mary Ann Brough, who later murdered six of her own children.

Perhaps the strangest custom in the early modern period was

that after a royal birth the mother was not allowed to attend the christening. She had to wait for a decent interval to be cleansed and purified by a priest after her ordeal. This links to the church's traditional dislike of sex and any other physical process that seemed to suggest that human reproduction was remarkably akin to animal reproduction. Nothing about giving birth seemed to suggest we were made in God's image. There was nothing spiritual about a bloody and dangerous event and the church had to find rituals to lift the experience from the earthy to the spiritual.

The use of wet nurses was also linked to an ancient bias against giving cow's or goat's milk to a royal baby. In his *De Proprietatibus Rerum* (*On the Properties of Things*), written in the 1240s, Bartholomaeus Anglicus refers to 'evil milk', meaning animal milk.

Hardly acknowledged and perhaps not fully understood, the use of a wet nurse had another great advantage for a queen: it meant a quick return to fertility. Breastfeeding is known to delay a return to fertility, so by not breastfeeding, a queen was quickly able to once again become pregnant. In an age in which children died so often and heirs were seen as absolutely vital by monarchs, anything that increased the royal rate of reproduction was welcomed. During this early period there was a better than average chance that the child would die well before the age of five. In an Exeter University study, Nicholas Orme estimates that at this time, '25 per cent of [children] may have died in their first year, half as many (12.5 per cent) between one and four, and a quarter as many (6 per cent) between five and nine'. The chances of reaching adulthood were roughly one in four. Such was the risk of death that by the twelfth century children were invariably baptised on the day of their birth.

In addition to being farmed out to a wet nurse, royal babies were also physically confined and restricted in a manner that today seems barbarous but was hallowed by centuries of unthinking practice.

Swaddling – the business of wrapping babies tightly in bands of linen, so tight that they could not even move their arms and legs – was thought to ensure a child's limbs grew straight. In fact, it was entirely unnecessary and must have caused agony for many babies as they had no chance to develop leg and arm muscles and if they were not changed often the effects of excreta would have been seriously exacerbated by their inability to move.

Once the young prince or princess was weaned and the services of a wet nurse were no longer required, royal childcare demanded the employment of other professionals. A governess would be employed (a governor for boys) to look after the growing child. Royal children might see their parents for a short formal meeting once a day – again a practice that continued until the 1950s and beyond – and if the royal parents had to be away then their children, even very young children, would simply be left behind with their staff. Prince Charles was left for months in the first year of his life while his parents toured their dominions.

But while their babies and toddlers were being looked after by others, what were these medieval queens doing?

Curiously, women in royal circles in Anglo-Saxon England had more rights than they were to enjoy after the Norman conquest. They could own and inherit property in their own right and they were not considered intellectually inferior to men – and indeed this was irrelevant since physical strength gave men their superior status. And though it was the duty of a queen to have children, this could not always be enforced. There is even some evidence that medieval queens might try to avoid having children – something that would have been unthinkable after 1066.

The chronicler William of Malmesbury records in *Gesta Regum Anglorum* (*Deeds of the English Kings*) that Æthelflæd, daughter of Alfred the Great, had one child and then refused ever again to sleep with her husband. The reason she gave was that childbirth was so painful and unpleasant that it was not justified by the pleasure she got from sleeping with her husband.

At the age of seven or eight, aristocratic boys and royal princes were almost invariably sent to live away from their parents – it was a way of cementing friendships and loyalty between two families or of linking the king more closely with his nobles, many of whom in this early period might well have harboured rival claims to the throne. As Justin Pollard explains in his biography of Alfred the Great, 'The children of kings and nobles ... were fostered out for long periods to other households. In an age when death might well overtake parents long before their children reached adulthood and where the more kin one had, the better one fared, this made a lot of sense.' The idea that a seven- or eight-year-old boy might be upset or psychologically damaged by being parted from his parents for so long seems never to have occurred to anyone. One of the few early kings who was not sent into another household was Alfred the Great himself. Instead, he was sent as a child on a pilgrimage to Rome – but then much about Alfred was unusual. According to Asser, a Welsh monk who completed his *Life of King Alfred* in 893, Alfred did not learn to read until he was twelve, but he thought so highly of books and learning that he promoted the value of learning to read and write as no earlier king had done. The normal practice, as Keith Thomas notes in his book *The Ends of Life*, was for a young prince to learn in another household. 'In 1576 the first Earl of Essex bequeathed his young son Robert to the Master of the Wards, Lord Burghley, "to bind him with perpetual friendship to you and your house".'

Despite its ubiquity, this was a practice that astonished foreigners. An anonymous late-fifteenth-century Italian report (intended for the Italian ambassador to England, Andrea Trevisano) and translated into English by Charlotte Sneyd in 1846 includes an account by an Italian nobleman of a visit to England: 'The want of affection in the English is strongly manifested towards their children; for having kept them at home till they arrive at the age of seven or nine years ... they put them out, both males and females, to hard service in the houses of others.'

As with so many ideas about childhood, the practice of farming out royal princes at age seven lasted centuries and arguably continues to this day in the institution of the boarding school.

The effect this banishment had on royal princes and princesses can perhaps best be judged by a modern example – Prince Charles's deeply unhappy experience at Gordonstoun in the early 1960s would no doubt have echoed closely the unhappiness of those medieval princes 'put out to hard service'.

But it is wrong to think that life for medieval royal children was all about duty and work – they did play with toys and games. Tiny toy metal horses dating from the end of the eleventh century have been found along the muddy shores of the Thames in London and occasional references in early documents suggest wooden dolls, ships and models of houses were made for children from the eighth century onwards. Balls made from pigs' bladders were also certainly being used at the time, although then as now football was considered a rough game and unsuitable for those of noble blood.

Royal princes would have taken part in hunting from as early as four years old. Riding to hounds didn't mean modern foxhounds but rather sighthounds, the ancestors of today's greyhounds. A deer would be followed by the hounds until exhausted and then the mounted followers would despatch it either with bow and arrow or with a sword. The practice of keeping dogs of all kinds is an ancient one and closely associated with English royalty and the aristocracy. Frederick the Great of Prussia (ruled 1740–86) was so fond of his dogs that he was buried with them. Queen Elizabeth II was surrounded by dogs as a child; corgis, terriers of various sorts and Labradors have been royal favourites for a century and more. Elizabeth II owned more than thirty corgis, all descended from a childhood favourite called Susan for whom the Queen designed a headstone when the dog was buried in Queen Victoria's elaborate pet cemetery at Sandringham. Labradors replaced sighthounds as royal sporting interests changed from chasing deer and boar to shooting pheasant and grouse using muzzleloaders and then, towards the end of the nineteenth century, breechloading shotguns. Labradors were essential to find wounded and dead birds that had fallen into dense undergrowth. And royalty was never squeamish about killing animals. Although Elizabeth II enjoyed working her dogs far more than she enjoyed the actual process of shooting the birds, her gamekeeper at Windsor explained how from her earliest years she had rarely failed to retrieve a dead or wounded bird, adding that she was highly efficient at wringing the necks of wounded pheasants.

The profound importance of hunting for a royal prince cannot be overestimated and what was true for princes was true for the sons of the nobility. M. D. Palmer in his biography of Henry VIII quotes a letter from one Richard Pace written in 1516. Pace argued that only a very few things were necessary for a noble child: 'Gentlemen's sons should be able to sound the hunting horn, hunt cunningly, neatly train and use their hawk.'

Hunting was a preparation for hand-to-hand combat and although combat has gone for individual royals – beyond in more recent times flying helicopters and captaining ships – killing birds and other animals continues, pre-eminently defined as a sport of the aristocracy and royals. And royal children see no contradiction between the love of shooting and hunting and the love of pets: that royals grow up surrounded by dogs and other animals and invariably hand this love to their children is a truism not contradicted by their love of hunting foxes and shooting deer, pheasant and grouse. The royal love of dogs in particular can perhaps best be judged by the fact that they have frequently been painted or photographed with their owners – Queen Victoria, who didn't like people much, adored her dogs and numerous portraits exist of her with Dash (her closest childhood companion) and other favourites.

The importance of hunting as a symbolic and practical preparation for adult warlike duties can also be judged by a curious and barbaric ritual that continued among royals and the aristocracy until the 1970s and 1980s. This is the practice of blooding a child – smearing blood from the child's first kill on their face. As a child Prince Charles and his siblings were 'blooded' after a successful fox hunt and he was blooded again after shooting his first stag. His family's pride and pleasure in this would have been almost identical with that felt by his royal ancestors more than a thousand years ago – a young prince was supposed to quickly dismount and stab a cornered stag without fear.

Of course there were other less violent pursuits for the offspring of royalty. In Anglo-Saxon Britain, for example, a popular game among royal and noble children was tafl, a strategy board game only supplanted by chess in the twelfth century. It was a game played across the old Scandinavian world from Ireland to Iceland.

* * *

Corporal punishment was an accepted fact of life at this period and boys and sometimes girls were whipped for what might seem minor misdemeanours today. The idea no doubt stemmed from the biblical instruction 'spare the rod and spoil the child'. But there was a problem with princes, especially when they were heir to the throne. If they had been divinely appointed to rule at some date in the future, how could lesser men – their tutors, for example – even think of whipping them? The solution was to employ whipping boys – a boy of the same age as the prince who would be whipped for the prince's bad behaviour. The idea was that princes, being noble, would see the suffering of their young friend and be so appalled that they would behave well in future. Of course, theory tended to be far removed from practice in this regard and historically reliable evidence about whipping boys is hard to come by. Writing in his 1592 book *De Educandis Erudiendisque Principum Liberis*, Konrad Heresbach mentions the rumour that a young English king had said blasphemous things in front of his tutor. The boy's closest friend was then whipped for the offence and the young king told this was a punishment that he deserved. In his 1724 work *History of His Own Time*, English writer Gilbert Burnet tells us that William Murray, Lord Dysart, was Charles I's page and whipping boy.

Whipping boys were clearly not always a guarantee that a young prince would escape punishment. As a young boy fresh from his wet nurse, the future Henry VI was handed over to the Earl of Warwick and the Duke of Exeter to be educated. Something of a sadist, the earl had no qualms about beating his young charge. But Warwick began to worry that when he became an adult the young king would seek his revenge. What on earth could he do? The answer was clear – according to the *Proceedings and Ordinances of the Privy Council*, first published in 1834 and quoted by Dulcie Ashdown in her book *Royal Children*, the earl approached the king's council and demanded a written guarantee that he would never at any time in the future be held accountable for what he had done to the prince.

If the earl stopped short of outright brutality, this was not always the case and punishing children, even royal children, could get out of hand. In her biography of the poet John Donne, Katherine Rundell discusses Richard Burn's 1755 book *The Justice of the Peace and Parish Officer*. Burns explains that 'when a schoolmaster, in correcting his scholar, happens to cause his death … he is at least guilty of manslaughter', unless he uses a sword or an iron bar and then 'he is guilty of murder'.

But corporal punishment was largely unnecessary because royal princes first came to consciousness with a sense that they were special and that their duty to their position required obedience to the traditions laid down for them. The teenage royal rebel was still some centuries away, and when he finally arrived, his behaviour or his misbehaviour, his conduct and his fate, were to echo down the centuries.

Edward II (1284–1327) was deposed, imprisoned and almost certainly murdered. Chroniclers looked back at his childhood and claimed to see the seeds of his later disasters in his 'unkingly' youth, for Edward, instead of enjoying hunting and hawking, sword play and other pursuits appropriate to a royal prince, was addicted to what were seen at the time as peasant pursuits – he liked rowing, hedging and ditching and helping with thatching. These were considered entirely unsuitable for a prince, as they would still be today. What was proper to a royal prince were what Levi Seeley in his 1899 *History of Education* calls 'the seven perfections of the knight' – 'horsemanship, swimming, use of bow and arrow, swordsmanship, hunting, chess-playing and verse-making'.

* * *

Childhood lasted only a short time in medieval England. If a child survived beyond the age of ten, they would be working either at their father's trade or helping their mother at home. For royal children, work was not an option. Marriage was an early duty of the first importance since it cemented political alliances. The necessity for marriage was something taken for granted for girls and for boys, although it should be said that in Anglo-Saxon England, daughters might alternatively be sent to run large religious houses – this was in a sense just another kind of alliance, for it ensured the second most powerful organ of the state, the church, was under the watchful eye of someone it could be assumed was loyal to the king. Edward the Elder's daughter Eadburh was 'dedicated' – in modern parlance, given – to the nunnery at Nunnaminster when she was just three. She spent the rest of her life there. Child oblation, the practice of giving a child to a religious foundation like this, was common in the Anglo-Saxon period, but it was relevant only to princesses. Princes were too valuable to be disposed of in this way.

Royal children were far more often used as political pawns to be married to foreign royalty at the earliest possible age, but this did not always mean that the age of the child was entirely ignored. One rather touching story recounted by Dulcie Ashdown in her 1979 book *Royal Children* explains that

> the King sent a ship to Norway to collect the six-year-old Queen Margaret of Scotland, his Norwegian-born great-niece, whom he intended to marry to his heir ... On Edward's orders the ship that went out to Norway was provisioned with all sorts of sweet things dear to childish palates: gingerbread, sugar loaves, figs and raisins.

Even in an age we have come to assume was overly violent and serious, there was still time for small acts of kindness.

Until the eighteenth century, child marriage or at least betrothal among princes and princesses was common, although the evidence suggests child marriages were not usually consummated until the partners were in their early teens.

Given life expectancy in this early period child marriage was perhaps inevitable, and lives shortened by sudden illness or accident in an age without modern medicine also meant that children, sometimes very young children, found themselves governing a country before they could hold a spoon: Edward III was fourteen when he ascended the throne; Edward VI was nine; Richard II just ten. Henry VI was nine months old when he came to the throne. In the Anglo-Saxon period pragmatism might have taken over and a powerful adult noble might have become king, but post-1066 the obsession with primogeniture meant this was no longer possible – at least without bloodshed.

The obsession with primogeniture stretched also across Europe – in France Louis XIV was four and a half years old when he became king; King Sebastian I of Portugal was just three when his grandfather died and he took the throne. And although of course a regent would be appointed for these child monarchs, the presence of a child on the throne created instability – one reason perhaps why the witan in earlier centuries sometimes thought it better to choose a king rather than rely on the accident of birth. The combination of a regent and a child was always tempting to an ambitious noble with a claim to the throne. The famous deaths of the princes in the Tower of London resulted from the desire of their uncle the Duke of Gloucester, later Richard III, to take the throne. This was made easy by the fact that Edward V, though the rightful heir, had not yet been crowned when he vanished into the Tower in 1483, never to be seen again.

And if royal children often came to the throne at a dangerously young age, it is surprising how often they went into battle while still children. Edward the Black Prince was just sixteen when he led almost 4,000 British troops at the Battle of Crécy in 1346. Henry

V (1386–1422) – unquestionably the greatest warrior king England has ever produced – led the English victorious forces together with his father at the Battle of Shrewsbury in 1403. He also was just sixteen. And whatever we might think about modern royals joining the army but being kept back from the front line, the same was certainly not true of their medieval ancestors. Henry V was in the thick of it at Shrewsbury – so much so that he was hit in the face by an arrow and only the skill of his surgeon saved his life.

Where princes trod the English aristocracy was never far behind – the profession of arms was always seen as the noblest and most princely of activities. Robert Devereux, Earl of Essex, is a case in point. Like most aristocrats he was related to royalty – he was Elizabeth I's first cousin twice removed. At age twelve he was sent to Cambridge University, but there was no glory in an academic career. It was a natural progression for an ambitious young aristocrat to fight. When he was twenty-one, he was appointed Master of the Horse and at the Battle of Zutphen, as Lytton Strachey remarks in his life of Essex, 'in the mad charge … he was among the bravest, and was knighted by Leicester after the action'.

For a nobleman, to be killed while fighting was perhaps the highest honour of all – youth made such a death even more noble, and this poisonous idea lasted and fuelled much of the carnage of the First World War. The idea of very young men heading off to battle explains why recruiting officers often turned a blind eye to men as young as fourteen joining up in 1914, and the idea that it was an honour to die for one's country at almost any age may explain why King Albert I of Belgium allowed his twelve-year-old son to join the army and serve as a private during the First World War.

This ancient love affair with physical violence continues today among royal males as all the children of Queen Elizabeth II were expected to serve – and when Prince Andrew, her favourite son, was offered a posting to the Falklands War in 1982 that would have kept him out of the action, she insisted this was not acceptable and that he must fight alongside his fellow officers.

* * *

Leaving your children in the care of others from the earliest age – whether wet nurses and governors or in more recent times nannies, nurses and public schools – is designed primarily to produce early maturity, toughness and resilience. A royal prince does not get upset or show emotion; such things are unmanly and unprincely. Keeping royal princes and the sons of the aristocracy close to their parents and failing to suppress all shows of emotion were assumed to produce weak, even effeminate, adults, but this obsession with manliness, as we will see, led to generation after generation of dysfunctional, sometimes reprehensible, adults from Henry VIII to Prince Andrew.

CHAPTER TWO

BED-PAN BABIES

'Every generation, civilisation is invaded by barbarians
– we call them "children".'

HANNAH ARENDT

In 1778 as Marie Antoinette was about to bring a new child into the world, she would have looked around and seen more than 200 courtiers and other officials eagerly looking on. The doctors and midwives surrounding the queen were directed to shout 'the queen is about to give birth' in time for the whole court to enter the bedroom. If there were sufficient witnesses then there could be no doubt afterwards that the royal baby really was, well, royal. In poor Marie Antoinette's case, the crowd around her was so vast that, unable to see precisely what was happening, many of the onlookers climbed on the furniture to get a better look. Several elderly courtiers were hurt in the crush and Marie fainted from the heat and the lack of air.

Despite her supremely elevated status, the queen was also, in this special circumstance, public property. Witnesses, preferably large numbers of witnesses, were essential if the legitimacy of the child was not to be questioned.

Checking the legitimacy of a royal birth reached a pitch of absurdity when George II (1683–1760) rushed to St James's Palace where his son Frederick's wife, Princess Augusta of Saxe-Gotha (1719–72), was about to give birth. George was convinced his daughter-in-law was not pregnant at all and that it was all a plan by the hated Frederick (1707–51) to sneak what had become known as a 'bedpan baby' into Augusta's bed. In the event, a girl was born and George II and his wife accepted the birth must be genuine – a girl was of no consequence in their view and therefore not worth counterfeiting. George's hatred for his son Frederick seems almost incomprehensible today – partly, no doubt, it was due to the fact that Frederick had grown up away from his father and partly that George had been heartily disliked by his own father, George I.

An even more significant factor was that there were rumours about Frederick himself – rumours that he was a changeling, a bed-pan heir secretly brought into his mother's bedroom at the conclusion of a fake pregnancy. These rumours arose because Frederick's father, George II, had insisted his wife should give birth behind locked doors and with only her female servants around her. This break with tradition gave rise inevitably, when Frederick fell out with his father, to the rumour that he was not George's son at all.

Traditions in the royal family, especially in respect of babies and children, die hard, and what began as a way of ensuring that royal babies really were royal ended as an embarrassing process in which the Home Secretary was summoned to every royal birth. Incredibly, this lasted until abolished by George VI in 1936, following the birth of Princess Alexandra, cousin to Queen Elizabeth II.

The fear that a non-royal baby might be substituted for the real thing stemmed from an obsession with primogeniture and from the idea that 'royal blood' gave a child virtues and abilities that ordinary mortals would not have. This belief survived into the modern era despite the obvious evidence that many monarchs were mad (George III), bad (James II, George IV and Edward VII) or incompetent (Queen Victoria, Edward VIII).

Of course, much of the obsession with royal blood bypassed royal princesses since they only rarely ascended the throne. The days when their early marriages to foreign princes helped cement alliances had largely vanished by the eighteenth century, and by the time Queen Victoria was trying to find husbands for her daughters, marrying foreign princes was simply an obsession with status and prestige – when Victoria's daughter Louise married the Duke of Argyll, Victoria was deeply disappointed at this lowering of standards.

More than three centuries earlier, following Henry VIII's break with Rome in 1534, royal princesses were no longer given to convents, nor were they encouraged to see a life of religious exclusion as an alternative to marriage. Without marriage, a woman, even a princess, was a dangerous anomaly. Marriage, with only rare exceptions, was unavoidable.

* * *

Henry VIII (1491–1547) may have been ruthless and a good example of absolute power corrupting absolutely, but he did have a relatively enlightened attitude to the education of his daughters Mary (1516–58) and Elizabeth (1533–1603) and this marked a shift in attitudes to aristocratic and royal princesses – education, especially a knowledge of languages and above all Latin, had become a matter of status. Henry would also have known that his former friend Lord Chancellor Thomas More (famously executed for refusing to accept Henry as head of the church) educated *his* daughters, especially Margaret who translated Eusebius's *Ecclesiastical History* from Greek into Latin. Henry's daughters had more need of an education, since they might have to deal with ambassadors for whom Latin was the lingua franca of the day, but this would have been a minor consideration for Henry, who was determined to sire a male heir. A king with only daughters was in this regard at least a failure and Henry could not bear failure.

Elizabeth, later Elizabeth I, was exceptionally well educated, but unlike her half-brother Edward VI (1537–53), who came to the throne aged nine and was destined to rule for just six years, Elizabeth was not taught about politics. Despite the fact that there was a genuine chance she would become queen, it was assumed she would rely on her male advisers far more than Edward. That said, Elizabeth was taught not entirely by women but, unusually for the time, by male tutors. In fact, she was taught by one of the greatest scholars of the age – the humanist Roger Ascham, whose book *The Schoolmaster* gives us glimpses of a teacher who believed far more in encouragement than in coercion.

Henry's desire that Elizabeth should be educated has to be seen in curious contrast to his decision to declare her illegitimate in 1536 when she was just two years and eight months old. In the short term, this meant she became a sort of non-person. One of her first nurses, Margaret Bryan, wrote to Thomas Cromwell to explain that as Elizabeth had been declared illegitimate by her own father following the execution of her mother, Anne Boleyn, she was no longer even being supplied with the basic necessities of life: Bryan explains that the child 'has neither gown nor kirtle nor petticoat, nor linen for smocks, nor kerchiefs, sleeves, rails [nightdresses], bodystychets [corsets], handkerchiefs, mufflers, nor begens [nightcaps]'.

Despite this setback, by the time she reached adulthood Elizabeth spoke Latin, French and Italian fluently – the importance of languages in royal education has never quite disappeared. Even Elizabeth II, whose general education was almost non-existent, was taught French as if fluency in the language was not just useful but absolutely vital. Languages have always been a key part of the royal family's fluctuating sense of identity – Queen Victoria spoke fluent German, as did her children and grandchildren. But after the Great War, the royal family became horribly embarrassed rather than proud of their German origins. They also ceased to teach their children German.

Even as queen, Elizabeth I had to put up with the condescending attitudes of her senior advisers and of foreign diplomats, but she occasionally got her revenge. When the Polish ambassador visited the English court, he spoke disparagingly about her in her presence, thinking he was safe as he spoke in Latin. She immediately put him in his place in rapid and fluent Latin. It is easy to imagine his surprise.

Elizabeth's sister Mary was also well educated – as author Dulcie Ashdown notes in her book *Royal Children*, Mary's mother,

Catherine of Aragon, approached the Oxford fellow Juan Luis Vives to ask what her daughter should read. The idea of reading for fun would have seemed incomprehensible at this period, so it is no surprise that the suggestions included Greek and Latin works that showed the virtues of the ancients (despite their lamentable paganism) as well as Thomas More's *Utopia* and of course the Bible.

Elizabeth inspired a remarkable degree of loyalty in those who taught and cared for her as a child. Blanche Parry, the queen's first nurse – Elizabeth referred to her as her 'cradle rocker' – stayed with her long after she had grown up and become queen. Elizabeth's third governess (more like a modern nanny) was Katherine Champernowne, later Ashley, who started caring for Elizabeth when she was four, became one of Elizabeth's most devoted friends and confidantes and stayed with her for the rest of her life. Katherine has her exact modern counterpart, as we will see, in Bobo MacDonald, the Scotswoman who looked after Elizabeth II from her earliest years and stayed with her until MacDonald's death in 1993.

Despite the care of her various servants, Elizabeth I knew that from her father's point of view she was at worst a disappointment and at best just a political pawn. Having made himself head of the church in order to obtain his divorce from Catherine of Aragon, Henry would no doubt have disowned any number of daughters and wives in his desperate attempts to produce a male heir.

The bitterness and sorrow of Elizabeth's childhood – repudiated by her father, divided by bitter religious differences from her half-sister Mary and knowing that her mother Anne Boleyn had been executed for treason – all this would have been hugely emotionally damaging and no doubt contributed massively to her decision when she became queen never to marry. It is a truism that those forced to endure difficult, harsh childhoods often become poor parents or they reject the whole idea of becoming a parent and never have children. This is certainly true of Elizabeth I's refusal to marry, but the decision was also highly political: had she married, she would have remained queen but been obliged also to accept the authority of her husband and his desire to influence events through her.

* * *

One of the oddities of this period is that the influence of the Italian political writer Niccolò Machiavelli gradually seeped even into the education of royal children.

Machiavelli's *The Prince*, first published in 1532, insists that princes are not bound by the normal rules of truthfulness and honesty. The book was quickly translated into English and sold widely, although many people in England saw it as confirmation of a long-held belief that Italians were innately treacherous. On the whole, royalty were far more tolerant than their subjects of the notion that treachery and double-dealing might be occasionally justified for the purposes of political expediency. But, as we will see, the idea that royal princes are somehow not bound by the same rules that bind the rest of us became deeply embedded down the centuries – and remains to this day, if we are to judge by Prince Andrew's behaviour.

Machiavelli's book justified a tendency that had always existed in the royal family. A king's word was not necessarily to be relied on, since his duty to be honest to others applied only to those of the same or a similar rank. It was perfectly permissible to lie to people of a much lower rank.

During the Peasants' Revolt of 1381, an insurrection caused largely by royal attempts to collect a poll tax in parts of south-east England, in order to restore calm, the fourteen-year-old Richard II agreed to many of the peasants' demands, but as soon as order was restored and the leaders of the revolt had been killed, Richard went back on his word. Magna Carta, the first real attempt to limit a king's power, was famously repudiated by King John in 1215 after the Pope's intervention. This sense that the elite may do as they please existed among the aristocracy too. Aristocrats believed that lies were permissible if told with the agreement of the king and for political ends – during the Pilgrimage of Grace rebellion in 1536 against the suppression of the monasteries, the Duke of Norfolk told all those protesting they would be pardoned if they returned to their homes. It was a lie that Henry VIII connived in because as soon as the rebels dispersed, the leaders were rounded up and executed.

The right to lie was in a sense codified by Machiavelli and the lessons learned from *The Prince* filtered into the royal schoolroom. Royal princes were encouraged to think of themselves as so far above ordinary mortals that they could do more or less as they pleased, whether this meant lying to quell a rebellion, to divorce a wife or to take a mistress. Being economical with the truth in this fashion lasted well into the twentieth century among royals and continues to this day. It sits uneasily with the notion that, as head of the church and head of state, the monarch, and by extension the royal family, exists in some sense to provide the rest of the country with a moral compass.

Thus, while Prince of Wales, the future Edward VII lied under oath when he gave evidence during divorce proceedings. He was cited as co-respondent in a divorce case – the legal term for the accusation that he had slept with another man's wife. Edward told the court he had not slept with the woman in question (Daisy Brooke, the wife of one of his oldest friends) when his friends, backed by future historians, agreed that he had indeed slept with Mrs Brooke.

Edward VIII was little better – he sued a newspaper for suggesting he had slept with Mrs Simpson before they were married. He was awarded substantial damages, yet he had lied in court. It was common knowledge that he had slept with Mrs Simpson while she was still married to Ernest Simpson.

By this time, Machiavellian behaviour existed merely to ensure royal princes could do as they pleased in their private lives; lies could no longer be used to trap and perhaps kill one's enemies.

* * *

Much of Elizabeth I's childhood and youth was marred by the constant and very real threat of imprisonment and even death. Mary hated the idea that her half-sister would inherit the throne in the event of her death; Elizabeth may later have said we must not make 'windows into men's souls' in an attempt to reduce the extent to which the authorities persecuted Catholics, but for Mary, Elizabeth's Protestantism – even if it was relatively tolerant – was anathema. These life and death tensions among royal children can only have been stressful and damaging, but they also instilled the lesson that life was dangerous and that for an adult prince, ruthlessness could be the only way to survive.

Elizabeth's cousin James VI of Scotland (1566–1625), who came to the Scottish throne aged just thirteen months and inherited the English throne on the death of Elizabeth in 1603, had no real memory of his mother, Mary, Queen of Scots, whom he probably saw for the last time when he was around a year old.

The absence (and later execution) of his mother and the murder of his father, Lord Darnley, made James's childhood difficult to say the least and he compensated for his lack of parenting by becoming excessively devoted to adult courtiers. The situation was made worse in his early childhood by the dour Presbyterianism of the Scottish court and of his nurse Lady Mar. She behaved towards James very much as Lady Glenconner's nanny behaved towards her and her sister when they were children in the 1920s. In her memoir, as we have seen, Lady Glenconner recalls how she and her sister were tied to their beds every night.

So many royal nannies have been unsuitable or downright sadistic that it is extraordinary how the royal family continues to insist on employing them. Like James and Lady Glenconner, George VI and his brother suffered at the hands of a nanny who would pinch them hard enough to ensure they screamed just before they were due to see their parents each day. The nanny would then further abuse George and his brother for crying, even refusing to give them anything to eat. This sort of abuse was always a risk when parents paid someone else to do the work and then simply let them get on with it.

*   *   *

For James VI, Lady Mar's harsh treatment seems to have killed in him any sense that women might offer the kind of affection he was never able to get from his mother. Instead, he became deeply attached to Lady Mar's son. And this was just the first in a series of passions for young and not so young men around the court – passions that led to scandalous gossip about James's sexuality.

Perhaps the greatest of James's childhood loves was Esmé Stuart, a French nobleman who was thirty-seven when he met the thirteen-year-old James. There seems little doubt that Stuart was a father substitute for James – although there was certainly also a sexual element to the relationship – but as a Catholic Stuart was disliked and distrusted by the court. Eventually he was forced into exile in France.

At this stage James, who was just thirteen, was increasingly desperate for affection and his relationship with Stuart now fixed in place a pattern of behaviour that was repeated again and again in his adult life, leading to centuries of speculation that he was gay. Later loves included Robert Carr, Earl of Somerset, and finally George Villiers, Duke of Buckingham.

The damaging effects of a childhood with neither mother nor father were of course the result of the violent politics of the time – James's mother executed by his cousin, his father murdered – but later royal males and females have all tended to lack close parental ties simply because of the persistent obsession with making royal children independent as early as possible. James compensated by clinging to male father figures just as in more recent times Prince Philip, a man also abandoned by his parents, clung to his uncle Lord Mountbatten.

James's reign marks a clear shift in the nature and character of English kings. He was as far from the admired warrior kings of Anglo-Saxon England as it is possible to be – timid and fearful, small of stature and physically weak. He also hated confrontation, aggression and even loud argument. He detested large groups and suffered numerous real and imaginary ailments, many traceable to his frightening and lonely childhood. S. J. Houston, James's 1973 biographer, explains how throughout his adult life 'James suffered porphyria. His physician said he also suffered from night terrors, insomnia and hallucinations.'

According to James's near contemporary Sir Anthony Weldon, James was

> naturally of a timorous disposition ... His tongue [was] too large for his mouth, which ever made him drink very uncomely, as if eating his drink ... he never washed his hands ... his legs were very weak ... his walk was ever circular, his fingers ever in that walk fiddling about his codpiece.

Not a very edifying picture and it is difficult to imagine that the Anglo-Saxon witan would have chosen someone like James to lead them. No one seems to have noticed that the royal obsession with marrying their children to other royals (who were often cousins) was weakening rather than strengthening each successive generation. But despite his physical weaknesses, James had a sense of his own importance that has been handed down the centuries to all royal males: in a speech to Parliament on 21 March 1610 he insisted that 'kings are justly called Gods'. M. de Fontenay, envoy to the Stuart court, summed James up neatly when he said James was 'an old young man'.

Despite his rumoured homosexuality, James fathered seven children, although only three survived to adulthood. It has been claimed most notably by Dulcie Ashdown in her book *Royal Children* that James I was an affectionate father and there is indeed evidence for this, but the curse of royal children being farmed out to paid staff darkened his relationship with Elizabeth, his sole surviving daughter, and with Henry, his heir, and Charles, his weak and sickly second son.

James's problem was that the conventions of royal childrearing combined with his own lack of parenting to create an adult who was perceived both as weak and needy – and his children sensed this. Children always notice their parents' behaviour and how others react to it; James's children hated what they saw as their father's faults and they determined to be their exact opposite.

It is hardly surprising that James hated confrontation and violence given that both his parents died violently; he was not a jousting, manly, warlike king and his son Henry noticed. Henry decided he despised a man who ran about fawning on royal favourites. He would have heard the whispers around the court that sometimes found their way into letters and cruel jokes – a Latin epigram circulated widely at the time, for example, ran: '*Rex fuit Elizabeth; nunc est regina Jacobus*' ('Elizabeth was king; now James is queen').

When James wrote to the Privy Council saying, 'I love the Duke of Buckingham more than anyone else', his sons would have been horrified. James had done his duty by siring them and making sure they had the tutors and governesses they were required to have, but that was not enough. The energies of James's affections were always elsewhere and his children despised him for it. As a result, his daughter Elizabeth looked up to her brother Henry in a way she did not to her father, because Henry was the manly man that kings and princes were meant to be.

As a result of these inherited tensions, Henry had a major disagreement with one of his father's favourites, Robert Carr, and the violence of the falling out would have been fuelled by Henry's sense of the inappropriateness of his father's relationship with this man. Though he died aged just eighteen and before he could ascend the throne, there is no evidence that Henry ever had the sort of passionate friendships with other young men that his father so frequently indulged. Ashamed of James's inadequacies, Henry had spent his short life trying to be as different as possible from his weak, despised father.

Henry was far more of a father figure to both Elizabeth and to his younger brother Charles than James ever was. In her 1973 study of royal children, Dulcie Ashdown cites a letter written by Charles to his elder brother Henry. It's the kind of letter he would never have written to his father.

Charles writes:

Sweet, sweet brother, I thank you for your letter. I will keep it better than all my graith [possessions] and I will send my pistols by Master Hinton. I will give anything that I have to you, both my horses and my books, and my pieces [guns] and my crossbows or anything that you would have.

After Henry's premature death in 1612, Charles (1600–49) found himself heir to the throne at the age of twelve. This would have been a shock for a boy who was physically frail and psychologically timid like his father and used to behaving in a subservient way with his elder brother and even with his sister Elizabeth.

Centuries of marrying close relatives had produced in Charles a short, physically weak, knock-kneed king who struggled to learn even to speak. Inherited physical and mental health problems echo down the ages – both Edward VII and George VI inherited the knock knees of James and Charles, and George VI struggled all his life with a stammer; haemophilia afflicted the closely related Russian and British royal families; the Austro-Hungarian royals frequently suffered from prognathic jaws (extended jaws caused by inbreeding). Other royals suffered from inherited madness: Ferdinand VI of Spain ran around biting people, refused ever to wash and liked to dance in front of his friends in his underwear. Despite this, Ferdinand remained king for more than a decade and numerous other kings stayed in command despite general agreement that they were entirely unsuited to the job.

But if Charles was physically weak, that did not lessen his conviction that he was divinely appointed. Despite his tiny frame and

weak legs – he was just 5ft 4in. and painfully thin – Charles behaved as if he were a giant bestriding the world. Like his father,
he believed absolutely in his divine right to rule and he became an
intellectually inflexible and unimaginative adult. The result was a
watershed in British royal history – the Civil War ended with the
execution of Charles and the end of the monarch's divine right to
rule. From now on, a monarch's power could and would be limited.
But the effect of this on the British royal family was to make them
increasingly concerned with personal power, status and wealth and
with their elevated status as Britain's first family.

Charles's inherited difficulties were exacerbated by his upbringing. When James came from Scotland to England in 1603 to take
the English throne, Charles was left in Scotland in the care of Lord
Fyvie and his nurses and governesses. A year later, he was sent
to England but not into the care of his parents whom he hardly
saw. Instead, he was looked after by Lord and Lady Carey. Lady
Carey was a kind woman who did as much as anyone could to help
Charles. She prevented his lingual frenulum (the thin strip of mucus
membrane under the tongue) being cut – a mad idea designed to
help his speech difficulties – and insisted he should not be placed
in leg irons to strengthen the weak legs he had inherited from
his father.

Largely abandoned by his father, Charles then lost his father-
figure brother Henry when he was just twelve; then when he was
nineteen, his mother died. As we have seen in recent times with
the death of Diana Spencer and the effect on her sons, especially
Harry, Charles would have felt this loss in a way that always made

it more likely he would seek father figures throughout his life just as his father had.

Charles found his in the Duke of Buckingham and in William Laud. He was persuaded to make Laud Archbishop of Canterbury, but Laud was an intolerant bigot who immediately tried to suppress the puritanism that had become widespread in Scotland. The result was a Scottish revolt and the Wars of the Three Kingdoms, which Charles lost.

Laud's disastrous influence on Charles's masculine side was matched by Charles's wife's influence. When Charles fell out with Parliament, Henrietta Maria (1609–69) insisted he dissolve Parliament and rule by diktat. Historians disagree about the extent of her influence, but few doubt her support of her husband's absolutist view of monarchy. The results were catastrophic, leading to the king's impeachment trial and execution. Easily swayed by father and mother figures who exploited his vulnerabilities and never doubting his divine right to rule, Charles epitomises the worst outcomes when royal intermarriage combines with absent parents.

When Charles I's son returned to England in 1660 to ascend the throne as Charles II (1630–85), he hunted down and executed many of those who had signed his father's death warrant, but he knew better than to try to emulate his father's insistence on his divine right to rule. Charles II's early years away from his father and then life as an exile in France gave him a taste for pleasure rather than business that has characterised many royal princes ever since, and it is Charles who represents the great shift: on the one hand, his father and all earlier monarchs believed in their right to rule; on the other, Charles II accepted that, ultimately, he could not rule the country. He could only really rule in his private life, and in his pursuit of pleasure, Charles has been matched by only one royal male: Prince Andrew.

*   *   *

Charles II had many children but no legitimate heir. He was never involved with his children's care, but much of his reputation as the merry monarch came from the fact that he liked his illegitimate children and ennobled many of them – at least five of our present dukes are descended from the bastard sons of Charles's mistresses.

Charles's brother, the Catholic James II, succeeded to the throne in 1685, only to be deposed in the Glorious Revolution of 1688. He was followed by the safely Protestant William and Mary, and then Queen Anne, but neither reign produced an heir and the result was a desperate scramble to avoid the numerous Catholic claimants hovering on the Continent. Dozens had a greater claim on the throne than the man eventually chosen by Parliament, but a Protestant had to be found and that Protestant was George, Elector of Hanover, soon to become George I. George's arrival on the scene heralded the beginning of a new century and more of the most disastrous royal parents ever to have been foisted on royal children.

CHAPTER THREE

MAD, BAD AND SAD: ROYAL CHILDREN FROM GEORGE I TO WILLIAM IV

*'Most of the trouble in the world is caused
by people wanting to be important.'*

T. S. Eliot

The Georges went one better than previous monarchs. Where royal children were once largely ignored, now they were sometimes actively hated. Yet it was during the Georgian period that the special needs of children began to be recognised.

What really began to transform attitudes was the publication in 1762 of *Émile* by Jean-Jacques Rousseau. Subtitled *On Education*, the book's central message is that children should be the focus of their parents' lives and parents should look after their children themselves. Ironically, Rousseau gave all his own children up for adoption as soon as they were born, but for the middle classes in

England, his book – which became a bestseller – caused a shift in the moral atmosphere; it ushered in the modern attitude where children are no longer seen as adults in waiting who need only to be kept out of harm's way by paid staff.

But if the message gradually altered the way the middle classes treated their children, the same is not true of the way the aristocracy and even more so royalty treated their children. For the upper classes, the old ways were the best. Nannies and governesses and nurses were and are still employed on the basis partly of habit and partly because of the deeply entrenched idea that childcare is not something royals do; paying others to look after children is also a statement about history and status.

One central idea expressed by Rousseau that took hold widely in Britain was the idea that mothers should breastfeed their own children, and by the early years of the nineteenth century, most middle-class families did exactly that. Only the most die-hard aristocrats and the royal family still employed wet nurses. Queen Charlotte, the wife of George III, was attracted to the idea of breastfeeding, but she couldn't quite bring herself to do it. But unlike George I and George II, she and her husband did at least spend an unusually large amount of time with their children.

George I's and George II's relationship with their eldest sons is almost too well known to need mention. It is not going too far to say that George I's hatred of his son was only exceeded by George II's hatred for *his* son Frederick. In both cases, the sons had spent most of their formative years in Germany with little or no contact with their parents.

The great problem for George I (1660–1727) was that he never felt entirely secure on the English throne. He knew he was widely disliked and mocked. He also knew that the British knew everything about his sordid treatment of his wife, Sophia (1666–1726). She had been unfaithful to him with a Swedish count and the weight of evidence, though not conclusive, suggests he took his revenge by having the count murdered. But if there is any doubt about the murder, there is none at all about the fact that he locked his wife up in a remote castle in Germany for the rest of her life.

But the wife he had locked up had given birth to a son and that tainted any relationship they might have hoped to enjoy. The younger George was a constant reminder of the woman the king wanted to forget. What made this worse was that, during his early years, the younger George was kept in Germany while his father reigned in Britain. It was an extreme example of that obsession with sending royal children away when young.

*   *   *

Born in 1660 in Hanover, the future George I was the son of the Duke of Brunswick-Lüneburg, the ruler of a tiny area of northwest Germany. He must have been astonished as anybody could be when, at the age of fifty-four, he was offered the throne of England. His only qualification was that his mother was a granddaughter of James I of England. He accepted the throne rather as one accepts a promotion one knows one is not qualified for. He needed the money and wanted the status. The fact that his subjects disliked him stemmed from his sullen, reclusive character. Like royals across Europe, he had been brought up by nannies and governesses and had seen his parents only infrequently. When he was four, his mother left for a year-long holiday in Italy. And from his earliest years, he was reminded that he and his family needed money and that he must marry someone who could provide it. The emphasis on duty and nothing but duty seems to have crushed his spirit and embittered his mind. Writing in her exhaustive study of the Georges, *The Strangest Family*, the historian Janice Hadlow neatly sums up everything that was wrong with George I's childhood:

> His father, Ernst August, was a man of calculating ambition, dominated by the all-pervasive desire to see his dukedom of Hanover elevated to the far greater status of an electorate. His many children were raised in an atmosphere of military discipline, expected to display absolute obedience to his will ... He seldom saw any of them alone or in informal circumstances; unsurprisingly, they were said to be 'solemn and restrained' in his presence.

The younger George married his first cousin, Sophia Dorothea of Brunswick-Celle, because she brought with her the adjoining duchy of Brunswick-Lüneburg-Celle – a duchy George's father had long coveted – as well as a large annual income.

But the couple were entirely unsuited – she enjoyed life and parties while he hated them. Like most royal princes, he took it as a given that he was entitled to take as many mistresses as he pleased, but when his wife took a lover, the consequences, as we have seen, were dire.

Sophia's son was never allowed to mention his mother in his father's presence, but by the time he joined his father in England, he made sure he had a portrait of Sophia that was kept well out of sight of the court in his private apartments. Young George had inherited some of his mother's sense of fun and determination to enjoy life and there seems little doubt that his decision years later in England to set up a court to rival his father's – something that caused a complete rift between the two men – had a great deal to do with his father's treatment of the young George's mother.

Childhood-based resentments in the heirs to the British throne up to the present day can be attributed to childrearing habits and traditions that intensified under the Georges.

George I had only been in England for three years when a minor disagreement over the choice of godparent for his grandson George William, the second son of the Prince of Wales, led to a row that further alienated father and son – to the point where George I considered imprisoning his son in the Tower. As a result of the row, Princesses Caroline, Amelia and Anne were removed from their parents' care and spent the next dozen and more years sitting watching their grandfather play cards every evening in the gloomy candlelit royal apartments at Kensington Palace. Their parents, George and Caroline (1683–1737), were forbidden even to see them.

According to R. L. Arkell in his 1939 biography *Caroline of Ansbach: George II's Queen*, the young Princess Anne complained, 'We are like charity children; nobody loves us.'

George I must have cursed the rule of primogeniture. No doubt he would have been delighted to ask the old witan to choose a successor – any successor – other than his son.

The details of the intergenerational feuds and cruelties of the Hanoverians are well known, but one or two examples give the flavour of decades of hatred.

George and Caroline were kept almost entirely apart from their children from 1717 to 1727, when George I died. By then it was too late for any kind of meaningful relationship between parents and children. In 1728 the situation worsened when George and Caroline's son and heir Frederick, who had been sent back to Hanover as a child, was invited to return to England. His parents had not seen him since he was seven in 1714.

Having complained bitterly about his relationship with his father, George I, George II quickly fell out with the son he hardly knew. Frederick had no intention of obeying a father who must have seemed a complete stranger.

George and Caroline's dislike of their son quickly reached a pitch of hatred. Frederick's hatred of his parents was equally venomous. When George's ship was feared lost in a storm in the North Sea, as he returned from a visit to Hanover, Frederick held a dinner party in celebration. Caroline called her son that 'hardened liar'; when she saw him walking below her window in the grounds of Kensington Palace, she shook her fist at him and called him a 'beast'; she even spoke disparagingly of him to her servants; in a final insult, she insisted he was not man enough to father an heir.

Even on her deathbed, Caroline made it clear which of her sons she loved and which she hated.

She wrote to Frederick's younger brother William:

You know I have always loved you tenderly and placed my chief hope in you; show your gratitude to me by your behaviour to the King; be a support to your father, and double your attention to him to make up for disappointment and vexation he must receive from your profligate and worthless brother. It is in you only I hope for keeping up the credit of your family when your father shall be no more. Attempt nothing ever against your brother and endeavour to mortify him in no way but by showing superior merit.

When Caroline died in 1737, her son Frederick was blamed – his perceived bad behaviour was seen by his father George II as having put a terrible strain on the queen. Placing the blame in this way echoes down through succeeding centuries – Victoria, for example, blamed her son and heir Bertie, later Edward VII, for the death of Prince Albert. The Queen Mother blamed the early death of her husband George VI on his brother's decision to abdicate. She seemed to think it had nothing to do with her husband's habit of smoking fifty cigarettes each day.

In the event, George II did not have to face the prospect of his hated son becoming king for Frederick predeceased him and George's grandson, whom he much preferred, became George III (1738–1820).

Despite being heartily disliked by his parents and especially by his sister Anne, Frederick seems to have behaved well to everyone;

he bumped into his father and mother at the theatre one evening and bowed politely to them. They ignored him. Even knowing that his parents much preferred his brother William did not embitter Frederick. In public, at least, he was his brother's greatest supporter.

Something of this more tolerant attitude – tolerant at least by the standards of the Hanoverians – seems to have seeped into Frederick's son George III. On ascending the throne, he decided to leave Kensington Palace, where the royal family had lived since William III's (1650–1702) time, and move to Buckingham Palace. Rather than be distant from his children as his ancestors had been from theirs, he decided to be a model father and husband – he doted on his fifteen children and though he had his favourites none was treated as his father and grandfather had been treated. But George III could not quite escape the dysfunctional legacy of the past. In his determination to be a good father who cared about his children, he went too far – his sons were kept under strict control and his daughters were made to feel that leaving the family to get married was a kind of betrayal. Indeed, George III was so obsessively determined to rule every aspect of his children's lives that they behaved just as badly as previous generations of Hanoverians had done.

George III produced some of the most profligate, deceitful, sadistic, selfish princes in British history – from the eccentric Augustus, who illegally married a Catholic, to the gross drunken Prince Regent, later George IV (1762–1830). If his sons rebelled, his daughters were crushed; they were so cloistered that rumours spread that they tried to have sex with any man who came within reach. The warm, close family George thought he had created actually produced a brood of children none of whom seemed in the least interested in doing anything dutiful, least of all siring an heir, which is why we ended up with Queen Victoria.

*   *   *

George III had fifteen children and was famously happily married to Queen Charlotte (1744–1818). He was the first British monarch not to take a mistress. But his overcontrolling nature and moral absolutism caused huge problems for his increasingly resentful children, and the more he restricted their freedoms, the more they rebelled as adults. It is ironic that a king who prided himself on his strict sense of morality should have had children who had countless illegitimate children; who were drunks and spendthrifts, sadists and bullies and even murderers.

The ultimate symbol of George III's desire for control of his personal world came when he insisted Parliament pass the Royal Marriages Act of 1772. This was designed to ensure none of his children married without his express permission – the monarchs of earlier centuries who had insisted on their divine right to rule the kingdom had degenerated into the divine right of a king to control his offspring. And the result? Well, two of his sons married Catholics, one became a soldier who had his troops executed on the flimsiest of evidence and the Prince Regent became one of the most loathed British monarchs of all time.

George III's obsessive desire to control no doubt arose from his own bizarre childhood. His father and mother made it clear they disliked him and much preferred his younger brother Edward, Duke of York. They insisted to everyone who would listen that

'Edward will one day be somebody'. In fact, Edward became a womanising drunk who achieved nothing. According to Lady Mary Coke (pronounced Cook), whose journals were first published in 1889, Augusta frequently belittled her son and heir. Often when he spoke during conversations with his parents and siblings, Augusta would shout, 'Hold your tongue, George; don't talk like a fool.'

Not one of George III's sons was able to sire a male heir, although between them they sired more than twenty illegitimate children, despite Parliament offering huge financial incentives for the sons to ditch their mistresses and marry suitable princesses. The Duke of Kent left his long-term mistress in return for a parliamentary bribe and in 1819 his wife, Princess Victoria of Saxe-Coburg-Saalfeld, gave birth to the future Queen Victoria (1819–1901).

Victoria's story has often been told. Born in Kensington Palace, she spent her first eighteen years virtually a prisoner. Her mother introduced what came to be known as the Kensington system – shorthand for a childhood where Victoria's every move was carefully watched; she was never allowed to be alone, only rarely mixed with other children and was aware from the earliest that her mother was being manipulated by a sinister figure called Sir John Conroy. Conroy was an Irish aristocrat who went quickly from being Victoria's mother's adviser to being someone who controlled her and, through her, Victoria. In later life, she described her childhood as 'melancholy' and she grew to hate Conroy, suspecting that his ultimate aim was to rule the country through her mother and her.

But if she was overcontrolled as a child, she was also indulged – looked after by nurses and governesses, on her daily walks through

Kensington Gardens she was always accompanied by a footman; the picture gallery at Kensington Palace was subdivided to provide her with an adequate playground; and she was surrounded by dogs, including her favourite spaniel, Dash. Dash may have been a favourite, but she also kept Dandie Dinmonts, fox terriers and Labradors. Like many children growing up in an emotionally cold environment, she invested her emotional life in animals – the same is true of her great-great-granddaughter Elizabeth II. Like so many earlier monarchs too, Victoria was hardly a splendid physical specimen – centuries of inbreeding had in Victoria produced a woman who was under 5ft tall.

Victoria may have been unhappy under the harsh regime imposed at Kensington during her childhood, but she learned little from her own painful early experiences. Just as she was overly controlled, she too tried and often succeeded in controlling her own children in a manner that, in the twenty-first century, would be seen as abusive.

The secret of Victoria as child and then parent lies in the old adage that we often turn into our parents even if we dislike them.

Victoria was cowed and repressed by her mother and John Conroy, but she learned brilliantly from them how to cow and oppress her own children.

Victoria was idolised by her nurses and her mother's ladies-in-waiting, and by her sister, Feodora, but her own mother, true to form, had nothing to do with the sordid business of actually looking after her baby. Victoria's mother was absurdly strict, but then she saw Victoria for only a short time each day. She began to fear that the paid staff were over-indulging the future queen. The evidence, as Lytton Strachey puts it in his biography of Victoria, was that as a toddler, 'from time to time, she would fly into a violent passion, stamp her little foot, and set everyone at defiance'.

This was a side of Victoria's character that never completely disappeared – it surfaced in later life in fearsome rows with Prince Albert (1819–61) and with her officials if they disagreed with her. A tendency to sudden rages came from her almost bipolar early years – a strict mother combined with indulgent nurses and governesses. Victoria's mother would hardly let the child do anything; her nurses allowed her to do whatever she liked. One of the biggest early influences was Fräulein Lehzen, as Lytton Strachey explains:

A change came with the appearance of Fräulein Lehzen. This lady who was the daughter of a Hanoverian clergyman ... soon succeeded in instilling a new spirit into her charge. At first indeed she was appalled by the little princess's outburst of temper ... then she observed something else: the child was extraordinarily truthful.

Victoria was fond of Lehzen and wanted to please her, but her mother's influence was still always there. After all, throughout her teenage years, Victoria had slept in the same room as her mother, who had insisted that Victoria must always hold either Lehzen's or someone else's hand when she walked downstairs. She must never ever walk down unaccompanied.

All her mother's efforts had one aim, as Lytton Strachey explains: 'The Duchess was determined that her daughter, from the earliest possible moment, should be prepared for her high station in a way that would commend itself to the most respectable; her good, plain, thrifty German mind recoiled with horror and amazement from the shameless junketings at Carlton House.'

Carlton House was of course the home of Victoria's embarrassing uncle George IV and his mistress Lady Conyngham, whose husband had been persuaded to accept the situation with the bribe of a peerage. Victoria's other uncles were not much better – William IV, for example, had ten illegitimate children by the actress Mrs Jordan. Victoria's own father had only left his long-term mistress to marry Victoria's mother after being paid a bribe by the government. Another uncle, the Duke of Cumberland – known as 'Butcher Cumberland' for his savage reprisals after the Battle of Culloden – had disgraced himself by striking a fellow officer. Victoria's mother's whole aim in life was to stop Victoria being anything like these reprobate uncles and that meant keeping Victoria under lock and key. But by trying to make Victoria the moral opposite of her uncles, the duchess created a woman obsessed with respectability and sexual propriety.

From the very first, Victoria's very existence was the cause of intense family and political rows. First there was talk of calling her Charlotte; then Alexandrina because one of her godfathers was the Tsar of Russia. Her second name would then be Augusta or Georgiana – a nod to her other godfather, the Prince Regent. When the Regent heard this, he was furious that his name should come after that of the tsar. Eventually, Alexandrina Victoria was chosen – Victoria was neutral enough and had no historical awkwardness attached. Victoria was always known as Drina as a child.

She was taught French and German, maths, history and Latin. She was good at maths and history but resented the fact that she was not allowed to speak to her mother in German in case she grew up with a German accent. Despite the plethora of children's books being published at this time, Victoria seems to have been largely restricted to very serious books. In one of her letters she writes, 'I am reading Russell's *Modern Europe* ... and Clarendon's *History of the Rebellion* ... I read Jones' account of the wars in Spain, Portugal and the south of France.'

The pressure on Victoria from the earliest was that she should behave as far as possible like an adult long before that was a reasonable expectation. In this respect she was treated very much as her ancestors had been treated, despite the fact that so much had changed in terms of childrearing outside the palace walls.

Aged just twelve, like some latter-day Elizabeth I, Victoria began to tour the country – the idea was to introduce her to her subjects since she was by now almost certain to become queen. This was seen by her uncle William – king from 1830 – as an insult to his dignity. He was unpopular and hated to see his niece being feted wherever she went.

Her early experience of being welcomed with cheers wherever she went had far more to do with the fact that she was a child and that she was not William than it had to do with her character, but it stood her in good stead many years later when she was booed by the crowd on her way to Parliament – she ignored the booing, convinced that the vast bulk of her subjects loved her as they had loved her when she was on that first tour. The sense that she was divinely chosen to reign if not to rule had been deeply instilled by her cossetted and controlled childhood.

But Victoria could easily have failed to become queen – in 1835 she contracted typhoid and though this threatened her life it also brought out for the first time Victoria's absolute belief in herself. As Victoria lay ill in bed, her mother's adviser Sir John Conroy tried to force her to sign a paper promising he would be private secretary when she became queen. Despite her weakened condition and pressure from her mother and Conroy, she refused – her strict upbringing was beginning to produce the exact opposite of what had been intended. Instead of having learned to do exactly what her mother and Conroy told her to do, Victoria had learned to issue commands. The assumption that Victoria could be controlled echoes a similar assumption made more than a century later about Lady Diana Spencer.

By the early 1830s, Victoria knew that only death could stop her becoming queen and exercising real power over her family and friends, and she was determined to exercise that power. Conroy had hoped he would be able to control the country through Victoria – we know this because as William IV's life reached its close in 1837, and after Conroy's failure to get Victoria to agree to his terms when she was ill, he urged the Duchess of Kent to lock Victoria in her room until she agreed he would be private secretary. The duchess, fearing she might lose her daughter for ever, refused and Conroy's final bid for power failed.

An acute observer might have noticed how early in her life Victoria had sensed her elevated status and the power that went with it.

Lytton Strachey describes how, when six-year-old Lady Jane Ellice was taken by her grandmother to Kensington Palace,

> she was put to play with the Princess Victoria, who was the same age as herself. The young visitor, ignorant of etiquette, began to make free with the toys on the floor, in a way that was a little too familiar; but 'You must not touch those,' she was quickly told, 'they are mine; and I may call you Jane, but you must not call me Victoria.'

Victoria later described her childhood in very negative terms, but she was luckier than many royal children as she had the company of her adored half-sister Feodora until she was nine. It was only later that her real solitude began. Victoria's 2014 biographer A. N. Wilson quotes a letter from Feodora written many years later to Victoria, in which she says, 'I escaped some years of imprisonment, which you, my poor dear sister had to endure after I was married.'

Victoria confided her unhappiness to her diary many years later: 'I had no brothers and sisters to live with, never had had a father … was not on comfortable or intimate or confidential footing with my mother.'

But like many people with controlling mothers, Victoria was deeply upset when her mother died in 1861 – part of this had to do with recognising that despite her stern parenting, the duchess's focus was entirely on her daughter. Indeed, it was a level of attention that Victoria came to expect from all her intimates, and even Albert could not replicate it.

The irony is that Victoria's childhood was far worse because she was the heir presumptive than it might have been had she been illegitimate – before he became king, Victoria's uncle William lived happily with Mrs Jordan and their vast brood of children and he was by all accounts an indulgent parent. From his point of view, he could be indulgent because none of his children ultimately mattered. They were not going to inherit power and influence. Victoria mattered very much indeed because she was his heir.

Victoria's father, the Duke of Kent, had died in 1820 before she was a year old and she would never hear a word against him despite his well-deserved reputation as an incompetent, sadistic soldier. And this was typical of an attitude she developed early in her life – she rarely changed her mind about people and rather than mistrust those who deferred and flattered her, she much preferred them. Despite or perhaps because of Conroy's attempts to control her, she was always highly susceptible to the influence of powerful male figures such as Lord Melbourne and later her gillie John Brown.

But if Victoria had a melancholy, overcontrolled childhood, it taught her nothing at all about being a mother, for as we will see, she was to cause her own children misery by her unthinking demands for attention and obedience.

CHAPTER FOUR

'MY DAUGHTERS HAVE TURNED INTO COWS': THE CHILDREN OF QUEEN VICTORIA

'Children have never been very good at listening to their elders,
but they have never failed to imitate them.'

JAMES BALDWIN

Queen Victoria made the royal family dull and respectable and we were never allowed to forget it; and apart from a short interval when her son Edward VII did a very reasonable imperson-ation of his philandering ancestor Charles II, successive monarchs have continued the tradition of dull respectability, or at least they did until the children of the late Queen Elizabeth II came of age and blew the respectable ship out of the water.

Despite being one rung below the royal family, the English ar-istocracy – descendants in many cases of the Saxon witan – have always seen themselves, in some senses, as superior to the royal family. The 7th Earl of Leicester, Lord Coke, whose family have been Norfolk landowners since the late sixteenth century, suggested in an interview with the present author, for example, that the British royal family were actually little more than German arrivistes. Queen Victoria echoed this when she confided to her diary that the British people thought her relatives were all 'German paupers'.

Though Victoria was obsessed with what she called 'dear Germany' and insisted her children should all learn German and, if at all possible, marry Germans, she recognised that as a rule the British population admired and looked up to the English aristocracy far more than they looked up to the royals. This was no doubt a hangover from a century and more of Georgian kings who were deeply unpopular with the public. Victoria was as determined as possible that both she and her children should be as little like her disgraceful, profligate, promiscuous forebears as possible.

One might be forgiven for thinking that having endured what she herself called a 'rather melancholy' childhood, where every minute of her waking life was controlled and watched, Victoria as a mother might have been inclined to allow her children more fun and more liberty.

Alas no. So terrified was she by the appallingly bad behaviour of the monarchs who came before her that she determined only the strictest upbringing would prevent history repeating itself in her children, especially as she believed that character was to a large extent inherited. Children with these most dangerous antecedents should be raised in only the most carefully controlled environment.

But just as in the story of Oedipus the king, the faster Victoria ran from her fate, the quicker it came towards her.

And there was another factor in the disaster that was Victoria as mother. It is a truism of psychology that we are more likely to repeat the parenting mistakes of our own parents because that is all we know – we may not have enjoyed our childhoods, but we fall naturally into the parenting habits we saw in our own parents, good or bad, unless we have the intelligence and the imagination to escape, and Victoria had neither the intelligence nor the imagination. Agnes Cook, who worked in the kitchens at Buckingham Palace in the years immediately following Victoria's death, recalled, 'The old hands in the palace, I mean among the servants, used to say that Queen Victoria didn't have the brains to be a decent pastry cook!'

Victoria's other difficulty was that she had inherited the Hanoverian tradition of actively disliking her children, especially when they were young. She confessed to her diary that even the prettiest baby is 'frightful'.

She confessed she had 'the greatest horror of having children and would rather have none'. She described having children as the shadow side of life; and pregnancy was, she wrote to her daughter Vicky, like being a dog or a cow. The problem was that she could not have sex with Albert without having children and she loved sex – after her wedding night she wrote in her diary, 'When day dawned (for we did not sleep much) and I beheld that beautiful face by my side, it was more than I could express.'

Her dislike of her children was especially acute when it came to her eldest son, Bertie, later Edward VII (1841–1910), in whom she saw signs of the debauchery she so loathed in her uncles.

Like her grandfather George III and her own mother, Victoria demanded obedience in all things from her children; she expected academic brilliance, military and sporting excellence and high moral standards. None of her children was able to match the standards she set for them, but then her standards were impossible.

There was never any question that Victoria would marry a German relative, and this she duly did when she married her first cousin Prince Albert in 1840 – first cousin marriages are common in many cultures even today, but scientists agree the offspring of such unions frequently suffer from inherited defects. Despite disliking her overcontrolled childhood, Victoria also married a man who was more controlled and controlling even than her mother. Historian Lucy Worsley has gone so far as to argue that Albert made sure his wife was pregnant almost continuously for more than a decade to keep her out of the picture, giving him room to behave more like a king than a consort. As a man, he felt it was humiliating that his wife should have political power and he none. It was the cause of most of the couple's furious rows – and there were many of those.

With parents like this it is perhaps no wonder that their firstborn son became as different from them as he could possibly be: Bertie was greedy, lazy, unintellectual and promiscuous. He was as wicked as the wicked uncles Victoria so despised.

Albert was a mixture of Victoria's mother, with her obsession with keeping Victoria away from anything she saw as a bad influence, and John Conroy, who, though hated by Victoria, had been a huge part of her early life because her real father had died before she was a year old. Throughout their marriage, Albert treated his wife as a wayward, over-emotional child, just as Conroy had done when Victoria actually was a child. Even in her marriage, there were deep echoes of her childhood relationships – modern psychology tells us that those who have been abused as children are drawn to abusers as adults.

Albert had grown up in the German tradition of discipline and self-control and he was determined to instil these German virtues in his wife and in his offspring. Victoria admired Albert's serious-ness and his need to control, and she was delighted that he took his children's education so seriously, but she herself was not prepared to be controlled by him. Victoria was a mass of complex paradoxes – in later life she described ideas about women's rights and votes for women as 'mad, wicked folly', but *her* rights were sacrosanct: she had no intention of submitting to her husband's desire to rule through her. This had too many echoes of Sir John Conroy. Thwart-ed, Albert determined that if he could not be the power behind the throne, he would be fully in charge of his children's upbringing and education.

Baroness Lehzen, who we may remember had looked after Vic-toria as a child, had been promoted to head of the royal nursery by the time Victoria and Albert's first child – also Victoria, but known as Vicky – was born in 1840. Albert hated the fact that Lehzen took control of the new arrival and ran the nursery just as Victoria ran the country. In 1842 when Vicky, by now the Princess Royal, was two, Albert persuaded Victoria to sack Lehzen and send her back to Germany. This was no real compensation for not being able to control his wife and, through her, events in the wider world, but it was something and for the rest of his life Albert chose his children's tutors and directed their studies and what he thought of as their moral development – he always knew this was a lesser role and his obsessively strict rule in and out of the classroom was perhaps a reflection of his anger and frustration at being kept out of the monarch's role.

Little more than a century later, Prince Philip found himself in a similar position and suffered a comparable crisis – he was to lament that he was the only man in the country whose wife and children did not take his name, and that complaint hid a deeper sense that, as a man, he should have been in charge rather than his wife. For Philip, compensation lay in insisting Charles, his heir, should attend Gordonstoun School, where Philip himself had been; Philip was convinced Gordonstoun would turn his over-sensitive son into a real man.

Albert insisted to Victoria that they chose Christian Friedrich, Baron Stockmar, to devise an education plan for Bertie. Stockmar appealed to Albert because he had all the virtues of German strictness and seriousness that Albert so admired. The plan was a complete failure, largely because Bertie's very earliest years had been the worst sort of preparation for any kind of academic effort – looked after by a series of paid attendants and with a mother who actively disliked him, Bertie was most likely suffering from what we would call attention deficit hyperactivity disorder (ADHD). Certainly, Bertie displayed all the classic symptoms – he found it impossible to pay attention and he could not control his impulsive, often destructive behaviour. But oblivious to the reality of her son's character – a character for which she and Albert were to a large extent responsible – Victoria lived in a fantasy world of hopes and aspirations.

She neatly summed up her view of what Bertie must become when she confided to her diary, 'I wish that he should grow up entirely under his father's eye, and every step be guided by him, so that when he has attained the age of sixteen or seventeen he may be a real companion to his father.' And typical of Victoria when she was writing in her diary, almost all of this is heavily underlined.

If Victoria and Albert disagreed about the extent to which Albert should be involved in the monarch's role, they were agreed about how their children should be treated. They believed absolutely that when it came to their children, they could not be wrong because they were queen and consort.

Bertie, the couple's second child and the heir to the throne, was born in 1841. In the months after his birth, Victoria suffered what we would now call postnatal depression; she felt a disgust for childbirth in general, and for Bertie in particular, and it was a disgust which stayed with her for the rest of her life. In a letter to her daughter Vicky written many years later, Victoria described this time. She suffered, she said, from a 'lowness and a tendency to cry … It is what every lady suffers with more or less and what I, during my first confinements, suffered dreadfully with.' Also, of course, Bertie was the heir and therefore the focus of far more parental attention than his brothers and sisters. Both Victoria and Albert believed that criticism and discipline were the means to create an honest, thoughtful, intelligent, morally upright adult. In Bertie, their parenting had completely the opposite effect. Bertie became everything his parents most hated – a gross sensualist like his Georgian ancestors, a liar, a cheat, a philanderer and a perjurer.

It is easy to blame all of this on his parents, but even Victoria's most sympathetic biographers agree that Albert and Victoria were appallingly bad parents. From their point of view, Bertie had to be the perfect son; ironically, of all their children, Bertie was least likely ever to be the son his parents wanted. As with so many generations of royal children, Victoria's daughters, especially perhaps Princess Vicky, would have made far better monarchs than Bertie.

In his 1989 book *Edward VII's Children*, John Van der Kiste makes the point that Bertie suffered far more from his dictatorial parents than his siblings: 'His three younger brothers all inherited, in some measure, the gifts of scholarship and temperament that their parents wished for [Bertie] ... He was singularly lacking in this respect.'

Over the seventeen years following her marriage, Victoria had a total of nine children. With her deeply rooted sense of duty – she had to have an heir – and her Hanoverian love for sex, Victoria was bound to have children, yet she claimed to loathe the whole process of pregnancy and childbirth as well as disliking small children. It's impossible to believe that her children were unaware of her feelings.

As Victoria had been controlled and bullied, so she controlled and bullied her own children. Like her grandfather George III, she expected her daughters to wait on her hand and foot and she was affronted when and if they asked permission to marry. Her pride in her children stemmed only from the fact that in later life they married into most of the great European royal families.

But Bertie was her real problem. She disliked him from the start, probably because she saw in him many of those traits she most disliked in herself, as John Van der Kiste points out: 'Bertie, as Queen Victoria perceptively recognised, was her "caricature". He took after her in his Hanoverian zest for life, aversion to studying, and hasty temper.'

Bertie was unlucky in that arriving in the world after his elder sister, he was always compared unfavourably to her. Where she was diligent and hard-working, he was or seemed to be lazy and inattentive. She liked schoolwork; he hated it. She seemed intelligent; he seemed stupid and uninterested. Some of this was no doubt simply down to genetic differences, but Victoria and even more so Albert made things far worse by employing increasingly harsh methods to make Bertie into something he was never going to be. And in that age-old tradition of getting paid staff to do the work, after the failure of Baron Stockmar, Albert engaged a series of tutors who were instructed to be as strict and forceful as possible. Rather than allowing these tutors to use their own judgement when it came to teaching Bertie and the other children, Albert interfered constantly if he felt Bertie was being treated leniently or indulgently.

But it wasn't all bad. Away from the schoolroom Albert at least could occasionally be fun. Historian Dulcie Andrews sums up Albert's efforts: 'He was not above turning somersaults for his children's amusement, or running and jumping and rolling with them in play ... He built snowmen and made them kites.' Victoria was less enthusiastic and later confessed in a letter to her daughter Vicky that when her brood was complete, and with so many of her children still either with nursemaids or with governesses, she visited them only once every three months.

At Balmoral in Scotland and at Osborne House, the couple's country house on the Isle of Wight, the children had the run of extensive grounds, they collected birds' eggs and wildflowers, rode ponies and had a miniature cottage in which to play. From his early teens, Bertie learned to shoot, and in shooting he at last found something he enjoyed – shooting became a passion that he indulged so often as an adult that he became very hard of hearing.

According to Brian Martin in *The Great Shoots*, Bertie was not just a wildly enthusiastic game shooter; he was also very good at it. A conservative estimate would put his lifetime total of birds killed (not to mention hares, rabbits and other small mammals) at several hundred thousand. With shooting as with his other pleasures – women, cigars and eating – Bertie had learned early on to be greedy.

Away from the pheasant-filled coverts and back in the classroom, Bertie's teenage years were filled with anger and frustration that echoed the darker side of his mother's personality. The extent to which Bertie wanted to escape the schoolroom where he was regularly thrashed either by his German tutor or by his father can be judged by a plea he made after a visit he and his elder sister Vicky made to Emperor Napoleon III in 1855. When it was time to go home, Bertie asked the Empress Eugénie if he could stay because 'there are six more of us at home, and they don't want us'.

Of course, Bertie was enjoying himself and would have said anything to avoid a return to the schoolroom, but his remark shows
an early example of both his charm and his determination to enjoy
himself; and enjoying himself became, as it were, Bertie's life's work.
Even where he has been praised as king for allowing his ministers
to get on with their jobs without interference, in contrast to his
mother, we should remember that his decision to stay out of politics
had much more to do with laziness than with political astuteness.

For Victoria, Bertie 'causes us so much anxiety', as she confided
to her diary when he was sixteen, but he had caused anxiety almost
all his life. A nurse and two nursemaids looked after Bertie and
his siblings from birth. While they were still toddlers, Lady Sarah
Lyttelton (a 'woman of rank' as Victoria describes her) taught them
French and German and then from age six they were taught by
a more professionally qualified governess, Miss Hildyard. There is
no evidence that Sarah Lyttelton was anything other than kind to
the children, but she was not their mother and relied heavily on
a team of maids. For her, looking after the children was simply a
job. Modern ideas about attachment theory – the idea that small
children need to bond emotionally with an adult caregiver if they
are to become mentally healthy adults – suggest that all Victoria
and Albert's children were damaged by a lack of attachment in their
early years.

The queen could bring herself to teach her children only one
thing: religion. As Victoria's 2014 biographer A. N. Wilson points
out, she gave all her children religious instruction except Bertie –
indeed, she could hardly bear to be in the same room as Bertie for

more than a few moments. Despite all her efforts to be nothing like her Hanoverian forebears, Victoria was identical in at least this one respect: she actively disliked her heir, just as George I and George II had disliked theirs.

From age seven, Bertie was taught by Henry Birch, a former Eton master. Birch made no progress at all with Bertie, who seemed impervious to persuasion and regular beatings; Birch was replaced by Mr Gibbs, about whom little is known beyond the fact that Bertie continued under his tutelage to fail to be the sort of boy his parents wanted him to be. Finally, in despair, Albert appointed Colonel Bruce as tutor, perhaps because he was a known quantity as he was the brother of one of the Duchess of Kent's most popular ladies-in-waiting. Bruce was far more sympathetic to Bertie and simply accepted his limitations.

Day-to-day life in the schoolroom was grim. Bertie threw books and pencils at his tutors, smashed things, hid under his desk and was continuously rude; he refused to learn anything he found uninteresting. Anxiety and stress led to an increasingly serious stammer, which in those days was often treated harshly – marbles might be placed in a child's mouth in an attempt to deal with the problem. Bertie's stammer worsened because his siblings taunted him about it – even his favourite sister, Vicky. The more difficult Bertie's problems became, the more his father beat him.

And it wasn't just recalcitrant sons who were treated harshly – Bertie's sister Princess Alice was whipped for lying, Vicky was condemned as sly and devious. But Bertie was always the least favoured child. Many of Albert's difficulties as a parent came from the fact that he had responded well to a strict, puritanical upbringing and he could never imagine it might not be possible for his son to respond to a similar regime.

Such predicaments have their modern counterparts – George V struggled to make David, later Edward VIII, take life seriously; Prince Philip struggled to make his son Charles into the tough manly military prince he felt he himself had become as a young man. George III wanted obedient dutiful sons; he ended up with promiscuous rakes.

Baffled that an effort of will could not turn their son and heir into a serious German intellectual with a taste for music and literature, Victoria and Albert even turned to phrenologists to see if there was something inherent in Bertie's skull shape that caused his problems – the phrenologist, quoted by A. N. Wilson in his biography of Victoria, concluded that the parts of Bertie's head devoted to 'destructiveness, self-esteem etc. are all large, intellectual organs only moderately developed'.

It was all nonsense, of course, but it confirmed Bertie's parents in their worst fears. And without the benefit of modern psychology, Albert and Victoria would never have considered the possibility that the fault lay at least partly with them and their obsession with what was proper for royal children. Bertie, so far as his parents were concerned, was a failure.

Bertie knew he was a huge disappointment – indeed, he was never allowed to forget it – but even as a child and teenager he saw how people deferred to him and he understood that his status would ensure that his hated childhood could be put behind him eventually and that once he was in control, his adult life could and would be filled only with the things he enjoyed. Like a number of more recent royal princes, he determined to do as he pleased in his private life and to control those around him for his own pleasure. After the puritanical diet imposed on him by his father, Bertie always ate and drank to excess as an adult; he smoked almost continually; he collected mistresses as most people collect stamps.

Had Bertie been alive in the early twenty-first century, he might have been described as a sociopath. Certainly, he never learned to empathise with those closest to him and he and his circle could be absolutely ruthless. One example will suffice. In 1868 Sir Charles Mordaunt's wife Harriet confessed to her husband that she had slept with the Prince of Wales and others. There was nothing unusual about aristocrats sleeping with each other's wives – it happened all the time – but Harriet, by confessing her adultery, had broken the rule of omertà. Her husband sued for divorce, determined to drag Bertie to court. At this even Harriet's sister Helen Forbes insisted that the main thing was not the truth of Bertie or anyone else's infidelity; for Helen, as for all those aristocrats surrounding the royal family, whatever the cost, the scandal must be suppressed. According to Jane Ridley's biography of Bertie, Helen wrote, 'Our great object is to prevent anything being brought before the public.' Despite Harriet's own doctors saying she was perfectly sane, the establishment closed ranks and Harriet was declared insane. The divorce did not happen and Bertie, though summoned as a witness, escaped a scandal that might otherwise have been far more damaging.

* * *

The damage to Bertie caused by his parents' rigid desire to control him was matched by an equal desire at least on Victoria's part to control his sisters. As with Bertie, their early years were spent with their nurses, governesses and nursemaids, but from the earliest they knew that their mother expected that as they grew their role in life was to entertain and amuse her. Each was allowed to marry only reluctantly and only when a younger daughter was ready to take their place as Victoria's constant companion.

The oppression of their childhoods stemmed from their mother's conviction that she was inherently a person of significance who deserved her role. As queen she believed that she could not be wrong. She had all the worst instincts of her more politically powerful ancestors and hated the fact that her ability to influence government policy was limited by the very settlement that brought her ancestors to England from Germany in the first place. Throughout her life, she interfered in politics and interfered in her children's lives.

Even Albert was occasionally shocked by his wife's constant complaints about the children. He wrote to her, 'The root of the trouble lies in the mistaken notion that the function of a mother is to be always correcting, scolding, ordering them about and organising their activities. It is not possible to be on happy friendly terms with people you have just been scolding.'

Albert was himself a terrific scold and Victoria was apparently enraged by the irony of being told by Albert that it was she who was the scold.

Vicky was always the closest to her mother, perhaps partly because she was Victoria's firstborn and when she arrived even Victoria enjoyed the novelty of motherhood. Vicky also responded well to her demanding parents; she was obedient and quick to learn – she was, for example, fluent in German and French before she left the nursery – and she was adored by her father, who had one of her teeth made into a brooch for the queen. Vicky survived the complaints and criticisms that so coloured her childhood and became the dutiful child her parents always wanted; after she left England to marry Frederick III of Germany, she wrote almost every day to her mother.

The youngest child was Beatrice (1857–1944), who was also Victoria's favourite, but even with Beatrice, who was always a calm and calming presence, Victoria needed to dominate – she was outraged at the least sign that Beatrice might want to spend any time away from her mother. Like her grandfather George III, Victoria felt it was perfectly reasonable to keep some if not all her children at home permanently. In George's case, an apparently close, loving family – George had no mistresses and adored his wife Queen Charlotte – still produced dysfunctional adults who grew up thinking they had been smothered as children. Victoria too, as we have seen, was smothered by her mother's protective controlling parenting, yet she repeated this with all her daughters, but perhaps most of all with Beatrice.

Victoria knew that once Beatrice had married there would be no younger daughter to replace her as secretary and companion; who would sit, hour after hour, day after day with the increasingly lonely, increasingly irritable queen? Victoria demanded and commanded love from Beatrice.

Ironically, it was Beatrice's very popularity with her mother that eventually saved the day. Beatrice was permitted to marry because

Victoria felt marriage was a woman's role and she did not want Beatrice to fail as a woman, but she still made it very clear that she felt this was a betrayal. The implication was that a dutiful child would sacrifice herself for her mother, especially a mother like Victoria who was convinced she had been the very best of mothers and therefore deserved to be treated by her children as she felt she should be treated – with absolute obedience and absolute deference.

Bertie was not the only child to rebel against what he once described as his 'eternal mother'. In Princess Louise (1848–1939), overcontrolling parenting produced a barely suppressed scandal not unlike the scandal that saw George III's daughters accused of throwing themselves at any man who hove into view – children who are locked away become desperate. It was a lesson Victoria all too often failed to understand.

Princess Louise, later Duchess of Argyll, was Victoria's sixth child and without question a rebel – always sceptical and questioning as a child, she was intelligent and as an adult became an ardent feminist, much to her mother's disgust. She supported women who wished for a career, especially a career in the arts. It says a great deal about Louise's powers of persuasion that she convinced her mother to allow her to study at the National Art Training School (now the Royal College of Art) at South Kensington. Art was the great passion of Louise's life but her friendship with the sculptor Joseph Boehm caused a scandal when, following a visit by Louise to the sculptor's studio, he was found dead from a heart attack. Though there is no evidence to prove it, gossips insisted that Boehm had died of his exertions while having sex with Louise.

Like her sisters, Louise knew that marriage was her only means of escaping her mother. She had been her mother's secretary for almost a decade by the time she married in 1871 and was frankly fed up with the restrictions this placed on her life. When Victoria realised that Louise was determined to marry, she began to look for a suitable German prince, but Louise once again put her foot down and insisted she be allowed to marry an English aristocrat, the Marquess of Lorne, later Duke of Argyll.

Princess Helena (1846–1923) was Victoria's third daughter and fifth child. Passive and obedient, she seems to have slipped almost unnoticed through the education system devised by Baron Stockmar. Still in her teens, she fell in love with her father's librarian, but the romance, which seems to have consisted entirely of passionate letter writing (many of the letters survive), was discovered by her mother, who immediately dismissed the offending official. Some time later, Helena was married off to a minor German prince, but this was allowed only on condition that Helena and her new husband live close to Victoria. The effects on Helena of her domineering mother can perhaps best be judged by the fact that when Victoria died in 1901, Helena cut herself off from the rest of the family for the rest of her life. She died in 1923.

And what of Victoria's other children? None was put under quite the level of pressure that Bertie endured, but all suffered one way or another from the repressive expectations of their parents and especially, after the death of Prince Albert in 1861, their mother.

Bertie's brother Alfred (1844–1900) – always known as Affie in the family – was the second son and fourth child. Born in 1844, he escaped the rigours of the schoolroom aged just fourteen and joined the navy. In 1862 he was offered the crown of Greece following the abdication of King Otto, and in a move that speaks volumes about the relationship between Victoria's children and their mother, it was Victoria who decided he should decline the offer.

Victoria and Albert's three younger sons were always calmer and more biddable than their elder brother – Alfred and Leopold (1853–84) were entirely compliant and easy going; Leopold, Victoria's youngest son, had genuine intellectual abilities. Prince Arthur (1850–1942), like his brother Affie, escaped the schoolroom as quickly as he could by joining the armed forces. He attended the Royal Military College at Woolwich from the age of sixteen. All knew, as more recently Prince Harry has known for as long as he has known anything, that for younger sons a life of leisure is almost a prerequisite of princely stature.

Likewise, Arthur and Affie's choice of a military career was simply a response to the limitations of royal life; for a royal prince then and now, joining the army or navy had far more to do with mixing with 'persons of rank' in the best regiments than it had to do with fighting. A military career was and remains the debased echo of that old idea of royals learning to fight.

Escape for the sisters was more difficult, as we have seen, but pressure in the schoolroom was always considerably less than it was for the boys – the girls learned to draw and paint, to play the piano and to speak French and German. By the time Princess Alice, born in 1843, had reached the schoolroom, tutors had come and gone, but as we have seen, Alice, like Helena, Beatrice, Vicky and Louise, was never under the sort of pressure that afflicted her brothers and especially, of course, Bertie.

Long after her daughters had married and left, Victoria's habit of criticising continued. If anything, it had intensified. Her diaries are filled with criticisms of her children's perceived inadequacies, and she was never afraid to criticise them to their faces.

When she discovered her daughters had breastfed their own babies, she wrote, 'It makes my hair stand on end that my daughters have turned into cows.'

Behind this visceral disgust lay a deeper dislike of her daughters' breastfeeding. Victoria hated change and this was a major break with tradition – the tradition that all royal babies were breastfed by wet nurses and looked after by nurses and nursery footmen.

All nine of Victoria's children were fed as babies by wet nurses, including Bertie, the last English king to have been wet-nursed. The fact that Bertie's wet nurse turned out to be a murderer is an extreme example but an example nonetheless of the risks of getting paid staff to do the childcare. The story is a bizarre one: Mary Ann Brough was brought in as wet nurse to Bertie when he was just a day old.

In May 1854, when Bertie had long ceased to need her but had kept vaguely in touch, Mary Ann was seen talking animatedly to a man who was not her husband. Unfortunately, George, Mary Ann's husband, who also worked in the royal household, had seen the two together and assumed they were having an affair.

Soon after, George told his wife he was leaving her and that she would not see her children again.

Having heard this, Mary Ann went home and, using her husband's razor, cut the throats of six of her seven children. She then killed herself.

* * *

Bertie suffered greatly as a child, but, as with so many members of the royal family, he continued most of the traditions of royal child-rearing. All his children were farmed out to paid staff, but Bertie was in at least one respect an improvement on his own parents. Where they interfered at every turn, he became a largely benign but almost entirely absent parent.

CHAPTER FIVE

BETTER DAUGHTERS THAN SONS: THE CHILDREN OF EDWARD VII

'It is not arms that constitute the surest safeguard of power,
but the ability to bestow favours.'

SENECA

Edward VII was a curious mix. Disliked, criticised and denigrated by his mother from as early as he could remember, he remained a child in many ways throughout his adult life. The puritanical regime inflicted on him in his formative years produced entirely the opposite effect from that intended. He was not as good or as noble or as intelligent as his revered father. He was also blamed for Albert's death. Victoria believed that Bertie's womanising had shortened her husband's life and she never let Bertie forget it.

The result of trying to make Bertie more like his father was that he actually became more like his mother – she was famous for her greed and her temper tantrums. Bertie was exactly the same: like his mother, he ate to excess and became almost as fat as his ancestor the much-hated Prince Regent; like his mother, he would fly off the handle if anything displeased him. Tantrums in the schoolroom led to beatings, but tantrums as an adult led to teams of people trying desperately to smooth his ruffled feathers.

Bertie was hugely narcissistic and lived his adult life almost as if the people with whom he became involved – especially women – had no lives independent of his need for them. All Victoria and Albert's efforts to beat a high moral sense into their son created a man who had no qualms about lying, cheating and even stealing to get what he wanted and, worse, what he thought was his due.

Recent biographers have emphasised his political astuteness – rather than interfere in politics as his mother had done, Bertie let the politicians get on with it. But this is surely being over-generous to a man who let the politicians get on with it not because he was shrewd but because he hated work and had no interest at all in politics. If others sorted all the political nonsense for him, then he had more time for shooting game, eating, sleeping with other men's wives and smoking cigars.

But just as he neglected his official duties – beyond appearing at important ceremonial events – he also neglected his children. He famously referred to his wife as his 'brood mare' – he meant that her role was simply to enable him to do the one part of his duty that he really enjoyed: producing an heir and a sufficient number of spares. He was never actively cruel to his wife, but he spent as little time with her as possible beyond having sex with her and made it very clear that he would do as he pleased regardless of her thoughts on the matter. In this respect, he was very much in the mould of his reprobate great-uncles, those wicked Georgians so deplored by his mother.

As British monarchs had lost political power over the centuries they had – and have – too much time to focus on self-indulgence; Bertie is the supreme example of this tendency, but unlike his ancestors who would dearly have loved more political power and who lamented its passing, Bertie was delighted that the rules insisted he should stay out of politics and simply enjoy himself.

Bertie had six children and he was to a large extent an indulgent parent – he had no intention of repeating for his own children the horrors he had experienced as a child, but his solution was not to be interested in his children's lives and to spend time with them. Agnes Cook, whose family members worked for the royal family for three generations, and whose unpublished memoir details the extraordinary behaviour of the royals, but especially of Edward VII, noted:

He was very sentimental about his children – when his son John [born in 1871] died at a day old, he wept openly for days. When his son and heir Albert Victor died aged just twenty-eight in 1892, Bertie was inconsolable, yet when the children were young and confined to the nursery and then the schoolroom, he took absolutely no notice of them at all. He didn't press their tutors to make them work harder; he seemed indifferent to their progress. By having children, he had done his duty and it was for others, his paid staff, to look after them and make sure they reached adulthood in one piece. Above all he hated spending time with his children because that meant time away from his various mistresses, from his life with his friends and from shooting, gambling, eating and all the rest of it.

In other words, Bertie used the royal and aristocratic traditions of childrearing to the full. He had rejected his mother's overcontrolling, super-critical attitudes and replaced them with benign indifference.

Perhaps at some level Bertie also knew that even with his own children, the long shadow of his mother's influence could not be escaped entirely because for the whole period of Bertie's young adulthood and middle age, Victoria was still alive and still insisting Bertie must do as she wished – and so it proved when, having married Princess Alexandra of Denmark (1844–1925), Victoria complained that it would have been far better if he had married a German princess. Then when Bertie had at least done his duty in terms of reproduction and fathered an heir in 1864, Victoria made it very clear that she would choose the child's names and Bertie had no choice but to acquiesce. Clearly Victoria's tantrums – or the threat of them – were enough to outweigh even Bertie's tantrums when he was told to obey.

Thus, Bertie's first son, born in 1864, was christened Albert Victor – his grandparents' first names. He was always known as Eddy. A second son born in 1865 was named George Frederick and Victoria took a great deal of persuading that it should not be Frederick George. She disliked the name George as it was too Hanoverian and no doubt reminded her of those wicked uncles. She also laid down the law about how all her grandchildren, those already born and those to come, were to be treated. Bertie, she wrote, to her daughter Vicky, 'should never do anything about the children without consulting me'. No wonder later in life, Bertie was to complain after a church service that it was all very well having an eternal father, but he was the only person afflicted with an 'eternal mother'.

As with her own children, Victoria swung wildly between sentimentality when she thought about her grandchildren and outright dislike, even disgust. She wrote a calm, reasoned letter to her daughter Vicky to say that Albert Victor was 'very placid, almost melancholy'; she occasionally even praised the children, but the habit of criticising was never far away and she even complained about Bertie's wife, Princess Alexandra. She protested bitterly that Alexandra did not believe in beating her children. Despite the failure of Bertie's continual beatings as a child, she still thought that sparing the rod would spoil the child.

Bertie's second son George, later George V (1865–1936), was shorter than his elder brother, spoke with a lisp and seemed worryingly puny – in another echo down through history, his speech impediment was combined with a serious case of knock knees, just like his ancestor Charles I, who, we may recall, had great difficulty speaking and walking. In relation to George, Bertie did manage at least one significant change in the relation between parent and child – where Victoria had kept Bertie completely out of her official work as sovereign, Bertie was happy to give George access to state papers and official documents.

Bertie and Alexandra were to have a total of six children, three boys and three girls. They were the first royal children not to be put out to wet nurses, but the nursery tradition remained for them just as it had been in past centuries. They saw their parents formally once a day if Bertie was not away (as he often was) and their needs were met by a team of nurserymaids, governess and nursery footmen. Once out of the nursery, they found themselves caught up in the same routine that their father had endured in the schoolroom but with far less beating and almost no parental interference. Conscious of who they were, as Victoria's children had been, they were mischievous – in her 1935 biography of Annie, Lady Rothschild, Helen Cohen quotes a letter written by Lady Rothschild in 1869 after she met the royal children. They were, she says, 'unruly and rather wild' – but they were far more biddable than Bertie had himself been.

George had his father's tendency to tantrums and enjoyed sometimes cruel practical jokes, but these were nipped in the bud to some extent by an incident that occurred when he was five. Told off by an old family servant called Mr Collins, George responded by kicking Mr Collins in the shin. Collins told the boy that if he did it again, he would be smacked. Clearly thinking that a prince was above being chastised by a mere servant, George kicked Mr Collins again. George was duly smacked and was astonished to discover that when he complained to his tutors, the blame for the incident was laid entirely at his door. A remarkably similar incident was to occur almost a century later when, according to a Windsor Castle gamekeeper interviewed by the present author, Prince Andrew had a tantrum and kicked a member of the castle staff, convinced that, as a prince, he would not be criticised or blamed.

Eddy, unlike George, did not kick or scream, but he seems to have done nothing else either. He could barely concentrate, was a poor reader and seemed unable to apply himself to anything in the schoolroom other than looking out of the window.

Dolly West, who worked as a maid at Buckingham Palace in the 1930s, remembered George in later life:

All the servants, even the senior servants, were terrified of him because he would lose his temper in a split second and scream at people. We never saw George in person – the butler and other senior servants organised things so George never laid eyes on us – but you could hear him roar from half a mile away. I once heard him screaming at what I assumed must be his valet – I couldn't believe the words he used. Fuck was the least of it.

George, it seems, had inherited the tendency to sudden rages that afflicted both his father and grandmother.

Bertie was open about the fact that he wanted his children to have a more 'liberal education' than he had experienced, but he had no real idea what this might mean. On leaving the nursery, the children were handed over to the Reverend John Dalton. Each day their lessons continued from 7 a.m. until 2 p.m., studying history, maths, French and the Bible. In the afternoons, they were allowed to play games and to ride in the park.

Bertie, we may recall, was taught by a number of tutors – one after another they left or were sacked because Bertie was so difficult. In the case of Bertie's own children, things were different and although their tutor John Dalton complained the children were 'silly, fretful and lazy', he nonetheless stayed for some fourteen years. And if Bertie was almost permanently absent on shooting weekends with his numerous mistresses – most famously Mrs Keppel and the actress Lillie Langtry – Princess Alexandra chose (perhaps partly because Bertie was always absent) to be far more involved in the early lives of her children, even to the extent of bathing them as babies. She also breastfed them, to the horror of her mother-in-law.

Bertie's third child, Louise, was born in 1867, followed by Princess Victoria in 1868. By now their grandmother Victoria was bored and irritated by her son's brood, writing that the new arrival, Princess Victoria, was a 'mere little red lump'. In 1869 Maud was born, then, in 1871 Bertie and Alexandra's last child was born at Sandringham, Prince Alexander John, who died a few hours after he was born. Worn out with childrearing, Princess Alexandra had become semi-disabled by now and was increasingly left alone by Bertie. Certainly, there were no more children.

During her third pregnancy, she had developed rheumatic fever which left her with a severe limp. The bizarre influence of the royal family could be seen even here – upper-class women began to copy Alexandra by pretending they too had a limp!

With the death of Prince John, the death in 1892 of her eldest son Eddy and the permanent absence of her husband, not to mention her own increasing ill health, Alexandra became a gloomy, almost permanently depressed figure.

* * *

Despite a far less rigorous regime than Bertie had himself experienced, his children – with the exception of Princess Maud – showed no enthusiasm for schoolwork. Like all royal children in the modern era, the fact that their birth alone gave status and wealth seems to have sapped any will to learn or do anything beyond, for the boys, joining the navy, and for the girls, making a good marriage. It was as if education was something that simply had to be got through but that meant little to children who knew from the time they knew anything that ambition and the desire to find some work to do was both unnecessary and to some extent undignified. Like the English aristocracy, the royal family saw work as a low-status activity; they were supremely members of the leisured classes and much of their status actually depended on the fact that they did not have to work to survive. It must have been a huge shock to the aristocracy and royalty when these centuries-old ideas began to be questioned. Shock waves hurtled through English society when Prime Minister Lloyd George, speaking to supporters in Newcastle upon Tyne in 1909, described the House of Lords, then filled with landed peers who did no work, as 'a body of 500 men chosen at random from amongst the unemployed'.

Edward VII's children were lucky in one respect. There is no evidence that their nurses and nannies were anything other than kind to them – as we will see, this was not the case for Edward's grandsons – and Alexandra enjoyed spending time with them. These were healthy attachments because at least one parent was involved with their early lives. Victoria was revolted by her daughter-in-law's break with tradition.

Given his continual and very public breaking of various commandments, it is extraordinary that Bertie insisted his children pray and read the Bible each day. The two boys were also taught about art and architecture but found both intensely boring. Bertie kept well away, beyond occasionally telling them to work hard, and this was a great relief to Alexandra, who dreaded that either boy should become like their father.

Alexandra took a close interest in all her children, but she was constantly aware that her mother-in-law would always insist on having the final say. The boys' tutor, the Revd Dalton, was under strict instructions, for example, to report to Victoria every week.

Bertie's brood were allowed to play only with other royal children – they played often with their cousins, the children of Mary Adelaide of Teck, who was the daughter of the seventh son of George III. They were boisterous, even unruly and like many extended family groups, they developed numerous in-jokes and nicknames – Princess Victoria was known as 'Gawks', Louise as 'Toots' and Maud as 'Snipey'. Bertie was so often absent with his various mistresses – Alexandra quipped when he died that for the first time ever, she knew where he was – but occasionally he would descend on the schoolroom and attempt to change everything.

As they were hopeless academically, Bertie decided that both his sons should join the navy – military service once again, as throughout royal history, seemed the right thing for royal sons. Did Bertie really feel his sons might go to war to protect England as their medieval ancestors had done? It is doubtful. Bertie was simply and unthinkingly acknowledging that royal princes do certain things and don't do others. Whether their sons are likely to be useful and talented soldiers and sailors is never the issue.

No sooner had he announced that the boys were to enter the navy than his mother insisted that they should go instead to Wellington College. Victoria seems to have had no idea that Eddy and George were so hopeless academically that they were unlikely to be able to pass the entrance exam. It was only when the boys' tutor explained the problem that Victoria gave up her plan. She shifted

her ground and thought Eddy might attend the college on his own
– still assuming that he would be admitted simply because for her
it was unthinkable that the heir to the throne should be rejected
by any institution. In this she was probably right, but one curious
aspect of Eddy's character made the idea completely unworkable.
He had achieved almost nothing in the classroom, but his tutor had
noticed that he would at least exert himself a little if his brother
George was in the room. If George was absent, no power on heaven
or earth could get Eddy to exert himself.

In the end, both princes did indeed join the navy. Victoria was
persuaded that Eddy would only learn in the company of his brother
and even in the navy some level of intellectual application would
be necessary. Joining the navy at the young age of sixteen (it was
often fourteen) might seem almost barbaric from the point of view
of the twenty-first century, but for the royal family at the end of
the nineteenth century, it neatly combined ancient ideas about the
value of sending princes to live away from their families as early as
possible with the royal obsession with the idea of the nobility of the
'profession of arms'.

In the navy, old patterns repeated themselves – Eddy, so said his
tutor John Dalton in one of his regular reports to Victoria, was
doing well but not really exerting himself. George, as ever, was
doing better. Both were teased by their fellow sailors – George
became known as 'Sprat', a nickname coined because his father was
Prince of Wales.

The two boys' time at Dartmouth College ended in 1879 and,
with Dalton still insisting Eddy would do nothing without George,
the two boys were sent – with Dalton as a kind of chaperone – on

a three-year tour of the dominions. Being sent away was combined, in Australia at least, with endless outings to shoot kangaroos and even albatross. Once again, as in all previous generations of royal males, the use of the gun to kill animals was somehow seen as a noble pursuit.

Despite the presence of Dalton, word began to trickle back to England that Eddy had a persistent habit at every port at which their ship, HMS *Bacchante*, called of disappearing with the ratings. It was assumed that he was visiting brothels, which was shocking enough, but later events were to be even more damaging: back in London, it was rumoured, as we will see, that his tastes ran to gay brothels.

Some idea of Eddy's difficulties in the academic sphere can be judged by the fact that his brother George, always more competent, failed to learn to speak either French or German despite intense tutoring. The joke in royal circles was that George was almost a genius compared to his brother, since Eddy could barely manage English. Typically, Eddy would begin a vague sentence and then, just as people began to listen to him, the sentence would fade away into nothing and Eddy, with a lordly wave of his hand, would walk off.

Eddy was physically very different from his brother – he was tall, very quiet and unobtrusive, even perhaps introspective. He was over-emotional, slow to anger and slightly effeminate with a shockingly high-pitched voice. His vaguely effeminate air and general similarity to his mother may explain why he was very much her favourite child. He was very close to his younger brother George, perhaps because George was such a contrast – loud, more obviously masculine, quick to anger and inclined to play slightly cruel practical jokes on people.

After the navy, there was a suggestion that Eddy should go to Cambridge, which he duly did in 1883, but he never completed his studies there. In fact, he was sent down – Cambridge code for expelled – for 'immoral acts', a phrase frequently used at the time to signify specifically homosexual acts. He was later awarded an honorary degree and must be one of few Cambridge graduates who, at least according to his admissions tutor James Stephen, was actually unable to read. Desperately trying to find something Eddy could do now, Bertie arranged for him to be commissioned into the 10th Hussars. Here, too, he failed to shine; in fact, he was a hopeless soldier – he could not learn the simplest drill exercise and showed an interest only in making sure his uniforms were perfectly pressed. He seemed to think soldiering was about dressing up, as one of his contemporaries wrote. George, meanwhile, remained in the navy.

All Bertie's children and grandchildren were expected to visit their grandmother Victoria regularly and like many strict parents, she softened towards her grandchildren. Princess Alice, the daughter of Victoria's son Prince Leopold, Duke of Albany, lived until 1981 and she recalled in her memoirs – *For My Grandchildren*, published in 1966 – how Queen Victoria would allow Alice and her siblings to build walls with her despatch boxes and play around her while she worked, an indulgence she would never have extended to her own children.

*   *   *

One curious fact remains to be told about Prince Eddy, who but for his premature death would have become king instead of his younger brother George. Eddy's father and George had both contracted typhoid and recovered when Eddy fell ill early in 1892 with flu – typhoid was a far more dangerous illness than flu, but Eddy's flu became pneumonia. Dolly West, who worked for the royal family in the 1930s, explained that rumours persisted down the decades about what really happened to Eddy when he fell ill:

My mother Gladys, who was in service in Edward VII's time, said that the servants were still convinced decades after Eddy's death that Eddy was such an embarrassment that he had not been given quite the care and attention he should have had. The family were devoted to him – I don't mean them. I mean the courtiers who control much of what goes on around the family. They thought Eddy was hopeless and awful. Servants tend to exaggerate when they gossip, it is true, but it is definitely also true that rumours about Eddy's liking for boys persisted through his adult life and long after he died. It wasn't just the Cleveland Street scandal that he had been involved in – you know where he was suspected of having been a regular customer at that homosexual brothel – it was also that everyone was worried that he would be a disaster if he ever became king. He couldn't remember anything for more than five minutes and seemed, some people said, slightly brain damaged, so when he got flu, so the servants said, it was allowed to run its course – I'm sure it was just gossip, but they thought the doctors didn't try as hard as they might have to save him.

I suppose it's not that different from George V's doctor giving him a lethal dose of morphine in 1936 when it was obvious he was going to die anyway and the king's entourage thought it was better the king should die at a time when the best newspapers could report it first rather than the gutter press. Just shows that the royal family may seem to have it all their own way, but there are always dark forces behind the throne.

Agnes Cook, another royal servant, several generations of whose family had worked for the royals around this time, agreed. She said, 'Among the servants, Eddy was referred to sometimes as a Nancy boy – not a very nice phrase, but I'm afraid people didn't think back then that a king in waiting should behave as Eddy behaved. He just seemed effeminate and fey.'

Dolly West's and Agnes Cook's family memories certainly tie in with much that later biographers have written. Philip Magnus's 1964 biography of Eddy even goes so far as to say that there was relief all round when Eddy died – Magnus insists that it was 'an act of providence'.

Whatever the truth of the rumours about Eddy's death, we should remember that his final illness was probably made much worse by his heavy drinking and smoking and the fact that he was already suffering from gout. He may well also have been suffering from syphilis.

With the death of Eddy, bad-tempered George became his father's heir, but what happened to those carefully sheltered sisters?

Known as the 'whispering Wales' from their habit of speaking quietly when they were among adults they did not know well, two went on to make the sort of matches that royal princesses were expected to make. One remained unmarried.

The curious thing about Edward VII's children – and this applies to so many generations of the royal family – is that his daughters would have made far better monarchs than his sons. Like their brothers, the three sisters, Louise, Victoria and Maud were not intellectuals, nor were they passionate about much beyond their own status, but they were less egotistical, less sure of their importance, less convinced that, in the private sphere at least, they could do as they pleased. If the purpose of the modern monarch is to be a figurehead who provides a moral lead but does not interfere in politics and does not get involved in scandal, then the daughters win every time. From the very earliest, Edward VII's daughters knew they were not, ultimately, the important ones and this instilled in them a degree of humility and a lack of egotism that would have made them far better monarchs than either of their brothers.

It is no coincidence that Britain's two greatest monarchs are, arguably, Elizabeth I and Elizabeth II.

The princesses' education was not that different from their brothers: they rode but did not shoot, kept numerous pets, learned French and German, history and architecture, as well as music and painting, all genteel activities in keeping with their station. There were eccentric pursuits too – they learned to make butter and cheese in the Sandringham dairies and they were taught fencing and golf, but they knew like their brothers that no amount of effort or striking ability would make any difference to lives whose purpose and destiny were fixed at birth. It was assumed they would marry well, probably to royal cousins or at least into the English aristocracy or into the other European monarchies – Maud married King Haakon VII of Norway; Louise married the 6th Earl of Fife. Only Victoria remained unmarried. She was very close to her mother, Queen Alexandra, and although Victoria's cousin the Grand Duchess Olga of Russia thought Victoria had wasted her life being a 'maid' to her mother, Victoria never seems to have complained and there is no evidence that Alexandra had tried to keep Victoria as her companion.

The three girls' grandmother, though occasionally indulgent, did not always warm to them, confiding to her journal that they were 'puny and pale'. They were taught by governesses, but in the nineteenth century the strict demarcation between the classes meant that governesses rarely became friends with their royal charges – such familiarities were seen as impossible before a more democratic age led to governesses such as Bobo MacDonald, the daughter of a railway worker, who looked after Queen Elizabeth II as a child and remained with her for the rest of her life, becoming one of Elizabeth's closest friends.

Edward VII's third child, Louise, later the Princess Royal, was probably the shyest of the three – she was almost as introspective as her brother Eddy. In 1889 she married the Earl of Fife, who was eighteen years her senior. She seems to have slipped through the rest of her life almost unnoticed, although she had a son and two daughters. She died in 1931.

Victoria, the liveliest of the sisters, was also the most eccentric. When she grew up, she retained many of her childish enthusiasms

– she always travelled with her pet pigeon in a small cage, for example. In fact, she would refuse to travel at all if her pigeon was not allowed to accompany her. She also enjoyed cycling – much to the horror of her grandmother – and was a talented photographer. She rejected several suitors. Her mother, Queen Alexandra, always insisted that she wanted all her daughters to marry but, isolated by her philandering husband and almost continually ill, she clearly aroused a deep sympathy in Victoria who found it impossible to contemplate leaving her. Alexandra enjoyed the company of her daughter for the rest of her life. Whether she felt that becoming her mother's companion until her death was a waste of life she never said. She died in 1935. Ghostly recordings of her playing the piano still exist.

Only one of Edward VII's children might almost be described as an intellectual: Maud. She was fluent in French, German and Russian and was the complete opposite of Victoria and Louise – where they were quiet and unobtrusive, she was loud and tomboyish. She married Prince Carl of Denmark and became Queen of Norway when her husband was offered the crown in 1905, following the dissolution of the union between Norway and Sweden in the same year. She died in 1938.

When Queen Victoria died in 1901, Bertie became Edward VII, but weakened by obesity, smoking and alcohol dependence, he was to reign for barely ten years. George was forty-five when he became king and he had already married and sired six children, including the future Edward VIII and George VI.

George V the man can be clearly discerned in George V the child; above all was his determination not to be like his father. He was embarrassed by very public reports of his father's drinking and philandering and he became just the sort of man his grandmother would have liked Bertie to be. He was a serious, sober adult who hated flamboyance or any kind of show; he combined a love of shooting and obsessively cleaning and checking his guns with a determination to live as far as possible out of the public eye. Terrified by the battering that royal families across Europe had suffered after the Great War, he decided to live in decidedly middle-class splendour in what by palace standards was the rather pokey York Cottage in the Sandringham grounds. And away from the shooting field, he made sure his only other great interest was as middle class as possible – he collected stamps.

CHAPTER SIX

THE RETURN OF KNOCK KNEES: THE CHILDREN OF GEORGE V

'Growing up is losing some illusions, in order to acquire others.'

VIRGINIA WOOLF

George V started off the way he meant to continue. He said to his friend Lord Derby, 'My father was frightened of his mother, I was frightened of my father, and I am damned well going to see that my children are frightened of me.'

Recent biographers have tended to downplay this as bravado or hyperbole (or even as an entirely invented story), but given widespread agreement about George's harsh, judgemental nature and legendary bad temper, one suspects George meant every word of it. In truth, George V was not a very nice man. He was as obsessed with stern morality and duty as his grandmother Queen Victoria had been and he was just as dull.

Certainly, he applied the rules of duty and domestic strictness as much to himself as to his children, but the disgust he felt as a result of his father's serial infidelities left him puritanically minded, overly critical and almost entirely humourless. If he was horrible to his courtiers – and he was – he was far worse with his children. He seemed to combine in one man the worst attributes of Albert and Victoria. He never played with his children when they were very young and saw them for just twenty minutes each day. Their nurse had to take care that the children were formally dressed for these meetings.

The children were also instructed to bow before speaking. He lectured them continually and the least infringement of the rules led to violent rages that terrified his wife, his children and the staff. Royal biographer Hugo Vickers reminds us that George's third son, Prince Henry, described him as a 'terrible father'. Queen Mary would defend the children if she thought her husband was being especially unfair or unreasonable, but her protests were always mild – she was a traditional Victorian woman who believed her husband was ultimately always right whether he wanted her to become pregnant again or wanted to chastise his children.

Dolly West, recalling her life as a teenager in the royal kitchens long after George had become king, said:

Everyone was afraid of him. We didn't see him, of course. In those days a king, especially a king like George, would have stepped over a dead servant if he'd seen one lying in the street. We were invisible to him, but he was not invisible to us, if you see what I mean. Servants always know what's going on in a big house. The talk among the servants was that he was a bit mad because he never smiled at anyone. It must have been terrifying for his children but especially his sons – I was told that they called him the ogre or the beast and dreaded it when he wanted to see them but that was very rarely. He was also obsessed with the idea that his people should only see a stern-faced monarch. I think he was nervous that if he smiled or made a joke, people would think he wasn't taking the job seriously, and as the monarchy nearly fell in 1914 what with war with Germany, he wanted to make sure that didn't happen on his watch. He wanted to seem like someone who never misbehaved or was frivolous. His father had had fun and misbehaved and George was ashamed of him, I think.

George's sudden losses of temper and his obsession with correct form and duty above all things produced one son with a permanently timid, frightened air – who also developed a terrible stammer – and a wayward, reckless heir who had all the worst qualities of self-indulgence and promiscuity that typified his grandfather Edward VII. Once again, as we saw with Victoria and her children, in trying to produce a serious, dutiful son as much unlike his own father as possible, George V produced yet another heir to the throne who drank, smoked, slept with other men's wives, lied and cheated.

Edward VII was not an ogre at least so far as his children were concerned, but if he was benign, he was also aloof and detached; his son George was also detached and emotionally distant, but he combined this with a hypercritical personality that was highly damaging to his children.

Victoria was a stern moralist in contrast to her wicked uncles. She was controlling and clingy like her grandfather George III. Her son became exactly like one of those wicked uncles. Her grandson George V reverted to type and was far more like Victoria – stern, rather forbidding, dutiful, bad tempered and permanently scarred by his father's infidelities to his mother. After the stern moralist that was George V, his eldest son David became a rake much like Edward VII, his grandfather. History for the royal family is rather like a mad dance in which the patterns endlessly repeat themselves.

If history tends to repeat itself, then in the royal family, history – to switch metaphors – always seems to repeat itself with the pendulum swinging wildly from one extreme to the other. Even while they try to be different from their parents, each royal generation finds it impossible to escape all the worst aspects of childhood, and even by trying to be very different, they tend to go from one extreme to another.

Perhaps the key reason for this is that until very recently the British royal family has mixed with and married into a very narrow social band. Childrearing traditions tend as a result to change far more slowly than they do for the middle and working classes, and central to aristocratic and royal childrearing is the idea, as we have seen, of paying other people to do the work.

The experience of George V's sons David (later Edward VIII) and George (later George VI) illustrates how badly the system can go wrong. Given over almost entirely to the care of nursery staff from day one, royal and aristocratic children are always being cared for by people whose commitment to the children's welfare is contractual and contingent. They do it not out of love but because they are paid.

And what begins in the nursery, that early contracting out of parental responsibility, continues with the modern practice of sending royal children to boarding school. Schools such as Eton and Harrow (lesser schools are rarely considered for royalty) are the modern equivalent to the medieval practice of sending royal princes to live away from home with other noble families. In these houses and boarding schools, many children were bullied and abused – including Prince Charles, now Charles III, as we will see.

The repetition of foolish childrearing practices stems to a great extent from embedded ideas about social class, which is why even today the children of Prince William, for example, will not attend a state school even in their earliest years.

Reputation, in the case of boarding schools, and letters of recommendation, in the case of nannies and nurses, can never eliminate the risk to the children.

Traditionally, nannies were always childless – they were expected to have either no children or grown-up children – as they were expected to live twenty-four hours a day, seven days a week with their royal charges. They were expected to devote their lives to the royal children and this meant psychologically unstable women were sometimes drawn to the profession; the demands were too great for anyone who wanted any sort of private life of their own. This is why figures such as Bobo MacDonald capture the imagination – like many royal nannies over the centuries, she devoted her whole life to royal service. For some women, this level of devotion, which truth to tell has something of the fanatic about it, was untroubled and untroubling, but for others it was asking too much and they took it out on their charges and this was spectacularly the case with George V's sons.

*   *   *

When George V's elder brother Eddy died, his wife-to-be Mary of Teck (1867–1953), popularly known as May, was quickly pushed in the direction of George, who dutifully agreed to marry her. This cannot have been a love match. The couple married because they were dynastically suitable, just as Charles marrying Diana was not a love match but something deemed suitable by others. In a wonderful mixture of the sublime and the ridiculous, when the family decided George should marry his brother's former fiancée, the code for the precise moment when George should propose was decided: George and May were staying at George's sister Louise's house, East Sheen Lodge near Richmond, with the rest of the family, and at the appointed hour, George was told to take May into the garden to show her 'the frogs'. He showed her the frogs (no doubt she delighted in them) and proposed. She, of course, accepted. It would have been unthinkable for her not to accept the man who was heir to the throne. Inevitably, they were cousins.

There were echoes of the past in George marrying a woman formerly betrothed to his elder brother; when Henry VIII married Catherine of Aragon, for example, he was marrying a woman who had previously been married to his dead brother Arthur.

It was a suitable arrangement and nothing more. For George, the death of his brother had brought his duty into sharp focus; he had to be king and he had to marry the woman he was told to marry, but he did not have to be a glutton and a philanderer as his father had been. Indeed, in his almost puritanical attitude to life, he was the exact opposite of his father.

George and May, by all accounts, became very fond of each other – some biographers have insisted they were deeply in love from the start, but this seems unlikely given how much pressure was applied, especially by Queen Victoria, who decided that May would be suitable as queen.

Long before he became king, George determined to be a very different monarch from his father, but in trying to escape his fate, in some respects, George ran towards it. He was never a pleasure-seeker, but his obsession with duty and respectability, though they would have made Queen Victoria proud, caused untold damage to the next generation.

George and May had six children, five boys and a girl. Their first child, the future Edward VIII (1894–1972), was born at White Lodge, Richmond. No sooner had he been born than his great-grandmother Victoria insisted on becoming involved in the decision about the child's name. She had already made it clear that she expected all her male heirs to be named Albert, and rather than battle it out with a woman of whom both George (later George V) and Bertie (later Edward VII) were afraid, they agreed the new arrival should be christened Albert. They dug their heels in when it came to choosing Albert as a first name, however, and the boy was christened Edward Albert Christian George Andrew Patrick David. In the family he was never known as Edward or Albert but as David.

George and May were not so lucky when their second child, also a son, was born a year later – he was born on 14 December, the anniversary of Albert's death in 1861, which may explain why when Victoria wrote enquiring after her great-grandchildren in the years that followed, she never mentioned this second child.

Sensing that his second son (who was given the first name Albert to appease Victoria) lived in the shadow of his elder sibling as he himself had lived in the shadow of his elder sister Vicky, his grandfather Bertie, with uncharacteristic sensitivity, made a point of writing regularly to him.

Like his grandfather, Albert was always known as Bertie. From the outset he was plagued by health problems. He had the royal knock knees that dated back to Charles I and beyond and his legs were seen as such a serious problem that he was forced to wear painful splints as a child – he was altogether physically frail compared to his brother.

Bertie's dreadful stammer, which he never fully overcame, and his hatred of public speaking and even of being in the public eye arose as a direct result of childhood experiences that mirror the difficulties George V (his father) experienced as a child. Emotionally cold, overly serious and deeply critical just like his grandmother, George was prone to sudden rages and he expected his children to be strictly formal at all times.

With an ogre for a father, the children inevitably suffered. Bertie began to stammer as his grandfather had done and every time his father bellowed at him, the young Bertie's stammer worsened. He was left-handed, but in keeping with the practice of the time this was seen as something entirely unacceptable (perhaps because of vague ancient ideas about left-handed people being in league with the devil – the Latin for 'left' is 'sinister') and Bertie was forced to write with his right hand. Coping with a stammer, the painful splints and the correction of his left-handedness turned Bertie into an adult barely able to cope with life – had he not been surrounded by servants and born into a particular role, it is difficult to imagine what he might have done.

Bertie's father George made all these problems more difficult because he was an emotionally cold and deeply critical man. Former maid Dolly West remembered the gossip among the servants.

He was as hard as nails, that was the view of the servants. People say we didn't know what they were like in private but we did – word always trickled down from the servants who looked after and waited on the children and occasionally saw and heard what went on between them and their parents. George would rather have died than kiss or hug any of his children.

If George was a terrible parent, his wife May was little better. She was profoundly unmaternal in ways that echoed Queen Victoria's own maternal shortcomings. Like her husband, she was cold and unemotional. Both were entirely lacking in humour or playfulness. Both were locked into the habits and practices of their class, so their sons and daughter, also Mary, were left, from birth, almost entirely in the care of teams of servants who it was continually emphasised should not be over-familiar with or over-friendly to the children.

In *Loyal to Three Kings*, her biography of her husband, royal aide Sir Alec Hardinge, Helen Hardinge quotes his comment about George V as a parent: Hardinge asked why a man who seemed reasonably kind to most of those around him should be 'such a brute to his children'. Hardinge's evidence is unimpeachable – he was a member of an ancient aristocratic family that had always hovered around and served the monarchy and he had worked as George V's private secretary from 1920.

Queen Mary's lady-in-waiting the Countess of Airlie, a woman who would never dare to criticise a queen, would only remark, as John Van der Kiste explains in his biography of George, that the problem for David and Bertie and their brothers and sister was that neither of their parents had 'any understanding of a child's mind'. Dolly West, a little more succinctly, said, 'George was a brute.'

Part of George's problem was inheritance: he came from a long line of royal parents who disliked their sons, and especially their firstborn sons. But Bertie and David had an extra difficulty – the nurse employed to look after them was probably mentally ill but was certainly sadistic.

The nurse, whose name has not been revealed, came with the highest recommendations, but it is highly unlikely that George and May would have had anything to do with employing the nurse. Others would have seen her references – supplied in this case by the Duchess of Newcastle – and offered her the job, but of course, references can be forged and what works for one employer may not work for another.

Whatever the explanation, the nurse turned out to be a cruel woman who made sure – as she was bound to – that no one noticed what she was doing to the children. Left more or less to her own devices with the children, the nurse quickly developed a loathing of the younger boy, Bertie, and she made sure he had less to eat than his older brother – well before he had finished eating or drinking, she would remove his bottle or his plate. But for different reasons Bertie's brother David was also abused. Just before the two children were brought in to see their parents for their once-a-day meeting, the nurse would pinch David until he screamed. Faced with a screaming toddler, George and May would immediately tell the nurse to take the children away. For the nurse, control may have been the issue – if the boys screamed when they saw their parents, she would always be needed to calm them down and the parents would begin to think that the children were just difficult.

A more junior nurse, Charlotte Bill, terrified of the head nurse, eventually became so concerned at how the children were being treated that she risked her career by telling the housekeeper what was going on. It must have been a great relief to her that rather than being sacked, she was believed and the sadistic nurse was immediately fired, but she had had plenty of time to wreak havoc – David was born in 1894 and the nurse was not dismissed until 1897.

Charlotte Bill (known as Lala to the children) was a far kinder nurse who treated the boys well, but she was not their mother and it is a truism of modern psychology that nannies cause insecurity because they are usually temporary; their affection is, by definition, conditional. They are employed and may leave to be employed elsewhere. The royal family have traditionally seen this as irrelevant – if a nanny leaves, she is replaced because monarchs have tended to think of nurses and nannies as important only insofar as the child's physical needs are met. In an interview with the present author, Prince Philip dismissed any importance being placed on the psychological welfare of his children – he thought this was mollycoddling and said, 'I think children should be toughened up and just get on with it. We fuss far too much about children's sensitivities and emotional well-being. It's largely nonsense.'

The abuse of children by paid nannies is not that unusual. Anne Glenconner, a maid of honour at Elizabeth II's coronation, recalls in her memoir how Miss Bead, her nanny, would tie her hands to the bed every night regardless of whether she had behaved well or badly during the day. Glenconner, tellingly, explains that she thought her mother must have ordered the nurse to do this.

And despite her own awful experience of being looked after by nannies, Glenconner in turn employed nannies for her children. The eldest two may not have been tortured by their nannies, but their father continually sacked the carers (Lord Glenconner was himself sadistic and mentally unstable) and so the two boys in their earliest years never experienced a stable, loving relationship with a significant adult. As an adult Charles became a heroin addict and died from hepatitis C aged thirty-nine; Henry died from AIDS aged thirty.

Like Lady Glenconner, George V, whatever his reservations about his own childhood, would never have considered looking after his own children. By 1902 Charlotte Bill's nannying services were being supplemented by the efforts of head nursery footman Frederick Finch. Finch, though no great intellectual, was able to balance discipline and tolerance in such a way that he became very popular with both boys – indeed, Finch stayed with the royal family until his retirement in 1935. But Finch was not responsible for much in the way of teaching beyond Bible reading and getting the children to bed on time. The boys' formal education was left to a former schoolmaster, Henry Hansell, who suggested it would be best if the two boys were sent away to school – a suggestion dismissed by George and May. Royal princes were always privately tutored – it was still a mark of status – and George and May were not going to go against tradition, whatever the arguments for and against it.

Hansell wasn't as popular with the children as Finch, but he dutifully put his charges through a lesson plan that had remained largely unchanged for more than a century. The boys learned French and
German (David was fluent in both languages), art and architecture,
Bible studies and mathematics. A suggestion that the boys learn
woodwork or some other craft was met with great disapproval –
working with one's hands was not for princes, as it had not been
for more than a thousand years. But there was one activity which
the boys were permitted to take part in occasionally to the astonishment (and disapproval) of royal officials. Now and then the boys
were allowed to play football with the local village boys at Sandringham. Hansell was approved of by David and Bertie's parents
not because he was a great teacher or particularly intellectual; they
liked him because he was the son of a Norfolk country gentleman
and therefore by extension a gentleman himself.

Neither David nor Bertie enjoyed lessons. Like their father and
uncles, they suffered from an affliction to which all royal males seem
prone – a strange kind of intellectual lethargy. It afflicts younger
sons most acutely and stems from the simple fact that whatever
royal princes do in the classroom or on the sporting field or anywhere else, their fate is essentially sealed at birth. Occasionally – and
William, Prince of Wales, is a good example – a royal prince feels
well suited to his role, but this usually only applies to direct heirs.
Younger brothers struggle with knowing they will never be king
but cannot go out into the world and do something other than be
a member of the royal family. The supreme examples are, of course,
Edward VIII after his abdication and, in more recent times, Prince
Harry's decision to live in the United States. As a cadet at the Royal

Naval College, Osborne, from 1909, David was consistently bottom of the class.

David and Bertie both disliked being princes. And that dislike made any real exertion in the schoolroom completely pointless, as it had for so many earlier generations of royals. They would always have riches beyond the dreams of most of their subjects, so work was never a necessity. Duty eventually became something real for Bertie, but this was largely because he felt he must step into the breach after the abdication of his brother. Had he spent his early life knowing that the crown would eventually be his, there is little doubt that his childhood would have been even more difficult than it was. David, despite his popularity when Prince of Wales, knew he was always going to be king and he hated it, largely because he had no choice in the matter and was constantly pressured by his parents to be highly moral, serious and hard working. The details were different, of course, but fundamentally, the pressure applied to Bertie by his parents was identical to that applied by Victoria and Albert to their sons.

*   *   *

Bertie imagined he would spend his life moving between various grand houses, enjoying country sports, supporting his brother occasionally by taking on some royal duties but generally staying out of the limelight with his wife and children. David (Edward VIII) was in many ways well suited to the role of king; he was more outgoing and sociable than Bertie and despite his childhood experiences had a charm that made him popular. Bertie spent his early years trying not to be seen – his shyness was legendary. If he was barely noticed, he could hardly be badly treated. Even his marriage to Elizabeth Bowes-Lyon, later the Queen Mother (1900–2002), was clearly a reaction to his difficult childhood – she became almost entirely a mother figure who bolstered him, looked after him and guided him, especially once he became king. Bertie was so damaged by his early experiences that being forced to be king when he had never expected it was enormously stressful for him. The Queen Mother always blamed David for her husband's early death and could never forgive him. The blame game echoes that of Queen Victoria, who, despite decades of widowhood, never forgave her son for the death of Prince Albert.

Neither Victoria nor the Queen Mother was able to look beyond the battles of their closed world; neither was able to step outside their strange cut-off existence to see that in Victoria's case, Albert's death had nothing to do with her son; and Edward VIII's abdication was not the reason for his brother's early death. George VI was an emotionally and physically fragile man who smoked cigarettes continually – cancer meant he had to have part of one lung removed in 1951 – and it is arguable that he was lucky to live as long as he did. Blaming the abdication for Bertie's death was a typical piece of royal histrionics, but one that says a great deal about a family whose overriding aim is not to serve the British people – though in many ways they do that well – but to survive.

It was George V, after all, who told the government not to offer sanctuary to his cousin Tsar Nicholas after the Bolshevik Revolution in Russia, in case this angered the British public and made them turn against the royal family – a family already unpopular because of its German origins and connections. Other relatives in addition to the Tsar were also repudiated and the British royal family renounced all its German titles.

Where Bertie grew into a young man in search of a mother figure, his brother David grew into a proto-pop star who, though less obviously perhaps, was also in search of a mother figure. David was more confident than his brother, he was better looking and he was the heir. Wherever he went, women threw themselves at him and he was quite happy to sleep with a string of married women and then unceremoniously dump them when a more attractive or interesting woman arrived on the scene. There was nothing new about this – David was behaving exactly as his grandfather Edward VII had behaved and for very similar reasons. He was bored and he hated work.

After he met Mrs Simpson (1896–1986), his former favourite Mrs Dudley Ward was never again put through on the telephone by the palace receptionist. She was dropped with no explanation. And like his grandfather, David was prepared to lie in court to protect his reputation: when a newspaper reported that he and Mrs Simpson had had sex before their wedding, he sued and won his case despite the fact that in doing so he committed perjury. Everybody knew that the two had in fact slept together while Mrs Simpson was still married to Ernest Simpson.

David wanted the social and sexual advantages of being the heir, but he hated the idea of being king – he disliked work and duty as much as his grandfather had disliked them. On the rare occasions he deigned to go through his red boxes, he left sensitive government papers strewn everywhere; he believed he should be allowed simply to do as he pleased. Servants of the time remember that he would often joke about finding a way out of becoming king – love for Mrs Simpson was certainly a factor in the abdication but not the only one. As Dolly West recalled, 'He was always saying to his friends he did not want to be king or even Prince of Wales, so it was no surprise when Mrs Simpson gave him the perfect way out.'

One reason he hated the idea of being king was that he had ever before him the image of his own father, who was consistent in one thing only – he was always horrible. As Craig Brown and Lesley Cunliffe remind us in *The Book of Royal Trivia*, when David hurried back from Africa having heard that his father was ill, George roared at him, 'Damn you! What the devil are you doing here?' Having spotted his son wearing newly fashionable clothes, George screamed at him, 'You dress like a cad. You act like a cad. You are a cad. Get out!'

As reports continued to reach George about David's increasingly wayward behaviour, the king confided to a courtier, 'I pray to God that my eldest son will never marry and have children, and that nothing will come between Bertie and Lilibet and the throne.' Those words might easily have been spoken by George I about his heir, by George II about his heir or indeed by Queen Victoria about her eldest son.

The irony is that under the wayward playboy image, David's childhood left him oddly vulnerable. Mrs Simpson, who was rumoured to be intersex, treated him as a naughty child, combining in her rough masculinity both a mother and father figure, neither of which David had ever had as a child. Both parents had been cold, judgemental and hypercritical. Mrs Simpson ticked him off now and then, which echoed his parents' behaviour, but she also hugged him.

The royal family is like a small business that has survived longer than most and no one – least of all the owners of the business – can bear the idea that it will all come to an end. Eldest sons must be made to realise this even though they might often be better disposed towards their fate if it were not continually rammed down their throats.

We can see this clearly in the very different treatment meted out to George V and Queen Mary's third child, a daughter, born in 1897.

Christened Victoria Alexandra Alice Mary but known in the family as Mary (1897–1965), she was always indulged, especially by her father, and treated with great kindness by both parents. This was in stark contrast to the treatment of the two eldest boys. The reason seems once again connected first with the obsession with duty and second with the ancient dislike of Hanoverian Saxe-Coburg monarchs for their sons in general and eldest sons in particular. It is as if the heir is somehow a threat to the monarch, which was actually the case in the early eighteenth century when George I's son set up a rival court to that of his father.

Mary, of course, was no threat at all, but she also had the advantage of being genuinely intelligent, unlike her two brothers who always struggled in the schoolroom. History was once again repeating itself – of all Edward VII's children, only Maud seemed genuinely intelligent; of all George V's children, only Mary. She was enthusiastic in the classroom, learned easily and was something of a tomboy. She rode, painted watercolours and was a skilful botanist and keen cyclist. Everything she did, she did with confidence and style. Her father made it clear she was the favoured child and even her mother seemed more comfortable with Mary than with her sons.

Mary's brothers sensed her deep confidence and, according to M. C. Carey's 1922 biography of Mary, David remarked on one occasion that she would make a better monarch than he was ever likely to be.

George and May's fourth child was christened Henry (1900–74). Always under less pressure than his brothers and perhaps in some way acknowledging the failure of the old nanny and tutor system, Henry was sent to school – he studied at Eton and then joined the army. He thus avoided a great deal of parental unkindness (apart from the simple fact of being sent away) but was always under less pressure anyway – he was neither heir nor spare. Like his brothers and his father, he was not an intellectual but was less troubled – no doubt partly because he was looked after by Charlotte Bill as a baby – and enjoyed his wealth and position since his role involved no real duties and he could slip through life relatively unnoticed as his sister did. His only real enthusiasm was for shooting, especially big game shooting during his various military postings.

After Henry's birth, the duty to produce children was proving too much to bear for his mother, despite her seriousness and dutiful nature. Like Queen Victoria, she was disgusted by the physicality of pregnancy and childbirth, announcing in 1900 that after Henry she had had enough. 'I think I have done my duty and may now stop,' she wrote to an aunt. 'Having babies is highly distasteful.' May was essentially a Victorian and probably more prudish even than Queen Victoria. She detested bodily functions – a servant story passed down the generations below stairs was that no one was allowed within 100 yards of Queen Mary's room for an hour or so each morning while she made up her mind whether to go to the lavatory or not.

Despite her dislike of pregnancy, dutiful May could not entirely escape the attentions of her husband, and a fifth child, George (1902–42), later Duke of Kent, was born. Of less importance dynastically than his older brothers – he was fifth in line to the throne – he was always under less pressure from his parents and their staff. But the pressure to be an adult as early as possible saw him joining the navy aged just thirteen. He later became a civil servant and then aide-de-camp to his brother Edward VIII. He died in a plane crash in 1942.

A sixth and final child was born in 1905. He was christened John and though he seemed perfectly healthy for his first few years, he developed severe epilepsy and after the age of eleven he lived with his own servants, including the children's old nanny Charlotte Bill, in a cottage in the grounds of Sandringham. His parents kept away and it is difficult to know if they did this because they were embarrassed by, or ashamed of, the boy's difficulties because they tended to keep away from all their children. John was looked after by paid staff until his death in 1919.

In a curious historical twist, May's mother-in-law Queen Alexandra had also given birth to a sixth child. He too was christened John. He died just hours after his birth.

George V died in 1936 and the short reign of his son David, Edward VIII, ushered in a new era that was initially brighter and more optimistic.

The contrast between cold, dour, repressed George V and his hedonist son was beautifully summed up by John Betjeman in his poem 'Death of King George V'. Betjeman describes George's life entirely in terms of his stamp collection and his love of 'well-shot woodcock, partridge, snipe'. Edward VIII, by contrast, cares little for such things and travels in the most modern way possible – by aeroplane. His youth and eagerness for change are signalled by the fact that he lands 'hatless from the air'. For his father, not wearing a hat would have been a serious breach of etiquette.

CHAPTER SEVEN

PRIDE AND JOY: THE CHILDREN OF GEORGE VI

'There is always one moment in childhood when
the door opens and lets the future in.'

GRAHAM GREENE

There is an enduring myth about the children of George VI (1895–1952). Margaret (1930–2002), we are always told, was the lively naughty sister, where Elizabeth (1926–2022) – always Lilibet in the family – was dutiful almost from the time she could speak. In fact, both girls were frequently mischievous but in very different ways and Margaret often got her sister into trouble; Elizabeth would happily take the blame for her sister's pranks but get her revenge at a later date. Elizabeth was naughty in subtle ways: she always loved practical jokes, even when they were at her expense – putting dog biscuits on a plate to see if any adults would take one and eat it was a favourite prank that she was still playing on pompous visitors when she was in her eighties. She was always very good too at subtle yet somehow devastating remarks, sharp little asides. Having said about a slightly overconfident young courtier, 'Well, he tries', she would pause and then say almost under her breath, '...if only he wouldn't'.

To a large extent sensing each other's developing role, each girl chose to be the opposite – which is typical of siblings, royal or otherwise. Where one chooses to be the entertainer, even the buffoon, another will choose to be a serious hard worker; where one takes an interest in sport, the other will focus on academia.

But beneath the old myths about Lilibet and Margaret there are details which paint a complex picture; a picture in which the future queen is both more selfless even than we had imagined and more inclined to try to take some of her sister's predominant role as the amusing, sparkling entertaining sister. The sisters always competed for their parents' and especially their father's approval. Lilibet did not always relish her role as the dutiful sibling and, as we will see, she frequently broke the mould and got into more trouble than her sister. The difficulty for Lilibet was that when she got into trouble, she was not quite so able to charm her way out of it. Instead, she was almost shockingly honest and straightforward. Margaret grew up thinking that her looks, wit and charm would always mean she could get what she wanted; Lilibet grew up thinking she would earn praise and approval by doing what was right – in other words, being the opposite of her sister.

Though their differences gave them space in the family to be themselves and space from each other, there were always resentments and difficulties. Lilibet wanted to be more amusing, which she could often be; Margaret believed she would have made a better monarch than her sister, but then she believed she was better at anything and everything once she put her mind to it.

But whatever their differences – and there were differences that led to rifts and misunderstandings – the girls benefited hugely from one major fact: they were girls. Like most royal princes, their father George VI would likely have struggled to maintain a positive relationship with an heir and a spare who happened to be male. Whatever the failures of his own father George V, Bertie would have been drawn – as we all are – to repeat them in some form, either by trying to be completely opposite (as Edward VII was from Victoria) or by conforming to type and repeating once again the near two centuries of monarchs disliking their first sons.

Lilibet and Margaret had another great advantage: they were not at birth in the direct line of succession. For the first few years of their lives, their parents imagined for them a life of leisure and wealth followed by marriage, countryside weekends riding to hounds and children. It was only the shock of their uncle's abdication that suddenly made Lilibet, aged just ten, a future queen, and by the time that became an unquestioned fact, it was too late for her parents to ruin her early childhood by adopting the obsessive and controlling practices monarchs have tended to introduce when the child in question is born as the heir.

But that said, the early lives of Lilibet and Margaret – despite the fact that they were born well into the twentieth century – echoed remarkably the early lives of their forebears. Once again, no one thought, 'Should we change this? Are we doing what is best for our children?' Instead, in a remarkably unthinking way, they repeated with minor variations precisely the childhoods they themselves had

had. For Elizabeth Bowes-Lyon, this would have seemed perfectly reasonable because she had enjoyed a happy childhood. For her husband, as we have seen, things had been very different.

Lilibet and Margaret's mother, Elizabeth Bowes-Lyon (more famously of course the Queen Mother), was born into an ancient Scottish aristocratic family – with connections to the royal family but not themselves royal. As with many English aristocratic families, centuries of marrying cousins had led to strains of eccentricity if not madness in the Bowes-Lyons – two of the Queen Mother's nieces spent their whole lives in psychiatric institutions. She herself was brought up to do nothing or at least nothing practical. William Tallon, Elizabeth's Page of the Backstairs and without doubt her closest confidant in her later years, said that she once asked him when she was in her nineties, 'Is it difficult to make tea?' He also explained how she relied completely on her dresser to decide what she would wear each day. 'These decisions are exhausting unless you are used to making them,' Tallon would quote her as saying, not perhaps entirely seriously.

The politician and diarist Henry 'Chips' Channon, who knew Elizabeth Bowes-Lyon well, wrote, 'Her indolence and general laziness are proverbial.'

The Queen Mother was born in 1900, a time when her family would have assumed that the world they knew, a world of vast numbers of servants, landed estates in different parts of the country, low taxes and widespread deference, would continue for ever. She grew up not simply believing in the established order – that would have taken some self-reflection – but living it unquestioningly: there would always be people to dress her and undress her, sometimes several times a day; there would always be people to cook and clean for her; there would always be coachmen and chauffeurs to whisk her away for Thursdays to Tuesdays (never anything as vulgar as a 'weekend') at grand houses up and down the country.

William Tallon, who worked for Elizabeth for more than fifty years, understood how her early life created an adult woman who never questioned her own position or that of her family.

> The child she had been in, say, 1910 was fixed firmly in the adult. That was a great part of her charm – she was all of a piece. She took everything for granted for good or bad. I know that in the 1920s, she was considered the most charming girl in London, even though she was perhaps not the most beautiful. Her role was to be charming, to be seen in the right circles and to dance with the right sort of partners. That was her work until she married a member of the royal family. Her upbringing had produced an adult perfectly tuned to the role she was destined to play as a married woman. Although she told me once that George V had worried that there was a strain of mental illness in her family, which there was, and he was worried that it would come out in any children his son might have with Elizabeth.

Mary Power, whose mother worked for the Bowes-Lyons as a sixteen-year-old, recalled the general atmosphere of Elizabeth's early life.

> Everything seemed fixed and unchanging – we just accepted that the family members were almost a different species from us below-stairs staff. They were so far above us, but there was no

resentment about that – we sort of admired them, even looked up to them, to be honest. We thought they deserved to be waited on hand and foot because in those days if you were nobly born, it meant there was something in your genes that set you apart. You had blue blood, which meant something then.

The Bowes-Lyon children, including Elizabeth, were dressed every day by servants, and even when they were old enough to dress themselves, they didn't – they still had dressers and the same was true for boys. Boys had valets to dress them. My mother remembered when one of Elizabeth's brothers was given a valet for his birthday! And all their clothes would reappear as if by magic in their rooms after being washed and ironed by us. Everyone, including the children when they were old enough, would dress for dinner. The children had their own servants, if you can believe that – sometimes a small team of them – though, of course, the nanny was the most important figure in the nursery and she had absolute control. If you got a bad nanny, it might take years to find out or you would never find out because the bad ones were very good at covering their tracks.

This was the environment in which Lilibet and Margaret's mother grew up. Just like their mother, the two girls first had lessons with their nanny and then later with tutors, but the emphasis was entirely on delicate ladylike subjects – French, music, art, a little history. Their mother – still implicitly accepting the world she had grown up in – assumed that even if the world outside had changed, her world was still the same and the attitudes and values of that childhood in the early years of the twentieth century were passed on not quite identically but almost so. Elizabeth and her siblings had had ponies and numerous other pets, especially dogs, but the main emphasis, the overwhelming emphasis for daughters was that they should grow up knowing how to talk to servants in one way and their equals in another; how to socialise on the endless social round; as John Betjeman put it in his autobiographical poem *Summoned by Bells*, 'how not to be a bore'. The aim of the social round, of parties with other landed families, was entirely that girls should marry well.

William Tallon said:

When we occasionally had lunch together – just the two of us – the Queen Mother would sometimes reminisce about her childhood and the childhoods of her own children; she would say, 'Sometimes, William, I am astonished at how extraordinary things are today. When I was a girl, we thought of nothing but parties and balls. Now everything is very different. There are no balls and we mustn't think of some people being in anyway superior to others. It was and is very difficult for my daughters to have to deal with this new world. As I have to, I suppose, at least some of the time.'

She would smile at me and almost wink. She never would have properly winked, but I took her glance to mean that it was extraordinary how she the Queen Mother was having lunch with me, a servant, just the two of us. Such a thing would never have happened when she was a girl.

But if some element of social change was unavoidable, at least one part of Elizabeth Bowes-Lyon's world remained very much the same. When her daughters were born, she simply did what her ancestors and those of her husband, the Duke of York, had always done. She handed them over to paid staff. Even that apparently most uncritical of observers Marion Crawford, the two girls' governess, recognised that for the Duke and Duchess of York, there was no question of Margaret and Lilibet receiving anything other than the traditional education – or non-education – afforded to girls of a certain class. Crawford wrote, 'The duke and duchess ... were not over-concerned with the higher education of their daughters.' In fact, their formal lessons amounted to little more than six or seven hours each week, although they also visited galleries and museums and there was a huge emphasis on the need to speak French fluently, which Lilibet managed easily. After the abdication when she became the heir, the provost of Eton college, Henry Marten, was brought in to teach her constitutional history.

Once again, the habit of royalty marrying other royals or aristocrats meant that, however inadequate, the traditional education system would always be handed down to the next generation. It would take a genuine outsider or two, as we will see, to shake up the outmoded, almost medieval attitude to education so deeply embedded in the royal family.

When Elizabeth Bowes-Lyon married the shy, diffident Bertie, the future George VI, she would have known that it was only possible because he was not the heir to the throne. In 1923 royal snobbery was perhaps at its peak, but it wasn't the strain of madness that ran through the Bowes-Lyons that would have prevented the marriage had Bertie been the firstborn son. The difficulty would have been that, on one side, Elizabeth Bowes-Lyon was descended from Durham mine owners.

But this really didn't matter when it came to Bertie. He could marry for love and he simply needed a strong woman with the right sort of aristocratic background. The Bowes-Lyons had their ancestral Scottish castle, another castle in County Durham, a fine house in London and St Paul's Walden Bury in Hertfordshire. They moved in social circles that overlapped with royal circles, they were immensely wealthy, at least in terms of assets, and they knew everyone they were supposed to know.

Elizabeth Alexandra Mary Windsor, the future Queen Elizabeth II, was born on 21 April 1926 at 17 Bruton Street, Mayfair, the London home of Elizabeth's maternal grandparents, the Earl and Countess of Strathmore and Kinghorne. It was a grand house certainly but by no means a palace, but then this hardly mattered as the new arrival was only third in line to the throne (after her uncle David and her father) and everyone expected, as Ingrid Seward points out in her survey of royal children, that David would marry and either before or after he became king would have children.

Elizabeth's mother, by now Duchess of York, for all her conventional upbringing did make a major change with her first child's upbringing. She breastfed her. The pressure not to breastfeed was huge if you were a royal princess, but the duchess, though aristocratic and now part of the royal family, had not inherited the dislike of breastfeeding that went back through Victoria to a time when all royal children were put out to a wet nurse.

But if that was a revolutionary change, it was almost the only one. The idea that this new child might one day have a job or marry a commoner probably seemed far more remote than that she would even become queen.

Elizabeth and her sister Margaret (born in 1930) were looked after in their earliest years by an unusually sympathetic nanny who adored both girls. Rather than accept the nanny recommendation of friends (which had led to the cruelties of her husband's early childhood), the duchess contacted the woman who had been her own and her brother's nanny. She was Clara Cooper Knight, who quickly became known as Alah simply because the children struggled to pronounce her name properly, and she was famously firm but kind.

But there was a dark side to Alah. Like so many royal nannies, she became over-attached to her charges and did not want ever to have to let them go. The younger daughter bore the brunt of this possessiveness, and though it was well meant – unlike the sadistic nanny who looked after her father – there is no doubt Alah's regime damaged Margaret.

In practical terms, Alah's regime was deeply rooted in the nineteenth century. She was, after all, a Victorian. She made the girls have their baths at the same time each day; they were fed at a precise hour and if either made a fuss or rebelled, they were ignored or left to go hungry. It was a disciplined but fair regime from which both girls benefited, although Margaret less so than her sister because Alah tried to encourage the baby side of Margaret rather than the increasingly mature side. It was a regime that instilled discipline, but even in Elizabeth it created a slightly rebellious streak. Margaret's rebelliousness was obvious; Elizabeth's more subtle. Because no picking was allowed between meals, Elizabeth spent her adult life sneakily eating biscuits and making sure she always had sweets, especially mints, in her handbag. She also insisted that small bowls of nuts should be left at strategic points in almost every room at her various palaces. William Tallon recalled how this occasionally caused problems:

Well, the various dogs in the household – but especially the corgis – always knew that nuts and biscuits were there to be had if they tried hard enough to find them, so occasionally a corgi would knock over a side table or jump on a sofa and from there on to a table and eat all the nuts. This upset their stomachs, which upset the footman charged with the duty of picking up the dogs' accidents. The palaces were so big that there was no real prospect of getting the dogs outside in time! Footmen were provided with napkins and soda water to clean up the corgis' puddles!

Many of Margaret's later problems no doubt stemmed from Alah's efforts to keep the little girl from growing up too quickly. Once Margaret left the nursery, that would signal the end of Alah's role. So, for far longer than was necessary, Alah refused to accept that Margaret could feed herself, that she could be taken out of her pram to walk. Even Marion Crawford, in her famous memoir, remarked that Alah 'longed to keep one baby in the nursery'.

Older habits die hard and even as the second and third decades of the twentieth century wore on with the start of air travel, and the motorcar sweeping the last few horse-drawn vehicles from the street, in Bruton Street it might just as well have been 1730 as 1930 when it came to parental involvement with the children's day-to-day care. Elizabeth and Margaret were carefully dressed each day for a visit to their parents in the morning and another in the evening. And that was it.

No one has ever doubted the enormous love and affection both parents had for their daughters, but their own relationships with *their* emotionally cold parents – and this, of course, was especially true of Bertie – had left a deep mark.

The royal family has never written or spoken in any detail about how they bring up their children and the effects this may or may not have on them, but Anne Glenconner, the daughter of Lord Coke, a close friend of Princess Margaret and one of Elizabeth II's maids of honour, writes movingly about her own and her children's damaged childhoods and her account can be taken as an authentic portrait of childrearing among the royals themselves.

In her memoir, Lady Glenconner describes how as late as the 1950s and 1960s she continued a tradition of childrearing she herself found deeply upsetting. Her comments reveal the madness of the nobility's determination to be distanced from their offspring. We have seen how her nanny tied her to her bed but that she still employed nannies (disastrously) for her own sons; and having been sent away from her parents as a child, something she found deeply upsetting when she was young – she then drops her own sons off at their boarding school. She is weeping and they are weeping, but she still does it.

Despite all the difficulties of his own repressed childhood, Bertie made every effort to be different with his own children. He and his wife may have found it impossible to consider the idea of actually looking after their two daughters without the aid of nannies and footmen and governesses, but they made every effort to engage with them, even to entertain and play with them. Recently released footage from home videos made by members of the royal family themselves show Bertie and his brother David linking arms before turning somersaults in the garden; the films also show Bertie making faces at the girls and making them laugh. Their mother, though smiling benignly, is less engaged. But what these remarkable recordings show above all is that Bertie was most at home in the company of his wife and children; he has none of the strained nervous look he habitually has in official newsreel film and photographs. Rather than repeat the stern, cold parenting he endured himself, Bertie seems genuinely to have tried as hard as possible to be different, and with his naturally diffident nature, that must have been difficult. Rather than being formed by his awful childhood, the duke's personality seems to have been all but erased, as Henry 'Chips' Channon noted in his diary: the duke, he said, had 'no charm, no wit, no learning, no humour ... and no vices'.

The duke and duchess may have tried to be more relaxed with their children, but there was a limit to how far they could go. Playfulness in front of the camera was one thing, but both parents had learned that displays of emotion and physical affection were slightly unseemly and undignified; they were to be avoided. To use a phrase made famous by the writer Nancy Mitford, they were definitely 'non-U' – non-upper class. Marion Crawford summed the situation up neatly when she wrote in her famous book about the royal children that George VI was always horribly embarrassed when the girls showed him any affection. She added, 'He was not a demonstrative man [and] Lilibet took after him.' The sense that even the youngest children must not be mollycoddled by their parents can be seen at its starkest when Elizabeth was a year old. It was 1927, and her parents thought nothing of embarking on a world tour that kept them away from their daughter for seven months. As we have seen throughout royal history, repeating the mistakes of the past is almost inevitable; decades after the Duke and Duchess of York set off for their world tour, Elizabeth (by now queen) and her husband Prince Philip left their children Charles (1948–) and Anne (1950–) for a similarly lengthy Commonwealth tour in 1953. But Lilibet was lucky. When her parents were away, as they often were in these early years, she stayed with her grandparents at Buckingham Palace, and George V, an ogre to his own children, seems to have mellowed with age. Charmed by the girls, he became an indulgent grandparent. Even the famously frosty Queen Mary thawed a little when the two little girls were brought into their majesties' apartments for their daily visits. But note the words *daily visits* – the half-hour visits were inevitably more like formal audiences and they ran strictly to time.

But it wasn't these newly warm grandparents who really saved the day. Elizabeth's universally admired nursemaid and later friend Bobo MacDonald and her governess Marion Crawford were the solid foundations of Elizabeth's emotional life. For Elizabeth's son Charles, by contrast, the early lengthy absences of his parents were deeply damaging.

History has not been kind to Marion Crawford, who was famously ostracised by the royal family after the publication of her memoir, but according to William Tallon, Lilibet had tried to persuade her parents that Crawfie had actually done nothing wrong. According to Tallon, Elizabeth always regretted the way the family treated her former governess but felt she could not openly criticise her parents' decision.

Margaret and Lilibet's distinctive personalities can be seen developing throughout their childhood. Margaret, desperate to be as different as possible from her sister, was turning into a wilful if amusing child. She did superb imitations of members of the family and others; she loved clothes, music and dancing and often made a point of distancing herself from her sister's enthusiasms. Lilibet's room was always obsessively tidy – she would sometimes wake in the middle of the night to check her shoes were polished – where Margaret's was untidy and filled with clutter. Lilibet was so keen to keep her bedroom clean and tidy that she insisted on having her own dustpan and brush – she was given a small bright red metal dustpan and a little brush which she used every day. When a small pile of newspaper and a bottle of vinegar were found in her bedroom, everyone was baffled until they realised that Elizabeth was cleaning her own windows. She was often found standing at her window, waving and smiling at passers-by – almost as if she had an uncanny presentiment of what the future held. Margaret was utterly different. When Elizabeth shot her first stag in the Highlands, Margaret was unimpressed and certainly had no great desire to emulate her elder sister. When, by contrast, Margaret flirted with the boys from the local scout troop at Windsor, Elizabeth was stony faced. William Tallon, who knew Margaret well throughout her adult life, said:

Half Margaret's antics as an adult – her drinking and smoking and flirting – were the adult version of her childhood habit of wanting not just her parents' attention but also and perhaps more importantly her sister's. She relied hugely on Elizabeth, almost as a sort of surrogate parent, and getting her sister's attention became a habit that lasted throughout her life, although as she got older, she had to be increasingly outrageous to be sure of the hoped-for summons to Buckingham Palace, where her sister would listen sympathetically and tell her gently that perhaps she could try tap dancing or gardening rather than jetting off to Mustique and getting drunk. Margaret liked being scolded but only by her sister.

One of the reasons Margaret found her sister so reassuring was that Elizabeth, throughout her life, hated confrontation or unpleasantness – her scoldings were always far more like quiet appeals. Good-tempered attempts to stop Margaret being overly silly or loud can be clearly seen in the earliest film of the two girls playing in the gardens of their various houses. As Margaret became more outrageous, so Elizabeth increasingly became thoughtful, restrained and organised. But avoiding confrontation was undoubtedly a factor in her own children's development, especially, as we will see, in the case of Prince Andrew.

Where Elizabeth was praised by her parents for her restraint and good behaviour, Margaret enjoyed not praise but a kind of positive feedback from her parents for being outrageous – her father, mother and even sister responded with gales of delighted laughter.

William Tallon said, 'She became the buffoon in a sort of feedback loop – the more her father laughed at her antics, the more she played up and the more her father laughed, which meant even more outrageous antics, even more laughter and so on.'

Even her grandmother Queen Mary described Margaret as 'a

little rogue'. Throughout the two girls' childhoods, of course this didn't matter, for Margaret was never going to be in the public eye. She would marry well and calm down.

A servant of the time who occasionally helped out with the day care of Elizabeth and Margaret said:

It was amazing, even before the two girls reached their teens, how you could see them developing as polar opposites. Margaret always misbehaved and the more she misbehaved, the more her sister determined to be the sensible one who kept her sister in check and behaved well herself. Margaret rarely did as she was told; Elizabeth always did – or almost always.

Margaret's occasionally wicked tongue did not always endear her to their governess Marion Crawford nor to the woman who went from being a servant to become Queen Elizabeth's dresser and arguably her closest friend.

Margaret 'Bobo' MacDonald's father was a Scottish railway worker, and like many girls from such a background, she went into service as soon as she left school in her early teens. Having worked in a hotel, she applied for a job as nursemaid at Glamis Castle, the ancestral home of the Bowes-Lyons. She began work soon after the birth of Princess Elizabeth, under Clara 'Alah' Knight, who had worked for the Bowes-Lyons when the Duchess of York was a child. Margaret, nicknamed 'Bobo' by the two sisters, never became especially close to little Margaret, but something extraordinary happened between her and the future queen.

With parents who spent relatively little time with their two daughters, Lilibet was always likely to latch on to an alternative mother figure at some point. Knowing the identity of your mother is no substitute for day-to-day intimate contact and that was something Elizabeth and Margaret had far more of with Bobo Mac-Donald and her sister Ruby, and with Marion Crawford. Margaret MacDonald perfectly filled the gap – she would have carried out all the basic nursery tasks in Elizabeth's first few years. Even her nickname, Bobo, came from games the young nursemaid enjoyed with Elizabeth. Margaret would chase the toddler around the nursery and shout 'Boo' when she caught up with her. Elizabeth would shout 'Boo Boo' back and that game became a favourite. By the time Elizabeth was aware of anything, she was aware of Margaret Mac-Donald as her primary caregiver. When, strictly speaking, Bobo was no longer needed – a number of years after the birth of Princess Margaret – there was talk of her being redeployed elsewhere or even leaving. This was one of the very few occasions when as a child Elizabeth put her foot down. Her love for Bobo MacDonald, the railway worker's daughter from Inverness, was now so vital that the thought of losing her was as frightening as the thought of losing her mother or father.

After the birth of Princess Margaret in 1930, Bobo and Elizabeth slept every night in the same room. This continued well into the princess's teenage years. And in 1993, when Bobo died aged eighty-nine, she died in a suite of rooms close to those of the Queen at Buckingham Palace. She was famously the only non-family member allowed to call Elizabeth 'Lilibet', and well into her eighties, she was still laying out the Queen's clothes each day. In her final years, she became too frail to work and remained in her rooms, visited daily by the Queen, who simply could not live without her advice and company.

William Tallon explained the magic of Bobo MacDonald and her importance to Elizabeth as a child and as an adult.

They were, I think, as close as two people could be. Elizabeth was always slightly baffled by her sister and though they were close in some ways, Margaret was so wayward that Elizabeth was always worried about her or stressed about what she might do next. With Bobo, Elizabeth felt completely at ease. It wasn't a servant–master kind of relationship either – even though Bobo was paid, the money was irrelevant. Bobo would never have left the Queen. She had everything anyone might want in the ideal mother and sister combined!

The Queen Mother often remarked in a joking way that Bobo MacDonald was far more like her daughter's elder sister than a servant. In fact, Bobo was one of the very few people Margaret was never allowed to mock or impersonate. Nor was anyone ever allowed to be rude to her or in any way to put her in her place – any treatment of Bobo that was not completely respectful would lead to an icy stare from Elizabeth if the culprit was a member of the family, and it might lead to dismissal if the culprit happened to be a member of staff. But even Margaret loved Bobo in a way that meant she couldn't bear to hurt her. Bobo had this magical quality, I think, and was fiercely loyal to the children and especially Lilibet in a way that no one else ever has been.

A former Buckingham Palace maid agreed:

She was definitely someone very special. She was kind to everyone and had a warmth about her. She could be a bit stern and
protective about the Queen, but then everyone thought of her as
the Queen's best friend. She and the Queen had all sorts of private
jokes – they had little phrases that only they understood. Even
the Queen's horsey aristocratic friends were friends only through
their love of horses. Bobo was a friend because the Queen knew
she could not live without her – it would have been like losing
your best friend and your mother in one go. When Bobo died,
it was as if a little bit of the Queen also died. She looked a bit
smaller and less robust, sort of shrunken. She carried on, because
she always carried on, but Bobo was a great loss.

The character that Lilibet developed as a child – conformist, obedient, serious and dutiful – left an emotional gap. Her father, as we
have seen, was embarrassed by emotion and affection, so Lilibet had
to find somewhere else to invest her emotional life and she invested
it in Bobo MacDonald.

An idea has grown up, however, that Elizabeth as a child was
always dutiful and obedient – as if the seriousness of royal childrearing, the paid-for childcare and emotional distancing of her
parents produced exactly the early maturity that such childhoods
were designed to produce a thousand years ago. It is certainly true
that in general Elizabeth was far more serious than many children
and concerned to do the right thing from the earliest age, but this
was not always the case.

Even Elizabeth could not always be completely in command of
herself – she famously poured a bottle of ink over her head to avoid

a hated French lesson, but interestingly she poured it over her own head, not her governess's. If it had been Margaret, the ink would have been thrown at everyone in the schoolroom. Perhaps most significantly, Winston Churchill, on meeting Princess Elizabeth when she was just two, said, '[She has] an air of authority astonishing in an infant.'

Meanwhile, Margaret found herself not praised for her seriousness but for her character as an entertainer. The laughter and praise of her family, especially that of her father, meant she grew up thinking everyone else would find her equally amusing, equally beautiful and equally sparkling. Her whole character was based, as was her sister's, on a remark made by her father when the two girls were still very young. He said, 'Elizabeth is my pride, but Margaret is my joy.' The remark sounds innocuous enough, but it is easy to imagine that for very different reasons both girls may have found it deeply hurtful. Is the dutiful child someone who cannot inspire joy in her father; is the amusing child someone in whom the father can feel no pride?

Margaret's role was to amuse and sparkle and to look wonderful, which may explain her obsession with clothes – an obsession that began in the nursery and ran in later life to jewellery, suntans, endless parties and a circle of apparently adoring hangers-on. As Ingrid Seward remarks in her 1993 book *Royal Children of the Twentieth Century*, 'from a young age, she would spend hours drawing sketches of beautifully dressed ladies'. And in an interview with the present author, a former lady-in-waiting said that Margaret 'always disliked the sensible tweed skirts and leather shoes so beloved of her sister'.

But for all her sparkle, Margaret forgot in her adult years that the laughter of her friends and ladies-in-waiting was often provoked not by her talent to amuse but by her status as the Queen's sister. She misread the praise and adulation for so long that when occasionally reality broke in on her fantasy, she found her life almost unbearable.

Kept as a child strictly within the confines of the royal family and only rarely allowed to play with ordinary children, Margaret grew up to believe the world would value her as her father and mother valued her, but she was mistaken. As an old African saying has it, 'every mosquito thinks its child is a gazelle'. Margaret was not a mosquito by any means, but she was not a gazelle either and her tragedy was that she thought she was.

The extent to which she could be crushed by reality breaking in on her fantasy can be judged by an incident that occurred when she was singing one evening with a group of specially invited celebrities – Margaret always loved actors and musicians and artists because they fed her ideas about her own artistic nature. Unfortunately, one of the celebrities on this particular evening was the painter Francis Bacon. After she'd sung several songs to the rapturous applause of the audience, she began another. Bacon, who was not afraid of anyone, shouted something – memories differ about what exactly was said – but the gist of it was that he told Margaret she couldn't sing a note. A crimson-faced Margaret immediately left the stage and stormed off. The incident raised that old terrifying spectre – was she talented and amusing or had she been tricked by her father's laughter and praise? Margaret's defence against any risk that she would be hurt was to get her own attack in first. As one of her former maids recalled:

Most royals, oddly enough, are only rarely rude to servants – quite rightly they see it as attacking people who can't defend themselves. Margaret wasn't like that. She was constantly hoping to catch her servants out so she could shout at them. She even used to check her television at Kensington Palace when she returned from a night out. If it was still warm, she knew the servants had been watching!

But Margaret didn't stop at servants. She was rude at some point to almost everyone. Elizabeth was asked by one of her ladies-in-waiting how she managed to put up with her sister's rudeness. 'Oh, I've just got used to it,' came the smiling reply.

Rudeness was not always a successful shield, however. Francis Bacon, as we have seen, was not cowed by her status and nor was Cherie Blair, as recounted by Craig Brown. When Mrs Blair introduced Princess Margaret to the MP Chris Smith 'and his partner', Margaret responded, 'Partner in what?'

Lightning fast, Cherie Blair replied, 'Sex, Ma'am.' Beaten at her own game, Margaret turned on her heel and stalked off.

On many occasions the waywardness encouraged in the young Margaret seemed to know no bounds. When the French ambassador dropped his fork and splashed gravy on her dress at a dinner, Margaret shouted 'Wipe it!' at him and made him get down on his knees to do it.

The kindness and solidity Elizabeth gained from Alah, Marion Crawford and above all from Bobo MacDonald seems to have bypassed Margaret. And without that solidity, she found that for much of her life she was alone. True, there were love affairs and marriage, but the lack of a strong maternal figure in her earliest childhood was deeply damaging. It explains why, though Margaret wanted to marry Group Captain Townsend and was given the chance to do so if she renounced her royal title, she could not do it. She trusted her royal status in a way she could never trust another individual.

*　　*　　*

After the abdication of their uncle Edward VIII in 1936 and the realisation that her sister would now be queen, Margaret always insisted she herself would have hated the responsibility of the role, but few believed her. Like so many royal spares, but especially a royal spare who had never found a role in life, Margaret envied not just the importance of the role her sister would play but also the fact that Lilibet's path was fixed and certain. Lilibet would never now be left in an uncertain world of unfulfilled ambition and desire. And always Margaret suffered a terrible sense that she was somehow second best. A student at Keele University, where Margaret returned every year for decades to present degree certificates, once joked that he wondered if she had brought her sister along. Margaret smiled but looked both angry and deeply upset.

Throughout her childhood and indeed throughout her later life, Margaret was always prone to behave spontaneously and outrageously. She was also prone to tantrums and sudden anger and her sister was one of the few people able to calm her and persuade her to be more level-headed. Elizabeth's role as the calm adviser and organiser – a role that has a great deal of the maternal about it – can be seen clearly in the earliest home videos made by members of the royal family. Elizabeth calmly pushes her sister's hand away when Margaret tries to upset something on a table. She smiles maternally while Margaret dashes off across the garden.

After Elizabeth married in 1947, things were far more difficult for her sister. Separated from Lilibet, the years passed and she began smoking cigarettes; she drank, went to nightclubs and began a lifetime of partying, but it was a life that never seemed to make her happy.

She felt that she had talent – artistic and musical – and that if she hadn't been saddled with the royal family, she could have had a wonderful career in the wider world. After she met and fell in love with Peter Townsend, she had the chance to escape, but she lacked the courage to renounce her royal status, as William Tallon, who knew Margaret well, explains:

Despite her reputation for the cutting remark, Margaret could be very kind. Her bad temper, which got worse as she got older, all came from a sense that she had wasted her life. Nothing in her teen years or adulthood ever matched the pleasure she got as a child in her immediate family when she was the adored, mischievous talented girl who could make everyone laugh. Keeping her in that narrow world gave her very little to prepare her for adulthood and she paid the price, I'm afraid. It was a case of the tears of a clown. Elizabeth had nailed her colours to a very different mast – her seriousness and desire to behave suggested, to me anyway, that she almost had a premonition her uncle would abdicate because her childhood, with the support of Bobo

MacDonald and her own serious nature, was perfect for what fate eventually placed in her lap.

Elizabeth is a rare example of how the age-old system of royal child-rearing can be spectacularly successful, but the explanation for this lies not so much with the system nor with Elizabeth's parents but with that railwayman's daughter from the Black Isle. Without her warmth and loyalty which lasted until she died in 1993, Elizabeth might not have become the most remarkable monarch in British history. Elizabeth I, another shrewd and widely admired monarch, would have understood why her descendant was so successful as she herself had been. Elizabeth II had Bobo MacDonald; Elizabeth I had Kat Champernowne.

Because her own childhood had been happy, despite the emotional distance and physical absence of her parents, Elizabeth saw no reason to change the childrearing regime that had always been part of the royal family's world. When her children were born, they too were left to nurses and nannies, but, as we will see, there was no Bobo MacDonald for the next generation, and the consequences of that were perhaps beyond anything the royal family might have imagined.

CHAPTER EIGHT

CHANGE AND DECAY: THE CHILDREN OF ELIZABETH II

'Desire is fuelled by prohibitions.'

OVID

'Rex nunquam moritur.' ('The king never dies.')

COMMON LAW SAYING

Traditionally, in England, at a royal birth the Prime Minister or another senior minister (or several ministers) might be present along with numerous courtiers, but the one person always absent was the king. As late as 1948, when Prince Charles was born, his father was told in no uncertain terms that he must not attend the birth. Little more than a decade later, when his son Edward was born, Philip had clearly had enough of this nonsense and insisted on being there as his son was delivered. But Edward was the only one of his children whose birth Philip witnessed.

Change in the royal family is possible, but the need for change – even when that need is pressing – always meets fierce resistance, thanks to the simple fact that much of what makes the royal family viable is its strict adherence to tradition. Being resistant to change means the royal family is always a few generations behind everyone else when new ideas develop and the world sees that the old ways are not always the best.

There is no doubt that once the ten-year-old Elizabeth had become the heir to the throne in 1936, expectations about who she might marry changed. Given her upbringing among the leisured classes, for whom work was simply not an option, marriage had always been the focus, as it was for all the daughters of the nobility. But as the first in line to succeed, there was now an added imperative for Elizabeth. She had to marry to produce her own heir. Had her uncle remained on the throne, Elizabeth might have married the son of one of the numerous aristocratic families in her family's social circle, but now such a marriage was impossible. She would not be allowed to marry a commoner, even an aristocratic commoner. But luckily for the establishment, Elizabeth conveniently fell in love – and there is no doubt she really did fall in love – with someone who carried much of the same royal blood that she carried. Philip (1921–2021) was, after all, descended from Queen Victoria – Philip and Elizabeth in fact shared the same great-great-grandparents.

Much has been made of the fact that Philip was smuggled out of Greece in an orange box as a baby following the forced abdication of his uncle Constantine I of Greece, but Philip's blood was hardly less blue than Elizabeth's, as he was both a Danish and a Greek prince. When his father Prince Andrew was exiled from Greece for life, a British warship was sent to collect him and his wife, Alice, and the young Prince Philip. No doubt there really was an orange box, but it was not carried over the mountains on a donkey. It was placed carefully aboard one of His Majesty's ships which had been sent to the rescue on the insistence of George V, who no doubt continued to feel real guilt about abandoning another cousin, Tsar Nicholas, to his fate some years earlier.

Philip is frequently referred to as having been penniless as a child, but penniless in royal circles is a relative term – for Philip's family not to have servants would have been inconceivable and like all princes, penniless or otherwise, Philip also had his nanny. Nanny Roosie was devoted to the little boy, though she did not become a lifelong companion. Philip was lucky too in that he was able to stay in the grand houses of friends and relatives across Europe, although he suffered a great deal growing up as part of a dispersed family whose very reason for existence had vanished.

Following his exile, Philip's father disappeared to the casinos of the south of France and father and son lost contact. Within a few years, a further blow came when Philip's mother, Princess Alice of Battenberg, had a mental breakdown and spent several years in a Swiss sanatorium. She later founded the Christian Sisterhood of Martha and Mary in Greece, but her role as a mother was virtually non-existent. Even Philip's sisters were unavailable to provide an immediate family for him – all four married German princes who were to become enthusiastic Nazis. His favourite sister Cecilie and her three young sons were killed in an air crash when Philip was just sixteen.

So where did Philip turn for the emotional support and closeness that less exalted families often take for granted? He did not have an equivalent to Bobo MacDonald, but he was lucky in that, having lived in Paris for a few years, he washed up in 1930 in England and was taken in by his uncle Lord Mountbatten.

Poverty is no longer mentioned from this point, as Philip was first sent to Cheam Preparatory School and then, famously, to Gordonstoun in Scotland. Like so many royal princes, Philip was not academic or particularly driven, but he loved sailing and sport and the general rigours of life at what was considered a very tough school.

The artist Feliks Topolski, a friend in his later years, thought Gordonstoun was the formative experience of Philip's life. He said:

> Philip loved Gordonstoun not just because it emphasised all the rugged outdoor activities and sports he loved but also because its disciplines and regular routines gave him the security – the solid boundaries, if you like – he had never had before. It was like a big tough family into which he fitted perfectly.

Despite the fractured nature of his real family, Philip was always aware as he grew up of its importance. One woman in particular coloured the young man's attitude to sex and sexual fidelity. Edwina Mountbatten, the wife of his much-loved uncle Louis, took a seemingly endless stream of lovers and thought it was absurd, and absurdly middle class, to make a fuss about such things. Philip duly took note.

Lord Louis Mountbatten, the single most important figure in Philip's early life, also took a lordly view of sexual matters. Though married, he was predominantly gay and, with the full acceptance of his wife, spent a great deal of his time pursuing young boys. There is little doubt that Mountbatten's paedophilia was tolerated partly because of his status as a member of the royal family and partly because society at that time preferred to pretend such things simply did not happen; if they did happen, it was distasteful, certainly, but hardly a criminal matter. Mountbatten was also careful to abuse boys from ordinary backgrounds. As a former member of Mountbatten's staff explained to the present author, 'Working-class boys were acceptable targets of abuse where aristocratic boys would most certainly not have been.' Lord and Lady Mountbatten were, in short, notorious, but in Britain at the time such things were overlooked because of their status. The same did not apply in America, however, and the couple were described in FBI files as being persons 'of extremely low morals'. Lord Mountbatten, according to the FBI, was 'unfit … to direct any sort of military operations'.

Like almost all the royal princes we have discussed, Philip's absence of a close relationship with his family, combined with the tough regime at Gordonstoun and the cynical attitudes to human relations of his uncle, produced an adult who was repressed and embarrassed by any show of emotion; like so many royal princes, he hated affection that was physical and demonstrative. He believed in toughing it out. In fact, in this respect he was very much like his father-in-law George VI and even more so George V. This was undoubtedly part of his enormous appeal to the young Princess Elizabeth. Philip seemed to have many of the qualities of emotional reticence that reminded her of her father.

In Elizabeth, Philip saw qualities that appealed to a man who, having lacked close emotional bonds with his parents, felt comfortable only with women who did not make emotional demands on him. With her traditional upbringing, Elizabeth would not insist on intense shows of emotion or overt acts of affection; nor would she make a fuss about sexual fidelity.

For the young couple, everything seemed a good fit: both had royal blood, there was an emotional compatibility and there was great attraction. George VI gave his blessing to the marriage and the rest is history. But behind what seemed like a perfect dynastic and romantic relationship there were misgivings. Several family members, including initially George VI, as well as royal advisers and others felt that Philip was, in royal terms, too obscure (he came, after all, from a dysfunctional and dispossessed family) and too poor. It was Elizabeth's own insistence on the marriage and the pressure applied by Philip's uncle Lord Mountbatten that eventually carried the day. Lord Mountbatten's role has perhaps never been fully appreciated.

Bernard Aldrich, his long-term gillie at Broadlands, Mountbatten's home in Hampshire, said of him:

Long after the marriage between Elizabeth and Philip and then later between Prince Charles and Diana, Mountbatten still boasted of how he had made both matches – he would talk of the past often with his friends when they were down here and he definitely saw himself as a king-maker. He enjoyed his power. We used to joke that his only disappointment in life was that he wasn't himself the king!

Mountbatten's biographer, though conceding the warmth and generosity of his subject, wrote, 'His vanity, though child-like, was monstrous, his ambition unbridled.'

Mountbatten's instinct was right when it came to Philip's marriage to Elizabeth; she, like her future husband, was emotionally reticent, as we have seen, and dedicated to her duty as queen as no other monarch has been, with the possible exception of Elizabeth I.

Indeed, duty meant so much to Elizabeth that when Philip misbehaved and enjoyed the company of numerous party girls with his friend Feliks Topolski in the 1950s, she said nothing. She simply accepted that this was what men do – just as her ancestors had accepted that male princes and kings have mistresses.

Elizabeth's only allusion to her partying husband came when she referred to his 'funny friends'. This was a euphemism for the parties Philip attended in Feliks Topolski's studio near Waterloo Station. Here the handsome prince could meet discreetly with young women in search of a good time.

Many years later, one of these young women remembered how

Prince Philip seemed always to be there – he loved dancing with the girls and Feliks always made sure there were lots of very pretty girls for Philip to dance with. The studio wasn't just a studio either – lots of love affairs started there and for Philip, as I can confirm from personal experience, sleeping with the girls was part of the fun.

Mountbatten had always advised Philip on the traditional royal view of this sort of thing. It was fine to do it, but discretion was essential.

But if Mountbatten got it right with Philip, he completely failed to see that the world had changed out of all recognition when he made it his aim to make Prince Charles marry Diana Spencer. His interference and manipulation of a young, vulnerable and highly sensitive man led to one of the most disastrous royal marriages in British history – a marriage that led to a divorce that almost destroyed the royal family.

The disaster of what we might reasonably call the last arranged dynastic marriage in the British royal family did have one great benefit: it killed at last the idea that royal princes must marry other royals or at least aristocrats. Without the divorce of Charles and Diana, there would have been no William and Kate, no Meghan and Harry.

*   *   *

Mountbatten, who as we have seen, was primarily gay, had taken control of Philip the child and become the father Philip never had and it was a trick Mountbatten repeated with Prince Charles. Prince Philip was quite open about the fact that he felt hurt by his son's preference for his great-uncle. And prefer him he did, as Bernard Aldrich remembered:

Charles adored Mountbatten. He hung on his every word. Mountbatten could be very pompous and snobbish with lesser mortals, but he really loved Charles and they were far closer than Charles ever was to his father. When Charles and Mountbatten fished together here at Romsey, I always accompanied them and Mountbatten was always giving Charles advice about how he should behave, how he should treat the press and even who he should sleep with. He pushed hard for Charles to marry Diana and he always made the point that it was important to marry the right sort of person to ensure he had a son and heir. He used to joke and say, 'That part is about duty, but kings have always had mistresses and I'm sure your wife won't mind. Just be discreet.' I think Charles knew Diana wasn't right for him and this was Mountbatten's way of reassuring him that marriage was almost like an official duty just to be got through for the sake of appearances.

* * *

If the poet Philip Larkin was right when he wrote that 'man hands on misery to man', he might well have been speaking about Philip. As we have seen, royal childcare down the ages tends to follow a bizarre pattern: monarchs and consorts who have had difficult childhoods seem largely incapable of learning from their own difficulties. Philip effectively received no real parenting at all until Mountbatten stepped in. But Philip, for entirely different reasons, himself became a non-parent and Charles was also forced to turn to Mountbatten.

This lies at the heart of a curious paradox contained in the question: how did the apparently happy marriage of Elizabeth and Philip produce children whose adult lives have been so problematic?

With his own difficulties damaging his ability to parent, Philip's failures are understandable, but Elizabeth had had a happy childhood, at least by royal standards. Her difficulty lay in the fact that, like all royals, she inherited an unthinking acceptance of traditional childcare: she never seems to have questioned the idea that, for her children, nannies, nursemaids, governesses and tutors were best. Royals had farmed their children out to lesser mortals for a thousand years and Elizabeth was too much of a traditionalist to overturn that convention.

Philip's philandering and Lord Mountbatten's insistence that sexual fidelity was not as important as discretion created a prince who had enormous difficulties finding his own way. But Philip had other problems that affected the lives of his children: chiefly, he was deeply frustrated at his lack of a real role in the monarchy.

He complained he was the only man in Britain who could not even give his children his surname. In a conversation with the present author, one of Philip's closest friends from the 1950s explained just how frustrated Philip was by royal life.

At first it was exciting. He was recently married, very much in love with his wife, with whom he had two children by the early 1950s. His eldest, a son, was heir to the throne and he had done his duty, but he was bored and felt marginalised. Elizabeth was sympathetic but just as her ancestor Victoria had been powerless to allow Albert more say, so Elizabeth was powerless to give her husband a genuine role. With nothing to do except walk slightly behind his wife on endless tours, he became angry, restless and desperate for a life away from the palace. I'm afraid he became a bit of a playboy. No one cared that he was married – he was like a pop star who could have whoever he wanted. Elizabeth actually encouraged him to go off and enjoy himself because that was the only way the marriage could survive. It was a policy she later tried to get Diana to adopt when Charles was with Camilla, but Diana didn't have the aristocratic indifference to sexual fidelity that Elizabeth had. Diana was actually very middle class despite being an aristocrat – that was the real reason the marriage didn't work.

Even Philip's titles – or at least those other than the Greek and Danish titles he had renounced – all came as a direct result of his marriage to the future queen. He once joked, 'I'm Admiral of the Fleet but only because my wife says so.'

But what of the first few years of Charles's and Anne's lives during this difficult period in the early 1950s?

Philip, banned from the royal bedchamber when his wife was giving birth, had just finished playing squash when news reached him that a son had been born. Elizabeth, in a significant break with tradition, decided to breastfeed her new son, but only for a month. After that Charles was handed over to his nanny Helen Lightbody. Philip was largely absent and took no part in any of these decisions.

Elizabeth and Philip might have been vaguely aware that the

world was changing and that some aristocrats had abandoned nursemaids and nannies, even if only because after the Second World War servants could no longer be paid a pittance for devoting their lives to their employers. But very wealthy aristocrats and royalty continued the age-old practice of distancing themselves from day-to-day childcare. The idea that this might have been damaging to their children simply did not occur to them.

As one of Charles's former maids put it:

Charles's parents would no more have thought of looking after Charles and the other children themselves – I mean feeding them and changing their nappies – than they would have thought of sending him to the local comprehensive school. They didn't stop to wonder if being brought up by nannies was a good thing; it was just what they did, and if it had been good enough for generations of royals, it was good enough for Charles.

The fact that nannies and nursemaids had produced the Prince Regent, Edward VII and Edward VIII – to name just three immensely damaged royal men – seems to have gone unnoticed.

Like generations before him, Charles was taken to see his parents – more usually just his mother – in the morning and in the evening. Contact amounted to little more than one hour each day and Charles himself was later to complain that his mother had been almost entirely absent from his earliest years. It is ironic too that, according to Queen Elizabeth's friend Eileen Parker, quoted in Ingrid Seward's book *Royal Children of the Twentieth Century*, Elizabeth wanted her children to be brought up in a more 'normal' environment than the one she had herself experienced. Of course, normal for Queen Elizabeth meant that they should perhaps go to school and meet other children who were not royal; they should be more aware than she had been of the wider world. What she did not mean was that she would change nappies, play with her children every day, feed and bathe them.

Queen Elizabeth, like Prince Philip, had learned as a child that hugs and kisses were slightly embarrassing. Neither ever hugged or kissed their eldest son or the children they had later on, but then they themselves were never really hugged by their parents. Misery was in the process of being handed down across the generations.

Charles's nanny Helen Lightbody made up so far as she could for the lack of parental affection Charles suffered. But it was never enough and a boy who was probably born genetically predisposed to shyness and over-sensitivity became worse as he grew older. These difficulties were compounded because of course one nanny is often succeeded by another or by a governess. For Charles, this meant Catherine Peebles. No one seems to have thought that a child needs continuity – a carer who will stay permanently. Charles suffered the additional obstacle that he was far more like his over-sensitive maternal grandfather than he was like his father. Unfortunately, Charles was also rather like his *paternal* grandfather and Philip always despised what he saw as his own father's lack of manliness. Charles also had his grandfather's flat feet and that ancient royal legacy: knock knees. Philip, the tough, outdoorsy, sporty type, who was never ill, had a son who was neither tough nor sporty. Charles disliked sports and found it difficult to stand up for himself among other, often tougher, boys. Baffled by this curiously unmasculine son, Philip withdrew. Without parental input, especially from a father figure, Charles became much more like the women who looked after him.

Things were made far worse when, in 1953, when Charles was just five and his sister Anne three, Elizabeth and Philip set off on a six-month-long tour of the Commonwealth, leaving the two children behind. For Elizabeth, with duty always fixed at the forefront of her mind, the needs of her children were always going to take second place, especially as she saw these largely in terms of physical rather than emotional needs. The whole idea of emotional needs would have been awkward and perhaps rather embarrassing for both parents.

Even the most sympathetic royalist would have noticed a remarkable and rather sad incident that occurred when, during one of his parents' lengthy overseas tours, Charles flew out to Tobruk in Libya to meet them. The world's cameras were there to record the meeting between mother and son – a meeting that took place after several months apart – and rather than hug the little boy, Elizabeth shook his hand.

A former member of staff who knew Charles as a child said:

It wasn't just that he was shy and looked permanently as if he wanted to run away. He was almost effete. He had the look of a boy who would be the first boy all the other, tougher boys would pick on. He had no male role model early enough in his life to make a difference. His father was never around. In fact, if Elizabeth and Philip had been poor, they might well have been charged with child neglect! And even when Philip was around, he was constantly shouting at Charles – he hated what he saw as weakness, weakness that reminded him of his own father. I can remember on numerous occasions Philip losing patience with his son within minutes and storming out of the room. He wanted to be anywhere but in a room with his son. He even once said thank God we can pay people to do the dirty work – meaning the day-to-day childcare.

As is the way in so many families, royal and otherwise, it was the second child who determined to be different. If Charles was deeply in touch with his feminine side, Anne was equally deeply in touch with her masculine side. Where Charles identified with Helen Lightbody and the nurse maids who flitted around her, Anne quickly identified with her tough, no-nonsense father. Philip still went out of his way to avoid any physical affection with his daughter, but he liked her sarcasm and dismissive tone; she quickly adopted many of his sayings and mannerisms. Even as a child, she tended to tell Charles to stop complaining, pull his socks up and just get on with it. She stole his toys, she clouted him, she was rude to her nanny and she threw tantrums when she was told not to do something. She also disliked the corgis and, according to royal page William Tallon, regularly booted them out of the way. The footmen and maids would joke about the need to run past her to avoid being clouted. One of Anne's stable hands later remarked, 'I'm not surprised Charles was frightened of Anne – even her bloody horses were terrified of her! She behaved as if she had every intention of being the next monarch rather than her brother.'

In fact, that was the problem – like her Aunt Margaret, who

thought she would have made a better monarch than her sister, Anne thought she'd be a far better monarch than her brother. Anne herself has said on a number of occasions that she should have been a boy – that is perhaps a measure of the extent to which she identified from her earliest years with her father. Charles had taken, as it were, the feminine role in the family and Anne decided, as siblings are wont to do, that rather than compete with him for their mother and grandmother's love, she would aim to show her father that she had the qualities he admired.

But Anne was a girl and Philip tended to be automatically dismissive of girls, however tough they might seem. He wanted a son made in his image and not a daughter, which may explain why despite their superficially matey relationship, Philip spoiled her as a child but tended to be dismissive of her when she grew up. Rather than praise her brilliant horsemanship, for example, he couldn't resist sarcastic remarks that belittled her. He once said of Anne, 'If it doesn't fart and eat hay, she's not interested.'

As with Charles, there was a nominal attempt to make Anne's childhood 'normal'. That didn't mean sending her to the local school but rather to Benenden, a boarding school specialising in the daughters of the wealthy and aristocratic. Anne's experience here was far more positive that her brother's at Gordonstoun – she was tougher than most of the other girls and her genuine abilities at tennis, lacrosse and riding meant she was never bullied. She became house captain and a prefect and like her father took the lead role in everything. 'She was just naturally officer material,' recalled a contemporary, 'not because she was a princess but because of her personality. She just took charge.'

The irony is that Charles would have been far better at Benenden, which was sporty but not obsessively so, and Anne would have thrived at Gordonstoun.

But when the children were small, there were lighter moments; it wasn't all gloom. The Queen (though never his father) gave Charles piggybacks and at Sandringham the family played football and rode together around the estate. The Queen always insisted on being the goalkeeper – she was surprisingly good at it, recalled one of her gamekeepers – while Anne would be a centre forward and refuse to pass the ball to Charles or anyone else. Philip was always the most aggressive player because he thought he was really good.

Both Anne and Charles continued a long tradition of anti-intellectualism that has always existed in the royal family – a tradition closely linked to the old idea that the really well born show their quality by doing nothing at all beyond riding and shooting, with their echoes of the medieval monarch's central function of fighting.

Charles famously entered Cambridge with very poor A levels (something about which the university is still very embarrassed) and though Anne did better in her exams, she firmly rejected the idea of university. 'It's completely overrated,' she is reported to have said.

Anne's abilities as an Olympic three-day eventer inspired a genuine sense of admiration in her father, but although riding was and still is one of the select few activities seen by the royals themselves as important, Charles was never particularly good at it. He loved hunting and shooting, which he was taught very early on, but the family tended to be low key about their interest, aware as they were that the public was turning against blood sports. Indeed, Charles's

love of shooting was eventually to lead to a significant area of conflict between him and Diana, Princess of Wales, who was always
more in touch with the public mood than other members of the
family.

At Buckingham Palace in the 1950s and 1960s, the joke among
the servants was that Anne was the son Philip always wanted, as a
former member of the palace domestic staff commented.

But if Elizabeth saw little of Anne and Charles, Philip saw less,
as former housemaid Sally Coombs recalled.

He had absolutely no idea how to be with children. He tried
being bluff and hearty and they looked baffled; he made jokes and
they didn't understand them. He looked permanently as if he was
desperate to be gone. Awkward and embarrassed. They were the
words you'd use. But then he had never really been allowed to be
a child with playful parents, so he couldn't do it.

Eileen Parker, again quoted by Ingrid Seward, remembered that
Philip was cold with Charles and that Charles 'was frightened
of him'. The truth is that Philip was embarrassed to find himself
saddled with what he considered a physically weak son. One royal
aide remembered Philip roaring at Charles, 'Stop being so bloody
namby-pamby about everything.'

What saved Philip from his own rootless childhood was his
uncle Louis Mountbatten and school at Gordonstoun on Scotland's remote Moray Firth. Philip was embarrassed by his son's
lack of obvious masculine qualities and rather than try to get to
know the boy himself and perhaps encourage an interest in sport

through his own example, he simply farmed Charles out to others. Nannies did the work until it was time for Charles to go to school and despite his mother's misgivings about sending her sensitive son to a notoriously tough school, she gave in to her husband, much as Queen Victoria had given in to Albert when he took charge of his children's education. For Elizabeth, this was a political gesture. Philip and Elizabeth's marriage survived the 1950s because he was allowed to live the life of a rich playboy, but he was also allowed to dictate how his children were educated. As Elizabeth was head of state and had a job to do but Philip had none, she felt she had to allow him to at least make this decision. So, for the sake of peace within the family, Charles was packed off to a school that could hardly have been less suitable. Charles himself famously described the school as 'Colditz in kilts', and although he later backtracked on his criticisms, it is impossible to believe that he was happy there. One contemporary remembered:

Charles had no real friends at Gordonstoun, nor at his previous school, Cheam, where he also boarded, because people didn't want others to think they were sucking up to him just because he was a prince. He was also unpopular because he was hopeless at sport – didn't matter which sport. He was just clumsy, lacking real vigour and had two left feet. He had flat feet and knock knees like so many of his male ancestors and so far as I can recall he always had a cold. To be fair to him, he was quite good when we had to build a wall or a put up a fence – but he'd have been better at a school which emphasised art and literature, drama, that kind of thing.

Another contemporary at Gordonstoun remembered that Charles 'looked permanently miserable. He did his best to seem invisible and made no real friends. It must have been absolute hell for him. Ever since, I've always been very cross with people who say the royal family has it easy. They don't.'

In a letter home Charles wrote, 'They throw slippers all night long or hit me with pillows or rush across the room and hit me as hard as they can.'

His deeply sad letter had no effect at all and Charles was forced to continue in an environment that was absolute torture for him. Anyone who has been to boarding school will know that if you are bullied, there is no escape, because day and night, week in week out, you must live among your tormentors.

But underneath the misery of Charles's childhood and teenage years at Gordonstoun, there was a solidity that had little to do with his family: it was the mere fact of knowing that one day he would be king. The downside to this knowledge was that, like his grandfather George VI and great-uncle Edward VIII, he knew there was no real point trying hard at anything. The curse of every heir to the throne afflicted Charles as much as it afflicted any of his predecessors – what was the point of having drive and ambition if one's destiny was fixed from birth?

His Gordonstoun contemporary again:

Despite the fact that he was unhappy, he knew who he was and we did – despite his father insisting he be treated like any of the other boys, it was different for him. He went to Balmoral in the summer, his grandmother took him out for tea now and then, arriving with an entourage. Charles revelled in the fuss made about him – not by the boys but by everyone else. You can grow up in a very dysfunctional family and be a reasonably happy adult if everyone else behaves toward you as if you are an important person and Charles had that. He was so timid that had he been ordinary, he would never have got himself a girlfriend, but because he was a royal prince and heir to the throne, by the time he was eighteen he had girls queueing up to sleep with him. He thought it was because he was charming and amusing, but we all knew the truth – one girl said to me, 'I'd rather sleep with Mick Jagger, but Charles is a very good second best.'

* * *

For most of the long history of the British royal family, the tradition has been that a king may have as many mistresses as he likes. His queen was expected to simply accept this – male monarchs, like dominant stags, were almost meant to show their sexual prowess in this way, as if sexual vigour was somehow synonymous with military vigour. The tradition of promiscuity among royal males long outlived the need for military prowess and it continues to this day, but with Elizabeth and Philip, the tradition was reversed. Instead of the monarch being promiscuous, it was her consort who enjoyed the company of a string of mistresses and it is testament to Elizabeth's adherence to the traditional values of the upper classes – a tradition that despises sexual jealousy – and her determination to put duty first that she allowed Philip to have what one of his friends called his 'bachelor decade'.

No one knows how many 'party girls' Philip slept with during the 1950s, but it was a considerable number, as a friend who also attended Feliks Topolski's parties remembered.

Philip was handsome and that partly explains his success with women who were often younger than he was. Before the 1960s, royalty and the aristocracy were still treated as rock stars were later treated. Because Philip believed in his own importance and attractiveness, and he knew everyone knew he was married to the Queen, it was a kind of aphrodisiac. Girls were just dazzled by royalty! There is no sense in which he mistreated them. They knew he was married, but they didn't care – they just wanted to have fun and Philip was fun. He had the arrogance and manner-isms of his great hero – his uncle Lord Mountbatten – because he had modelled himself on Mountbatten as he had no other father figure. His arrogance made him very attractive. It was an arrogance that his son Andrew inherited. It's curious too in that Philip would have known his uncle was essentially homosexual, but he was so in awe of him that that didn't matter. But there is an element of hypocritical insanity about this because if Charles had announced he was gay his father would have shot him!

After his years of philandering, Philip returned to the fold. Ac-cording to a former aide to Prince Philip, Elizabeth issued a mild ultimatum. She told Philip that he could no longer spend so much time with his 'funny friends'. She was worried that it was only a matter of time before his antics were written about – she sensed that as the 1950s ended, society was changing and the newspapers could no longer be relied on not to write about her husband.

'Philip was privately furious,' recalls a former aide,

but though it was never openly discussed, he knew that his wife knew what he had been doing and he knew when the game was up. Despite his bluster and love of the traditional masculine virtues, he knew his wife was actually the strong one. She had a certain steeliness which came out only rarely – when Philip was summoned back to the marriage, that steeliness was very evident. In fact, Philip was rather like Princess Margaret – just like Margaret, he had to be indulged a little, but if things were getting out of hand, Elizabeth would make it clear to him that enough was enough, just as she had done with her sister when they were children.

He knew when he had to toe the line. It hasn't really been noted, but Elizabeth treated Philip slightly as if he was a wayward child – but then he *was* a wayward child. He had grown up without a mother and there was a bit of him that responded to the strict maternal aspect of Elizabeth. She did not have the warm, cuddly side of the maternal, but she certainly had the firm boundary side of the thing.

Elizabeth always had to walk a tightrope: allowing Philip to feel he was making decisions but not letting him make decisions that were obviously wrong. Frustrated by the lack of a constitutional role, he tried to dominate when it came to bringing up the children – but as he had no experience of even half-decent parenting, this meant Elizabeth had to agree to childrearing ideas she knew were not ideal. She did not want Charles to go to Gordonstoun, for example, because she knew it was completely wrong for him, but it would have been risky to tell Philip that he was wrong at a time in the late 1950s when the couple were as close to estranged as they were ever to be.

A former aide to the prince summed up the difficulty.

Philip could be charming and very funny, but he wasn't the most intellectual of men and he thought people who worried about emotional development were complete frauds. Hugely influenced by Lord Mountbatten, he thought a royal prince should be a tough no-nonsense sort of character who was good at sport at school and then joined the army or preferably the navy while simultaneously sowing his wild oats. His view of what was good for a royal prince would have been perfectly comprehensible to a medieval king, the only difference being that a medieval king would have valued poetry, music and dancing as well. Philip thought these were suitable only for girls. The truth is that Philip worried that if Charles read too much poetry, he would become homosexual. Philip was not a sophisticated man!

But Charles *was* taught to dance – his teacher, Miss Vacani, had also taught his mother – and he enjoyed it just as the only subject he really enjoyed in the schoolroom was art. In the schoolroom, like almost all his male ancestors, he was slow – he was slow to read, hopeless at maths and so nervous that he was taught on his own for his first years. His sister Anne was so aggressive and bullying that even she was kept out of the room when he was being taught. With the exception of his sister, Charles always preferred the company of women and specifically his grandmother the Queen Mother, about whom he refused ever to hear a bad word. She represented the gentler caring, maternal figure he later found in Camilla.

Elizabeth worried that Philip's antediluvian attitudes would damage her son, and time proved her right, but she also decided that if Philip gave up his 'funny friends', she wanted more children. She also wanted to try again at something she felt she had got wrong first time round. With Charles and Anne, she had rarely visited the nursery and never once visited the schoolroom where her children were being given their first lessons. Charles was damaged by this and was later publicly to complain about his childhood, especially his parents' long absences on world and Commonwealth tours. Anne was far tougher and virtually unapproachable – her reaction to childhood deprivation was to retreat behind an impenetrable carapace.

For Elizabeth, trying new methods with any further children was always going to be difficult with a husband who thought, as Prince Albert had thought, that the mere fact of being male meant that his choices were inherently, unquestionably correct. She knew Philip would take careful handling with any new children, but she was determined to take that chance. The result was Andrew (1960–) and Edward (1964–).

Andrew was born when his mother was in her mid-thirties, rather late for a pregnancy at that time. But the pregnancy symbolised that

Elizabeth and Philip's relationship was back on a stronger footing again and that Philip's bachelor days were over – and for good. The pregnancy also excited the country – after all, it was a great surprise when the announcement was made, especially, as noted by many royal biographers, because this was the first child born to a reigning monarch in more than a century.

Despite her determination to do things differently with this new child, Elizabeth was not prepared to ditch all the traditions of her class. Although the world had changed and by this time many fathers were by their wives' sides when they gave birth, Elizabeth made it very clear she did not want her husband to be present. The Queen's obstetrician and nurse – Sir John Peel and Sister Rowe – helped to ensure an easy birth and Andrew began life the way he meant to continue, by being demanding and impatient and 'roaring when he did not get his way' as a former nursemaid recalled.

Elizabeth was determined to stay out of nappy changing and feeding, but she was equally determined to see a great deal more of this baby than she ever had of Charles and Anne. She knew she had caused problems for Anne and Charles a decade earlier by assuming all their needs could be provided by paid staff.

A Buckingham Palace housemaid of the time recalled:

The Queen was always with Andrew – well, at least for a couple of hours each day. She used to take the corgis for a walk around the Buckingham Palace gardens and she would also take Andrew. He was always in one of those enormous Victorian prams with springs like a carriage and she obviously enjoyed her walks with him – the gardens at Buckingham Palace are huge, so she could walk quite a way privately, but if the windows were open in the right place, the staff inside the building would often hear Andrew screaming blue murder in his pram! He was a very lusty, even stroppy baby. The Queen used to joke that taking Andrew out was just about bearable because she could also take the corgis! Given the events of Andrew's adult life, perhaps her joke revealed some hidden sense that Andrew was going to be difficult.

For the first month of his life, Andrew was breastfed by his mother. He was then handed over to Mabel Anderson, a much-loved Scottish nanny who had been taken on by her predecessor Helen Lightbody. Mabel supervised the small separate world in which Andrew began his life. Still heated by coal fires, the Buckingham Palace nursery had its own kitchen and bathroom and was filled with toys. To all intents and purposes, it might have been a royal nursery in 1760. There were nurses, nursery footmen, nurserymaids and cooks. Mabel just ran the show. From the earliest, Andrew recognised that he was special – he became expert both metaphorically and literally at throwing his toys out of his pram.

But, true to her new instincts, the Queen made more time for this new arrival. She would ask Mabel to deliver Andrew to her study or sitting room and allow him to play on the floor. But she could never quite bring herself to get down on the floor with him. Old habits were too entrenched for that. Her father's reticence and reserve were too deeply ingrained and there was only so much a queen could do, even in private. So, Andrew was brought to the Queen each day by Mabel. The Queen never visited the nursery, as a nurserymaid of the time reported.

It would never have occurred to her to go to the nursery – a message would reach us to take Andrew up to her for an hour or so and then a message would come that we should go up and bring him back, or we might have stayed with him. The Queen would no more have come to the nursery than come to the kitchen. She had been brought up to do or not do certain things unthinkingly.

From the very earliest, Andrew seems to have imbibed a sense of his own importance that outweighed that of any of his siblings – partly no doubt this was simply innate, but perhaps too it was the extra attention he received from his mother. Most likely, of course, it was a combination of factors – his mother could barely conceal that Andrew was her favourite and Andrew quickly realised that if he became a tough, no-nonsense bruiser of a child, he would gain his father's approval. But whatever the explanation, it is certainly the case that Andrew made every effort not to be like his elder brother Charles.

Whatever his other qualities, no one would ever accuse Andrew of being emotional, artistic or sensitive. Unlike his brother, he was only interested in nature if it was flying over his gun at Sandringham or Balmoral. He was also almost insanely convinced of his own importance, as a former Buckingham Palace maid recalled:

I knew Andrew when he was out of the nursery but still fairly young. It's very difficult to be fair to him because he was so horrible – he treated the staff as if they were dirt. Imagine a little boy walking up to a middle-aged man who had worked for the Queen for decades and saying, 'Bring me that horse,' referring to a toy on the other side of the room and the poor man would have to fetch it. His manner was always like this. He had screaming fits if he didn't get his way in everything. He would walk past the sentries again and again to force them to present arms. He teased the corgis mercilessly, smashed things when he didn't get his way and often tried to hit his nanny or the nurserymaid. He put porridge in the footmen's pockets and would stand in front of them again and again knowing that when he did it, they had to bow. The odd thing was that Philip adored him and would put up with bad behaviour that would have made him roar if it had been Charles or even Anne. I remember once Andrew threw a valuable toy out of a window and Philip just laughed. Everyone said Andrew got away with almost any amount of bad behaviour because both his mother and his father adored him.

The truth is that Philip indulged Andrew because Andrew was very much the ultra-masculine son Philip always longed for. Philip liked his son's bullying ways; he liked the fact that here was a boy he could mould. Here was a boy who would play sport energetically and reject the sort of 'namby-pamby' interests of his eldest son. Put simply, Andrew was a kind of mirror image of his father. Philip's elderly, chain-smoking mother, who had left the order of nuns she had founded so many years before and come to live at Buckingham Palace, was astonished at the resemblance between Andrew and her son.

Andrew ruled the nursery like a miniature despot, but there was a shock in store for him when, in 1964, his brother Edward was born.

If Andrew and Anne were like their father, Edward was far closer in character to his mother and Charles. Even as a baby he was quiet. 'He was like the child who gets left behind in the classroom when everyone goes home and no one notices or remembers him,' recalled a Buckingham Palace maid. Edward was also the only one of the children at whose birth Philip was present.

As with the three elder children, there was an attempt to normalise Edward's childhood by bringing in a few playmates, but inevitably the children he played with were the sons and daughters of aristocrats. Among the girls, for example, were Victoria Butler, the daughter of Lord Dunboyne, whose family had held their title since 1324. Edward was soon handed over to Mabel Anderson, while Andrew had progressed to the redoubtable Miss Peebles.

Andrew was enrolled in the Cubs in an effort to introduce him to some genuine ordinary boys, though the attempt at normality was somewhat undermined by the fact that the Cubs had to come to the palace. In any case, the experiment failed because Andrew disliked playing with children whose attitudes and values he found incomprehensible.

Like all the royal children, Andrew and Edward showed little real enthusiasm for their studies – any intellectual ambition or enthusiasm they might have had was quashed by the sense they developed early on that, whatever they did or did not do, their destiny was fixed: nothing they might learn in the classroom would change the roles they would have to play as adults.

Added to this sense of a future that cannot be altered is an inflated sense of importance that arises from the knowledge of status. Andrew was especially prone to behave like a spoiled brat, as we have seen, and as he grew older, this tendency only grew more pronounced, but even Edward, relatively quiet and unassuming as he was as a child, could be horribly self-important if he felt he was not being treated by those around him with the deference he felt he deserved; and this was especially true if the people around him were perceived as being beneath him. One chauffeur described how Edward insisted that on no account should he, the driver, turn and look at the prince. Andrew, as a young teenager, was often far worse. One aide said:

It is very difficult to describe Andrew as a teenager. He could be very nice to people he liked, but the number of people he liked shrank as time passed. He always had enormous respect for his nanny Miss Armstrong and for his parents, but I really think he looked down on Charles and, as with so many younger royal princes, thought he would make a much better king than his eldest brother. I think that, being like his father, he picked up Philip's slight impatience – to put it mildly – with Charles. Andrew was also always curt to the staff and dismissive of them – he treated them as if we were living in the middle of the eighteenth century and wouldn't hesitate to tear someone off a strip. Occasionally, this would get back to the Queen and she would talk to him, but I think there was a bit of her that admired his spirit even though she herself was never rude to the servants. She also hated to confront him with his own bad behaviour. She thought a gentle rebuke would work as it had worked with her sister. But it never did. I'd say that the Queen was unique among members of the royal family in that she was very jokey, even matey, with the footmen and other servants – she had in-jokes they shared with her often at the expense of visiting dignitaries but especially one or two overbearing and puffed-up Prime Ministers she found boring.

*   *   *

The irony is that Anne, Andrew and even Edward were better able to cope with the traditional methods of royal childrearing than their brother Charles. Anne and Andrew, in particular, adopted or absorbed the tough impatient arrogance of their father but became as a result slightly bullying, sometimes rude and impatient adults. Charles may have been damaged by his childhood and his unsympathetic father and distracted mother, but he became a man able to sympathise with others, far more self-aware and emotionally intelligent than any previous royal prince. In his memoirs the photographer Cecil Beaton, who knew the royal family well, recognised during a shoot at Buckingham Palace the essential difference between the various members of the family. Beaton 'realised soon that [Charles] was nice and kind and sensitive'; Anne was 'shrewish'; and Philip was a bad-tempered bully who expected Charles to be in a 'perpetual rugger scrum'.

Edward was so far down the pecking order by the time he reached his teens that there was never a sense that he resented his eldest brother. 'Edward knew he was not going to make his mark as a royal, but he had the sense to largely keep his head down and enjoy the trappings of wealth, privilege and status,' recalled a former member of the Buckingham Palace staff. 'But', she continued, 'he had the arrogance of his brother Andrew – he was ridiculously over-sensitive about being treated with the deference he thought was his due. He expected more bowing and scraping than his mother.'

Edward seems to have worried that he was treated like an also-ran. This was partly because he was a diffident child but also because he was the youngest and because he was bullied by Andrew. Everyone was appalled at this, but there was thought to be something in Andrew's nature that made him want to dominate. Charles and Anne were too old to be pushed around by him, but Edward was younger and less hard-edged and he was bullied. Even the formidable Mabel Anderson and Miss Peebles could do little to prevent it.

But both Andrew and Edward learned to be imperious, and at various stages in their lives, this would lead to unkindness. In an interview with the present author, a palace official explained how a driver was sacked for giving a royal child a sweet, another staff member was moved to other duties for wearing a loud tie made from nylon and a member of the domestic staff was transferred for what was considered an unsightly mole.

Two extraordinary incidents, recounted by Ingrid Seward in her book *Royal Children of the Twentieth Century*, speak volumes about Andrew's developing character. He was five and staying at Windsor. Bored, he wandered into the stables and began to tease the grooms and stable lads, even going so far as to hit the legs of the horses with a stick. When he felt like being annoying, Andrew never knew when to stop and after the stable staff had politely asked him not to make their lives difficult and suggested that perhaps he should go elsewhere, his behaviour became so awful that they threw him on a dung heap and shovelled horse manure on top of him. Enraged, he ran off shouting that he would tell his mother. The Queen, always an excellent judge in matters such as this, told Andrew it served him right and nothing was ever said to the stable staff. Andrew was furious they were not punished.

The Queen decided that Edward and Andrew should mix with ordinary children in a way that their elder siblings had not, but as usual 'ordinary' turned out to be a relative term – their early playmates were Princess Tanya of Hanover and Lady Sarah Armstrong-Jones. When it became time for school they were despatched to board at Heatherdown near Ascot.

From Heatherdown, the boys moved on to Charles's old school Gordonstoun, which seems extraordinary given how disastrous the experience was for Charles, but Philip was never quite able to give up this one area of life where he could be in charge and there was always his favourite phrase: 'If it was good enough for me, it's good enough for my sons.'

By this time, Andrew had largely given up the traditional pastimes of royal princes – he had not inherited his mother's love of horses and he shot only occasionally. He enjoyed Gordonstoun but was often disliked for his arrogance and boorishness. One contemporary remembered how he met Andrew after joining the school late in the year and at first didn't realise who Andrew was.

Here was this slightly chubby, very arrogant boy, who was clearly used to throwing his weight around – I thought he was some working-class oik who had somehow got a scholarship to the school. Andrew had no manners, he was loud, laughed continually at his own jokes, many of which were terrible sexual jokes.

The strange thing was he never changed his behaviour because he never noticed how other people reacted to him.

To everyone's surprise, the quiet, sensitive Edward did not suffer at Gordonstoun as his eldest brother had suffered. The school had mellowed over the years – no doubt stung by Charles's criticisms of the place – and girls had been admitted. Edward, though not overly athletic, enjoyed the various sports on offer and was by royal standards something of an intellectual. He managed three A levels but with grades that would not under any circumstances have got an ordinary mortal into Cambridge. But dazzled by the prospect of a prince attending the college, the Cambridge authorities accepted Edward anyway, just as they had admitted his brother Charles.

Andrew took the route of so many royal princes and joined the military, where the highlight of his career came when his mother insisted during the Falklands conflict that he should not be given a safe role: he should take the normal risks expected of a helicopter pilot.

The royal obsession with military service, with its echoes of medieval kings advancing at the head of their troops, also forced Edward into the armed forces. He joined the marines when he had finished at Cambridge and this proved as great a disaster as sending Charles to Gordonstoun. The great love of Edward's childhood and early teen years was listening to the radio and reading – he was the least physically robust of the royal children and the least temperamentally suited to the tough life of a royal marine. It was Philip, once again, who had pushed his son into a world to which he was temperamentally and physically unsuited; Philip refused to accept that you cannot easily turn a quiet, inward-looking boy into a tough soldier. For Philip, tough soldiering was always the ideal for his sons and as with his eldest so he failed with his youngest. Edward's later decision to work in television horrified his father, but by then there was little he could do. Edward left the marines – in fact he was asked to leave by his commanding officer – before he had even completed his training. One of his fellow trainees recalled, 'He was such a nice chap but absolutely the wrong man for the marines or any part of the army. He was more the arty type, the sort who enjoys dressing up and appearing in plays, a sort of cross between Cecil Beaton and Isadora Duncan!'

By the time all their children had reached adulthood, the Queen and Prince Philip were baffled by the extraordinary brood they had brought into the world. Indeed, the joke in the royal family was that the Queen loved her children but preferred the company of human beings.

Damaged by childrearing practices unchanged in centuries yet aware of the new world they were growing into, the four children of the monarch found themselves wildly unsuited to, and incapable of dealing with, the new realities. In the past, the four would have married and whatever problems arose in their marriages they would have stayed married, but the modern world had other ideas, and liberation and freedom and the idea of personal fulfilment as the most important goal in life (rather than duty) took effect. Three of the four were to divorce in the coming years; Edward became involved in a scandal around using his royal status to get work for his television company and Andrew, the favoured son, the boy most convinced of his own brilliance, became a pariah, a man for ever tarnished in the eyes of the public by (hotly denied) allegations of the sexual abuse of a teenage girl. For those looking back at the childhood of these royals, there are fascinating lessons to be drawn; here was the evidence that being brought up in a system unchanged for centuries does not sit easily with the modern world and modern values. Charles, Anne, Andrew and Edward grew up with one foot in the past, where royalty could pay lip service to duty and fidelity in marriage, and one foot in the present, where the world judges their behaviour against the standards they nominally adhere to. In the eyes of the public, the privileges of royalty do not mean, as they did in the past, that one can do as one pleases without fear of criticism; suddenly, the privileges of royalty mean more is expected of royal children than of lesser mortals. It would have been a shock for this generation of royal children to realise that the world would not treat them as their nannies and nurses, nurserymaids and footmen treated them – but then the royal family seems always half in love with the old ways and half aware that they must cope with a new world.

When Prince Charles married Diana Spencer, the clash of past and present became extraordinarily acute, especially when it came to the next generation of royal children in the direct line of succession: William and Harry.

CHAPTER NINE

ANCIENT AND MODERN: THE CHILDREN OF CHARLES AND DIANA

*'That men do not learn very much from the lessons of history
is the most important of all the lessons of history.'*

ALDOUS HUXLEY

The marriage of Prince Charles (1948–) and Diana Spencer (1961–97) was the last gasp of an ancient system of royal arranged marriages, and in the modern world, where such marriages are always going to be up against the modern desire for individual happiness and fulfilment, it was an arrangement doomed, perhaps, from the outset. Charles and Diana were virtually forced into the marriage by elderly relatives who were Victorian in their attitudes and values. What made a bad situation worse was that both Charles and Diana were needy and emotionally damaged while they were children and it is a truism of modern psychology that a marriage between two needy people is not likely to go well. Both sides expect to be bolstered by the other and two weak characters added together do not add up to a strong character. In fact, the reverse is almost always true: two weak characters end up blaming each other for their inadequacies and seeking more solid, reassuring characters elsewhere. In the case of Charles and Diana, their arranged marriage and damaged childhoods produced two children who were, in turn, damaged in ways that were remarkably similar to the ways in which their own parents had been damaged.

Diana's childhood included all the elements that we have seen as key to the unchanging system of bringing up the children of the nobility. She was handed over to nannies and governesses (Mary Clarke and Gertrude Allen were just two of a long series of nannies). Diana later said there were 'too many' nannies and the whole thing was 'very unstable'. Some of the nannies were probably unstable themselves – Diana's brother Charles, now Earl Spencer, quoted in Ingrid Seward's *Royal Children of the Twentieth Century*, remembered one nanny who attacked his father with a knife and then ran off shouting, 'To the river, to the river!' It never seems to have occurred to members of the royal family and the aristocracy that the desire to be a nanny, to devote your whole life (at the expense of your own life) to looking after someone else's children, might attract oddballs and eccentrics. When Nanny Crawford told Queen Mary she wanted to leave to get married after twenty years of service, Queen Mary was baffled. She told Crawfie that it was quite impossible and asked how on earth Margaret and Lilibet would manage. Not one word about Crawford, her life, her desire to marry or her future husband. Like Charles's parents, Diana's father and mother were formal, emotionally reserved and distant, seeing their children only once or sometimes twice a day when they were very young. But Diana had a far bigger issue to deal with: all her young life, she knew that her birth had been a disappointment to her parents and especially her father because having already had two daughters, the earl and his wife expected Diana to be a boy, the longed-for heir to the title.

Johnnie Spencer's disappointment no doubt matched that of aristocrats down the ages; aristocrats who were brought up to see girls as charming, perhaps, but also unimportant and expensive to marry off.

The really curious thing is how Diana's relationship with Charles echoed almost exactly her own parents' relationship. Both marriages were poisoned from the outset by the royal and aristocratic obsession with marrying people deemed to be suitable in terms of their social class – with no thought given to any other considerations.

Johnnie Spencer no doubt loved his three daughters – Diana herself was ambivalent about him, sometimes saying she was his favourite, sometimes blaming him for many of her problems – and he thought that providing the traditional upper-class childhood was enough. Certainly, Diana and her sisters enjoyed a materially rich childhood just as their royal cousins always do, but as with so many families, the Spencers believed that money (and plenty of staff – there were more than forty at Althorp) can make children happy.

It's a myth to imagine that Diana's childhood was entirely *unhappy* – she enjoyed swimming, though she hated riding and other country sports, and above all she loved parties and people. The seeds of her future as the people's princess can be seen in Diana the child because apart from swimming, her one real skill was talking to people.

In a brief interview with the present author, she confessed, 'I've always loved being around people. Even when I was a child, parties and people were my thing, not sports – especially country sports – ugh! – and definitely not books and studying.'

The Spencers were among that select group of English aristocrats from which the royal family draws its friends. Diana was born at Park House at Sandringham, leased by the Spencers from George V, and here Diana mixed with the young Prince Andrew and Prince Edward and she would certainly have been aware of Charles even though he was more than a decade older.

Diana later said that throughout her adult life she would often fall asleep only to have a nightmare – always the same nightmare – in which she could hear her parents screaming at each other, as they did relentlessly for months in the run-up to their divorce. Diana was only seven and already disturbed by a life in which her father – described by someone who knew him well as 'occasionally an absolute bastard, completely horrid and nasty' – was largely absent and her mother was unhappy, so unhappy in fact that she eventually embarked on an affair with Peter Shand Kydd, a man with no aristocratic pretensions, whose fortune came from the family wallpaper business.

The problem was that Johnnie Spencer had married a young aristocrat because she was suitable, but she was twelve years younger and was completely unprepared for the dull life that Johnnie felt that, as his wife, she should simply accept. Frances Roche was the daughter of the 4th Baron Fermoy, a close friend of Queen Elizabeth II's father George VI. Like Diana, Frances was born at Park House, Sandringham. Her marriage to Johnnie was the kind of marriage that echoes down the centuries – one need only remember George I and his young, vivacious wife Sophia. Bored by her older dull husband, she embarked on an affair, as we have seen, and was locked in a castle for the rest of her life.

Diana's mother and later on Diana herself were latter-day versions of Edward VII's Queen Alexandra – we may recall that Edward described his wife as his 'brood mare'. A year before Diana was born, Frances gave birth to a boy. He was christened John and died just a day later. Frances was sent to a private clinic to see what was wrong with her. It never occurred to her husband that he might be the problem. One suspects that Diana knew from the outset that she too was likely to be treated as a brood mare – one of her closest friends said that Diana wanted to abandon her wedding to Charles the night before it was due to take place because she knew her husband loved someone else, but the pressure of what she came to call 'the Firm' was too great for her to call the whole thing off.

By the time Frances's next child – the longed-for male heir Charles – was born in 1964, she had had enough. So, when she met Peter Shand Kydd, a completely different character from her rather staid husband, she embarked on an affair that destroyed her marriage. She sued for divorce, citing her husband's cruelty, but this was the 1960s, an era in which high court judges and aristocratic landowners had often been to school together, and there was no chance that Frances would get a balanced hearing. She was the adulteress, so Johnnie Spencer was awarded custody of the children despite his indifference to their daily needs and his violent temper. Frances quickly married Shand Kydd, but that marriage eventually ended too; Johnnie Spencer married again and just to prove that dysfunction breeds dysfunction, when he died and his son Charles inherited the title, he, his sister and the staff at Althorp threw all his stepmother's things into bin liners which were then hurled out on to the gravel drive at Althorp.

Like so many English aristocrats who know that from a financial point of view their lives will be easy, the Spencer daughters did not work hard at their lessons. Diana was famously uninterested, almost actively anti-intellectual. But she was at least sufficiently self-aware to acknowledge this – according to Craig Brown's *The Book of Royal Trivia*, when Diana had her head measured for a new hat and was told her measurement was seven and a quarter inches, she said, 'My head may be large, but there isn't much in it.'

But a lack of ambition, intellectual or otherwise, inevitably put her at the mercy of stultifying tradition and the plots and plans of relatives who were essentially Victorians. The real villains of the piece were Lady Fermoy, Diana's grandmother, and Lord Mountbatten, Charles's great-uncle and substitute father. Both saw Diana as easy to manipulate and so innocent that she would happily stay at home while Charles had as many mistresses as he liked; Lady Fermoy said that Diana reminded her in this respect of Edward VII's Queen Alexandra. 'Alexandra knew that queens are above petty jealousies and that husbands stray. It's in their nature and absurd to make a fuss about it. Diana has sufficient breeding to know how to behave,' she is reported to have said.

If Diana had been bookish and determined, she might have been able to look up and see the strings by which she was being pulled like a puppet; she might have realised that being manipulated into a dynastic marriage was the worst possible thing for a woman who craved affection and love after her empty childhood and least of all needed a man brought up in the same traditions that produced her own unhappy early years.

The late Bernard Aldrich, Lord Mountbatten's gillie at Broadlands for more than thirty years, remembered how Charles would come to fish with his great-uncle:

Charles and Mountbatten would have lunch together. I was sometimes there during lunch, sorting rods and other bits of tackle, not actually having lunch with them, but I would often hear them talking. They frequently discussed Mountbatten's plans for Charles. The prince was completely in awe of his great-uncle – in fact in many ways, listening to them, you would have thought Mountbatten was soon to be king and Charles was just there to do as he was told!

Diana was thought suitable for Charles because she was aristocratic, young and above all innocent and compliant. It was assumed that she would do as she was told because she had been educated in a manner that matched the correct upbringing for a royal princess. Writing about another royal bride, Charlotte of Mecklenburg-Strelitz (later George III's queen), historian Janice Hadlow might have been describing Diana: 'Young, inexperienced, untutored in the ways of courts or politics, her naivety emerged not as [a] disadvantage … but as her most powerfully attractive quality, an enticingly blank page for a man to write upon.'

Diana was certainly timid and shy and she was no intellectual – once, staying at an expensive country hotel, she found the sound of a weir close by kept her awake at night so she rang reception and asked if the weir could be turned off. She often seemed uncertain and desperate to hide, vulnerable and easy to control, and all these aspects of her character had been largely the result of her broken childhood. And yet there was a steely side to her nature that was perhaps linked to her ancestral inheritance, her sense of who she was – Diana knew she had been born into one of the oldest aristocratic families in Britain – which had been forgotten by Lady Fermoy, Lord Mountbatten and the Queen Mother. Even in her childhood, while she seemed so fragile, there was an underlying strength: her nanny recalled how Diana would refuse to work if she didn't feel like it; on one occasion she locked her governess in the bathroom; she smashed things and refused to be cowed. In her biography of Raine Spencer, Tina Gaudoin explains how, when Diana discovered that her father had secretly remarried without telling his children, she walked into his bedroom and slapped him across the face. In 1989 so furious had Diana become at the behaviour of her stepmother that she pushed her down the stairs at Althorp. And the vendetta didn't stop there – when her father died and her brother inherited the title, Diana, as we have seen, helped throw her stepmother's things into bin liners and then kicked them down the grand staircase at Althorp. She was also a shrewd judge of character – according to Craig Brown and Lesley Cunliffe in *Royal Trivia*, Diana said of Queen Elizabeth, 'She's not exactly cuddly, is she?' And her characterisation of Prince Philip has never been bettered. She said, 'I think of him motionless by a lake, spearing fish with that nose.' Perhaps most telling of all was her comment about Prince Andrew: 'I liked him when we were children, but something must have happened as he grew up!' This insightful side of Diana was the side that eventually emerged after her relationship with Charles broke down.

Diana has sometimes been accused of showing an interest in AIDS patients and the sick and needy because it bolstered her public image. In fact, her caring side was bolstered far more by her own experience of loneliness and unhappiness as a child. Her need to help others came out when she was at her boarding schools, first Riddlesworth in Norfolk and then West Heath near Sevenoaks in Kent. Both schools catered for the daughters of the very wealthy and the very aristocratic and academic prowess was of secondary importance. 'They taught us to speak in what they thought was a very refined way and they taught us to get out of a car without showing our knickers!' recalled one former pupil. At West Heath, Diana volunteered to visit old people's homes and children's homes. A contemporary remembered:

Apart from sport and dancing, at both of which Diana excelled, the one thing at which she was absolutely brilliant even back then was talking to people and making them feel better about themselves. She would sit with an elderly woman and never seem to get bored, returning again and again. If there had been an A level in looking after people, she'd have got top marks. She was told off once for pulling an old man out of his chair to dance with her – he was delighted! But she wasn't completely a goody-two-shoes – I remember her several times sneaking out of school dressed in a ridiculous tank top and short skirt and she would get back and have love bites on her neck. There was a bit of a rebel in her despite the apparently demure young lady front she usually presented to the world.

But there were to be no A levels and few O levels. Diana simply had no interest. She knew that there was no need to strive; there would always be enough money for holidays and clothes; someone else would buy her a property in London (her parents duly bought her a flat for her eighteenth birthday) and she could be a babysitter and later a nursery worker and no one would dare judge her – she was, after all, the daughter of an earl and therefore a lady, even if she was cleaning lavatories (at which her sister insisted Diana was rather good). She was also an old-fashioned romantic who wanted to marry and have children of her own – 'She always loved babies,' said her father – and succeed at parenting where her own parents had failed.

Diana's need for love and romance was not evident only from her school-era love bites. Soon after she got her own flat, she dated several eligible young men – one, at the time a promising young rugby player, said:

Diana was delightful, but she was desperate for affection and I'm afraid a lot of the time she confused sex with love – she was very passionate, but soon after our love affair started, within weeks I mean, she started talking about marriage. She needed the security and thought that once you'd had sex with someone, marriage automatically followed. She was not a very modern girl in that sense, at least not at that time. Her neediness scared men off – we were young and didn't want commitment at that time and so she had several lovers like me who dropped her fairly quickly. She just wanted too much. But what was really interesting was that at round the time she became engaged to Charles, who I knew slightly, I received a visit from someone from the palace asking me to be discreet and not to talk to anyone about my time with Diana. They wanted to give the impression she was a virgin when she married Charles, which was nonsense of course. I have no idea who the chap who came to see me really was – I was taken completely by surprise – but he definitely had a sinister air and I felt intimidated, which is why I have only talked about it since then on the understanding I won't be named.

Ominously, the age gap between Charles and Diana was almost the same – more than a decade – as it had been with Diana's mother and her father. Worse, Charles was like Johnnie in that he seemed somehow old-fashioned, rather dull and awkward, addicted to the embarrassing pursuits of the past. Diana, like her mother Frances, wanted fun, not marriage to, as a friend put it, 'a dry old stick who wore tweeds and parted his hair in a style that hadn't changed since 1956'.

But the older generation stuck to their guns despite ominous signs before the marriage.

A friend of Diana's from her days working in a London nursery recalled how

Diana loved the idea of marriage, but it had to be perfect. We used to talk about it and her fear was that she expected too much – she used to say that she wanted a fairy-tale marriage not just a

fairy-tale wedding. She was terrified that she would marry someone and be unhappy because her experience of marriage – her
parents' marriage – had been so awful. She famously said that in
the end she married Charles because he was the one person she
thought could never divorce her. How ironic was that!

So, the marriage went ahead even though Charles was still sleeping with Camilla Parker Bowles (1947–). Charles and Camilla's
affair began as early as 1971 and continued despite her marriage
to Andrew Parker Bowles in 1973 and Charles's marriage to Diana
in 1981. Charles had wanted to marry Camilla but was told this
would not be permitted as she would need to divorce her husband
to marry the future king. Charles married Diana solely to appease
his parents, his great-uncle and Diana's grandmother Lady Fermoy
and he knew the marriage would enable him to do his duty and
sire the next heir to the throne. Considerations of the couple's happiness or otherwise simply did not come into the picture. It was a
marriage created according to rules that would not have been out of
place in royal circles 800 years earlier.

Charles believed the propaganda of his father and great-uncle,
who had hinted that Diana was perfect because she would happily
allow Charles to continue to enjoy a bachelor life once children
had been born. Charles genuinely believed this because it was a
family tradition. His father had been allowed his bachelor years, his
great-uncle had never been faithful to Lady Mountbatten, Edward
VII and Edward VIII had enjoyed the company of strings of mistresses; the whole history of the British monarchy told Charles he
could do as he pleased once the children were born and it was this

attitude that led to yet another generation of damaged royal children: Harry and William.

*   *   *

Married aged just twenty to a man she had met only a dozen times and a man who was twelve years older than she was, Diana quickly became pregnant. Charles had done his dynastic duty. Diana later confessed to a friend that sex with Charles was

> very odd. I was very shy and inexperienced – but not completely inexperienced – and I thought Charles would be in command. In fact, he was as nervous as I was and a bit of a fumbler – I think it was difficult for him to really take part because his mind and his body were elsewhere. It was all over before I really had a chance to know what had happened!

But whatever those early difficulties, Diana, having married in 1981, gave birth to William little less than a year later in June 1982. It was the realisation that she now had her own child that brought out the first glimpse of the steely Diana. She had already gone against royal protocol by refusing to have her children at home – they were born in the private Lindo Wing at St Mary's, Paddington – and having won that battle she determined that William's early life would be absolutely nothing like her own.

Diana might have had the traditional upper-class early life – a childhood indistinguishable from that of the royals – but she realised that the royal family and the aristocracy did things the way they did them because of convention rather than any concern for the welfare of their children. She said to a friend, 'If only my parents hadn't had enough money to do stupid things like employing endless nannies, they might have done something for us themselves. Stupid people are bad enough but rich stupid people are the absolute worst.'

Charles, obsessed with good form, insisted on a string of aristocratic godparents for William. Diana, bored with what she thought irrelevant, let him have his way. She thought it was typical that he should spend so much time and effort on such things rather than spend time with the child himself.

Despite this, Charles was initially an enthusiastic father who tried to play with his infant son, even climbing into the bath with him – but the dead weight of tradition and his own lack of close parenting meant he was soon bored and he was shocked by the tedium of day-to-day care. 'Far better to leave it to the professionals,' he confided to an aide.

But there was another element to this. Charles, underneath it all a decent man, was so damaged by his childhood or lack of it that he didn't really reach anything that could be even loosely described as maturity until long after his marriage to Diana was over. One of the reasons he was unable to involve himself in the day-to-day lives of his new child was that he was himself, even in his early thirties, arguably still a child.

This was something Diana herself instinctively realised. When she met the tennis professional Chris Evert Lloyd at Wimbledon, Lloyd asked her if her husband was coming to the championships. Diana replied, 'No, he isn't coming; he can't sit still for long enough. He's a big baby.'

Having no example of good parenting from his own childhood, Charles had not learned to understand small children, but he had learned that as heir to the throne, he would get to make the decisions about his own children, and this is where the real friction began with his wife.

Despite his complaints that his parents had been largely absent from his own early years while he was looked after by a nanny, Charles simply assumed that when he told Diana they should employ Mabel Anderson (Charles's own former nanny), she would agree. Diana refused, however, and it was Charles who gave way. He later told Mountbatten that Diana was not quite the little mouse he had supposed.

With her dislike of unquestioned tradition, Diana was determined to play a large part in looking after her own children – and this included changing and feeding them, hopping into the bath with them when they were very young, chasing them around their apartment at Kensington and putting them to bed – but she was not such a radical that she planned to dispense with all help. She employed Barbara Barnes, Olga Powell and Jessie Webb over the years to help with William and later Harry, born in 1984, but she was deeply upset when William seemed to fall head over heels in love with Barbara Barnes, even to the extent of climbing into bed with her every morning. Barnes, the daughter of a Norfolk forestry worker, was far more in favour of the old-fashioned and the prim and proper than Diana. According to royal biographer Robert Lacey, Barnes would not allow comfort blankets and insisted the boys wear button strap shoes, banning trainers. Olga and Jessie were more distant carers so didn't create the same problems for Diana, but her constant jealousy when it came to her sons increased as her marriage began to fail; Charles annoyed Diana occasionally by trying to be too hands-on with the children and then disappearing to be with Camilla.

It's a truism that parents who feel unloved by their own parents sometimes invest too heavily in their own offspring. Diana loved her sons but like so many anxious parents wanted desperately for them to love her and love her more than they loved their father or indeed anyone else. This was perhaps understandable given that Charles spent so much time with Camilla and as a result was to some extent an absent parent. Diana was alone with her children and their carers. When the children were very young, she had no one else, so inevitably her relationship with them was intense; this is said to have made William and Harry feel safe and secure but also less well able to be parted from her.

A little more than six years after she started work, Barbara Barnes resigned, although some newspapers reported she had been forced to resign. Both Charles and Diana were relieved but for different reasons. Charles disliked the fact that Barbara was treated almost as a friend by her former employer Lady Glenconner – she was even invited to the Glenconners' private island for Lord Glenconner's birthday party, which Charles thought very bad form. Charles liked his employees to know their place and Barbara Barnes had crossed the line. Diana disliked the fact that William and Harry were increasingly focusing all their attention on Barbara and that Barbara was too old-fashioned in her attitudes. One insider said, 'Barbara would have those boys sleeping in tweed pyjamas

– she loved the shooting and fishing side of their lives and disliked Diana's insistence on taking them out for hamburgers and pizzas.'

Luckily for William and Harry, Olga Powell, who was considerably older than Barbara, stepped into the breach and stayed on till the boys were in their teens. She caused fewer problems for Diana because, as one former maid put it, 'she was very balanced – she would not put up with any nonsense or rudeness from the princes, but she let them run wild a bit, which was good for them'.

Olga herself, who died aged eighty-two in 2012, said, 'If they saw a muddy puddle, they wanted to jump in it and if there was something to climb, they wanted to climb it.'

As William and Harry grew up, they became the focus for arguments between Charles and Diana that were really about other things. Diana knew that Charles had never stopped seeing and sleeping with Camilla and she resented the fact that when she complained to the senior royals, both the Queen and Philip urged her to ignore Charles's infidelities.

Philip famously said he couldn't understand why Charles chose Camilla over the universally admired and much younger Diana, but Philip was also a traditionalist who told Diana that she should leave her husband alone to do what he needed to do. According to a friend of Diana's who did not want to be named, Philip told her that 'husbands do this sort of thing, and it only makes it worse to make a fuss about it. He will always return to you whatever he gets up to.'

Of course, for Diana, infidelity reminded her horribly of her own childhood, with the endless rows between her parents and their eventual painful divorce. She was not prepared to put up with it and unconsciously began to use William and Harry as weapons in her war with her husband.

The biggest area of contention was field sports, especially shooting and hunting. Despite his love for nature and the environment, Charles also loves killing things, whether stalking red deer in the Highlands, fishing for salmon on the Dee at Balmoral or pheasant shooting with his chums at various estates around the country. But Diana had grown up with all this and she loathed it – in a brief conversation with the present author she said:

> I just don't understand why shooting is such a passion with royalty and the English upper classes. In my mind, I associate it with all the tweedy bores who would come to us when we were children to shoot hundreds, sometimes thousands, of birds in a day. I used to hear injured hares screaming and I hated it. I suppose they thought it was exclusive and manly and of course it's just what people from certain backgrounds do.

Charles wanted William and Harry to enjoy field sports and for precisely the reason identified by Diana – field sports (or blood sports if you don't like them) are part and parcel of being a royal male and Charles is a stickler for tradition. Even his infidelities were seen as acceptable – to him – since having a mistress or several mistresses was part of a long royal tradition.

By contrast, Charles was horrified when Diana insisted that William and Harry should not learn to shoot and stalk (stalking is the practice of shooting deer, especially in Scotland). And things became much worse when Diana insisted that William and Harry would not have sensible haircuts with side partings and that she would not dress them as if they were being brought up in the 1950s, which was what Charles wanted.

A friend of Diana's from this time said:

[She] really didn't realise just how deeply conventional Charles was and how deeply committed to all the traditions that make the royal family both fascinating but also very dysfunctional. Despite his terrible experiences at Gordonstoun, he toyed with the idea of sending his boys there, until Diana put her foot down. And he thought it was a good thing if from their earliest years the boys wore tweeds and sensible shoes. For Diana, this represented a return to the horrors of her childhood, with her children being brought up not to enjoy music and dancing as she did but to shoot birds and animals.

The truth is that with his stiffness and old-fashioned attitudes and appearance, Charles was like a dark shadow from her past; for Charles, Diana was trying to be something she was not. He expected an obedient, uncomplaining, complaisant wife, not someone who wanted to wear the latest fashions and spend her evenings dancing in nightclubs.

Many of the most disturbing battles between Charles and Diana stemmed from their different views on how the children should be brought up and the extent to which they should embrace the modern world; in both spheres they were light years apart, but through the battles there were always lighter moments, as a friend of Diana recalled:

> The staff at Kensington Palace were often exhausted and on edge because of the constant battles between Charles and Diana and the tension filled the air – they liked Diana because she was always nice to them, but they thought Charles was like something out of the eighteenth century. The joke in the palace was that when Charles wanted to have sex with Diana, he would say to her, 'May one give one one?' Staff also used to say, 'Do you think they do it with their eyes closed and through a hole in the sheet?' Some of the staff – generally the older ones – sided with Charles, others with Diana. Charles couldn't help being what he had been brought up to be. Diana thought he should have chosen to rebel – she was a rebel, the ultimate rebel I think, and Charles the ultimate conformist.

Diana's rage against Charles led to some very odd behaviour; behaviour that led both the Queen and Prince Philip to consider trying to persuade Diana to spend time in a sanatorium. Diana's friend again:

> The senior royals undoubtedly wanted Diana at one stage to be sectioned. That was probably after she cut up several of Charles's suits and threw them out of the window at Kensington. Diana laughed her head off as she told us that after she'd thrown the

suits out, she spotted palace officials running like Olympic sprinters to retrieve the suits before anyone spotted them!

A retired member of Kensington Palace staff recalled how

Diana would sometimes even hug the maids and the footmen because she was friendly and didn't like the 'us' and 'them' attitude at Kensington, but she was a bit sneaky too and did it a lot more when Charles was there because she knew it really annoyed him. Charles always spoke to her as if he was making a speech to the Commonwealth and she used to say, 'Why are you talking at me, why are you lecturing me?' Then when he turned away, she would stick her tongue out at him and waggle her fingers to suggest his big ears, which made one footman explode with laughter. He apologised and excused himself, but we could hear his laughter as he disappeared along the corridor.

Another former member of the Kensington Palace staff said:

Charles and Diana were not different from ordinary couples who fall out – they used the children in their battles even though they were largely unconscious of the fact that they were doing it. Diana often thought the nannies were on Charles's side – especially Barbara and later Tiggy Legge-Bourke, who Diana thought Charles was in love with. Where the nannies and Charles wanted the boys to be very grown up from day one and to eat and behave sensibly, Diana deliberately let them run wild – she used to say,

'Let them have as much ice cream as they like and eat with their fingers. I don't care if they eat fried chicken till they are sick if they are having fun.' Charles, on the other hand, worried they should learn to hold a knife and fork properly.

The children were aware from as early as they were aware of anything that the differences between their parents were irreconcilable. William and Harry were forced to live in two different worlds and the divisions this caused can be seen in the splits that have developed between William and Harry as adults.

These splits are of course also linked to age-old patterns of behaviour that afflict all royal children. Parental influences mix with childhood experiences and the knowledge of who they are to create what Princess Margaret once called 'the luxuriously damned'.

As we have seen, generations of royal children going back a millennium and more have been brought up in an environment that is materially rich yet emotionally poor; they've also been brought up trapped in the knowledge that effort and ambition are pointless – and the result is a curiously half-formed adult who floats through life being advised and manoeuvred and steered. It's no wonder that Edward VIII when Prince of Wales said, 'I hate this princing.' He could find no other word for the pointlessness of his life.

Diana tried her best despite her own background to give her children a genuinely normal upbringing; not the 'normal' upbringing to which Elizabeth II referred in relation to Charles and his siblings. For Queen Elizabeth, normal meant mixing with the sons and daughters of noblemen, courtiers and English aristocrats. For Diana, normal meant mixing with children far lower down the social scale and even being aware of children and adults right at the bottom.

Visits to shelters run by the homeless charity Centrepoint and to various other charities, including organisations set up to help those with AIDS, had a profound effect on both William and Harry. William took over his mother's patronage of Centrepoint in 2005 (his mother had become patron in 1992), while Harry continued his mother's work with AIDS charities even to the extent of having himself tested live on television.

But if Diana inspired her children to be the first royal princes to really become involved in the lives of the seriously underprivileged, she also insisted that they should have fun: she famously took them to McDonald's and dressed them in T-shirts and jeans, to the horror of older royals, their nanny and their father. McDonald's always delighted Diana because she thought that far more than any other location, it was where real people could be found. She never forgot the time a counter assistant at McDonald's in London's Kensington High Street said to her while she was waiting, 'I've definitely seen you on television, but I can't remember what you were in.' Diana replied that she'd never been on television. 'You also look like Diana,' came the reply, followed by, 'Well, on second thoughts you don't really – I think it's the weird light in here!'

Batted back and forth between the worlds of rock music and McDonald's on the one hand and tweeds and pheasant shooting on the other, the boys' natural diffidence developed in curious ways, ways that reflect so much of what royal siblings in previous generations experienced. We should also remember that despite Diana's and Charles's genuine desire to be good parents, the long shadow of their own childhoods meant William and Harry were often left alone with domestic staff. In his book *Spare*, Harry recalled his loneliness and isolation during weekends at Highgrove. Charles may have hated the absence of his own parents when he was young, but he still often left his sons alone with his staff. Diana too had her life to live and the boys were often alone during their weekends with her at Kensington. For both Diana and Charles, the habit of relying on staff was just too deeply ingrained.

For the first few years of his life, William was the mischievous one. He had tantrums, broke his toys and even swore at Diana on one occasion. He famously pinched one of his teachers' bottoms and there were concerns that he would become something of an uncontrollable tearaway. Harry was much quieter. Diana worried about him, but by the time the boys were a little older, it was as if they had switched roles. Harry was sticking his tongue out at any and every gathering of reporters (something he continued to do as an adult!) where William, increasingly aware that he would one day be king, became more serious, more considered and more self-conscious.

William is probably the most academically industrious of all the royals of the past century. He hated the idea that people would think everything was given to him on a plate and he was embarrassed his father had been admitted to Cambridge simply because he was the Prince of Wales. So, to the astonishment of his teachers, William worked hard at Eton to earn his place at St Andrews University, where he studied geography. An Eton contemporary recalled:

William got on well with the other boys. He didn't lord it over anyone or pull rank and he wasn't teased or bullied as I recall – the school no longer encouraged bullying as character forming as it had in the past and the sadistic business of fagging had come to an end – but William also avoided anything risqué. One boy used to write pornographic stories and sell them to other boys. William never handed over his shilling, but rumour insisted he peeked over other boys' shoulders to get a look!

A St Andrews contemporary said, 'It's a very odd thing but the geography department was filled with boys from landed estates who had picked the subject – geography, I mean – because it is the ultimate safe, non-political subject.'

William also made the decision to go to St Andrews rather than Oxford or Cambridge, perhaps feeling that if he was accepted at an Oxbridge college with his A, B and C at A level, he would be accused of using his royal status to gain entry, given that the usual minimum Oxbridge requirement is three A grades.

Harry developed in a very different way – as a child he seemed often to be lost in his own head. When a courtier announced one Christmas at Sandringham that the Queen would be arriving at teatime, Harry piped up, 'Who is the Queen?' At Eton, Harry was good at sport, but academically he fitted the traditional royal mould and simply could not apply himself to his studies. The broadcaster Jonathan Dimbleby, an old friend of Prince Charles, said that Harry was 'not the brightest'.

Vague and unfocused in the schoolroom, there was a sense that Harry would always have a slightly lost air about him, an air that increased dramatically after the death of his mother in 1997.

True to the oldest traditions of the royal family, both princes did a stint in the armed forces after university – that echo of ancient battles and the need for royal princes to show they will fight for their country – and it is no coincidence that so many pictures were released when the boys were very young showing them riding on tanks and armoured vehicles.

Harry was always more likely to stumble drunk from a nightclub than his increasingly serious brother. William had kingship to lean on; Harry needed a strong woman and his early loves didn't quite have the solidity he needed. Harry was in need of another Camilla, and Chelsy Davy and his other early girlfriends did not have her maternal qualities nor her strength of character and will to control events.

Even before their mother's death, the two boys were aware of Diana's precarious mental state. One palace insider said:

Of course they sensed when their mother was at her worst – when he was little more than a toddler, I once heard Harry say, 'Why is mummy always crying?' Both Charles and Diana tried to protect the boys and of course they had their nannies and staff and their grandparents, but no parent can hide completely how they feel when they are often feeling suicidal, as I believe Diana sometimes was. But she was underneath it all a very strong person and would never have done anything really damaging to herself because that would have left her boys alone.

But if their mother's fragile mental health affected the boys so too did her frenzied search for happiness with a string of men, many of whom were already married.

A retired member of Diana's staff said:

Diana worried that her sons would inevitably find out that she was seeing various men so she never mentioned them when the boys were with her, but you can't really hide that sort of thing. They would never have judged her – when we are young, we accept our parents as they are – but later on it is different. As Oscar Wilde said, 'First we love our parents, then we judge them, sometimes we forgive them.' And that is so true and especially true when it came to the boys' relationship to both their parents. They were often embarrassed by their mother's antics but they sensed she was doing what she needed to do to be happy.

William and Harry grew up aware that they were special – surrounded by servants and deference, how could it have been otherwise? – yet both were conscious, as so many of their ancestors have been, that deep within, they were not special at all.

As a result, they reflect in their life decisions and personalities the characters and characteristics of both their parents and their grandparents, but perhaps especially of their grandparents. William has accepted his role and intends to play it exactly as his grandmother Queen Elizabeth played the role. Unlike his brother, he is acutely aware that he cannot control the press so his behaviour must be whiter than white. Sensing that Kate Middleton had all the solidity he needed – but without the hunting, shooting and fishing background – he knew that, despite their trial separation in 2007, he could not do his job as king without her or someone very like her. She has Diana's sensitivity and Camilla's uncomplaining strength.

Harry, with no official role to contain him, demonstrated early on that he had a great deal of the rebel in him. The nightclubs, the drunkenness and the dressing up as a Nazi for a party all pointed to a man trapped in dysfunctional childhood. But Harry also inherited his great-aunt Princess Margaret's inability to reconcile being a royal with being a spare. If anything, Harry was always closer to his mother than William. Certainly she encouraged his rebellious side – 'She delighted in it,' recalled one Kensington Palace aide – and he felt even less comfortable than his brother each time he was dropped into the essentially eighteenth-century world his father inhabits.

His escape, as we know, came via Meghan Markle, an immensely strong woman who does not share power. Her sense of her own destiny, her absolute conviction about how she and Harry should live, gave Harry for the first time an identity outside his status as a royal with nothing to do. But, of course, there was a price to pay for this. Like his ancestor Edward VIII and his great-aunt Princess Margaret, Harry felt he had to escape. In adopting the world view of his wife – a world view that seems to believe, for example, that it is fine to make speeches about climate change while flying in private jets – in short, in adopting 'Meghan's way', Harry has left himself open to the sort of press attention he has always hated, the press attention he believes hounded his mother to her death. The problem for Harry, as the broadcaster Jonathan Dimbleby put it, is that many people believe Harry is 'led by the nose' by Meghan, which means that he often spouts her views but stumbles when questioned about them. He and Meghan have fallen into the trap of believing that if you are famous, your opinion counts on every subject from climate change to nuclear disarmament, regardless of your qualifications.

Every generation of royals includes individuals who toe the line and individuals who spin out of the usual royal orbit and William and Harry are in this sense true to type. But how will the next generation cope with a world that is changing – even for the royals – faster than ever before?

CHAPTER TEN

MODERN LOVE: THE CHILDREN OF WILLIAM AND KATE

'I think that God, in creating man, somewhat
overestimated his ability.'

OSCAR WILDE

One of the biggest problems with the royal family is that obsessed as they were until recently with marrying their children to other royals to whom they were invariably related, each generation grew smaller and smaller in stature. No one seemed to notice this was happening, but it resulted in members of the royal family seeming almost stunted in the way the working classes were traditionally seen as stunted.

By the time Queen Elizabeth and her sister Margaret were born, they were so small that bigger people, as one courtier quipped, were in danger of tripping over them. Margaret, perhaps because she was so unkind to people – even, occasionally, to her friends – became known as the 'royal dwarf' or the 'poisoned dwarf'. Her biographer

Theo Aronson described her as looking rather like Minnie Mouse. But the general loss of stature is hardly surprising given that Queen Victoria was only 4ft 11in. tall – close to being classified, in those less politically correct times, as a dwarf.

Prince Philip helped buck the trend, pushing Charles to a respectable 5ft 10in., and Diana, also at 5ft 10in., ensured her children avoided the curse of miniaturisation. As we have seen, the senior royals had set their sights a little lower – metaphorically speaking – by the time Charles needed to marry, but an ancient and very senior English aristocratic family was the lowest level to which they were prepared to stoop and a former courtier told the present author that discussions were initially had within the family (before Diana was considered) about trying to find a foreign princess. It was only when they realised that there were none left, or at least none who were not Catholics or mad or in some other way disqualified, that they gave up and made do with Diana.

Prince William's (1982–) decision to marry Catherine Middleton (1982–) represented a further step down by the royal family from aristocrat to wealthy middle class. Kate was acceptable because William insisted but also because there was a sense that she would fit in and give an increasingly critical world a sense that the royal family was prepared to evolve in line with changes in society. The decision to allow the marriage likely had little to do with her height (a healthy 5ft 9in.), but the usual precautions were taken before her marriage to William. These are always carried out to ensure a future queen is able to have children. If Kate had not been fertile, there is little doubt the marriage would have been off. Diana complained in a brief encounter with the present author that she had in all

innocence thought her premarital check-ups had to do with general
health, only realising later on that she had actually been tested for
fertility. 'I was so innocent I just went along with everything at that
stage,' she said.

Catherine Middleton, far sharper than her husband-to-be and
indeed far sharper than the aristocratic oddballs surrounding the
royal family, must have known precisely what was going on, but
she is not nor has she ever been a rebel. Part of her attraction for
William may have been that she has a kind of solidity untainted by
centuries of mad Hanoverian and Saxe-Coburg blood. Her attraction for the royal family was that she was not tainted by their history and did not fit into any of the categories for which she could be
mocked – dim and aristocratic, dim and foreign. Although that did
not prevent her mother, a far kinder and more intelligent woman
than most royal women, being mocked by the aristocratic courtiers
at Buckingham Palace and Kensington, where she was known as
'doors to manual', a reference to her time as an air steward.

The royal family sensed that in Kate they had found someone
who was very unlikely deliberately to embarrass them. Upwardly
mobile like her parents, Kate was never going to do anything other
than adopt the ways of the royal family, just as her parents had
adopted the ways of the upper middle classes. Even gossip about
William being unfaithful to Catherine after their marriage was
unlikely to disturb Kate's apparent Buddhist calm. Of course, privately, William and Kate, like all couples, fall out, row, shout at each
other and say unkind things to each other, but Kate is an appeas-
er by instinct and William always gives way as he had more than
enough emotional turmoil, divorce and disruption as a child. He

hates confrontation and signs of annoyance can only be detected in the tone in which he calls his wife 'darling' when he is cross with her. One former member of the palace staff who knew both Kate and Meghan Markle said:

Kate is Meghan Markle without the messianic complex. Kate is also thoroughly modern and can be a tease. She calls William 'babe' rather than 'Binkie' or 'Twinky', 'Tiggy' or 'Fruity' or any of the other sorts of nickname one might expect in the royal family. (William calls *her* the 'Duchess of Doolittle'.) Kate herself teases the ladies-in-waiting, gentlemen of the bedchamber and other more self-important advisers by deliberately using the word 'lounge' instead of drawing or sitting room and by occasionally ignoring what they see as vital etiquette. On the other hand, she has nothing of the radical playfulness of Diana. Diana enjoyed slumming it and was in many ways downwardly mobile – she wanted to escape her aristocratic childhood. Kate wants to escape her middle-class childhood. She dislikes burgers and chips and wouldn't dream of taking her children to McDonald's, and she doesn't rock the boat when the vast weight of traditional royal pursuits bears down on her children. Prince George, for example, has been taken to the annual Boxing Day shoot at Sandringham, and he's been grouse shooting in Scotland with his father. Like Diana, Kate found the killing of hundreds of birds in a day upsetting – she was reduced to tears on her first outing – but she accepts that if the royals do it, then she must live with it. Kate knows that taking up causes is fraught with difficulty so she doesn't do it except in so far as she is able to support charities that help people. She is not the sort to join the League Against Cruel Sports or campaign vigorously to stop people flying and thereby reduce global warming. Unlike her sister-in-law, she has the sense to realise that campaigning on global warming is likely to result in huge criticism for the royals, who famously fly by private jet or helicopter.

As we have seen down the centuries, killing animals as a training for fighting is as old as the royal family itself, and the truth is William enjoys shooting despite his late mother's disapproval. Both he and Harry were taught to shoot and stalk as boys, and it is a tradition he will likely hand on to George and Louis. He did it partly to please his grandmother and father and partly because he enjoys it.

George (born in 2013), the heir, Charlotte (2015) and Louis (2018) will also learn, as their mother has learned, that the core values of the royal family cannot be changed. As we will see, Meghan tried to change those values, failed and was forced into exile. Kate will not make the same mistake, but she is already worried that the curse of the royal spare will fall on Louis as it has fallen on his uncle Harry.

In this environment, and with these parents, how will William and Kate's children fare?

As each of Kate's children was born, the Queen was told first via a specially encrypted phone call – this is standard practice – but then rather than wait for the traditional printed message to be placed on an easel outside Buckingham Palace announcing the news, Kate and William told the world via Twitter, to the disgust of the old guard at the palace.

Born in 2013, George was looked after in his first months of life on Anglesey, where his father had been stationed, largely by William and Kate themselves. They were keen to let the world know that during this early period, at least, they wanted to experience the sleepless nights that plague all new parents. A former member of staff at Kensington Palace, to which the couple quickly relocated in 2014, explained that they were so appalled by how tired they were that they gradually discarded this early enthusiasm, increasingly leaving the bulk of the childcare to paid staff. It is not for nothing that there are nine staff bedrooms at the top of their apartment at Kensington, not to mention a whole flat – bedroom, kitchen, sitting room and bathroom – for the nanny. By comparison, their new home in the grounds of Windsor Castle, where the family took up residence shortly before the death of the Queen in 2022, is relatively modest. Now that the children are all out of nappies, their parents have prioritised outside space over staff quarters, and Adelaide Cottage (so called though it is not a cottage by any normal definition) was chosen specifically to give the children more space to play: they will be able to ride their ponies and drive their miniature motor cars unseen and unaccompanied in the huge private grounds of Windsor Castle. Kensington Palace will remain William and Kate's official residence, but they will spend much of their time at Windsor and at Anmer Hall, their Georgian mansion at Sandringham.

George, as the heir, has quickly become aware that he is special, and with his sensible side parting and jackets and ties, he might easily be a boy from the 1950s, the last decade in which the royals felt they were secure. A former teacher at Thomas's, his school in Battersea, said:

George, though delightful, knows that he is different from all the other children. People talk nonsense about him being treated just like the other children at the school – it just isn't true, although the differences are subtle. But over time even the most subtle differences are noticed by children and I think George *knows* – he is aware of his difference and as a result has a slightly lordly or laid-back air about him. He already knows that one day he will be king, and children read story books where the king is always the special one. I overheard him ask another child, 'Where is your palace?' He quickly became aware that he was the only one with a palace, though God knows the school has enough oligarchs and other mega-wealthy people from around the world.

That laid-back air echoes the greatest curse of all royal princes: by the time they are aware of anything, they are aware of their privileged position and that whatever they do, this will always be the case. Kate makes no effort – unlike Diana – to bring the children down to earth, because she doesn't want them to have a 'normal' childhood in the sense that Diana wanted it for William and Harry. She is aware that Diana's modernising ideas created problems, most especially with Harry, whose rebelliousness and dissatisfaction with his role seem to stem at least in part from his mother's dislike of the constraints and rigidities of royal life. Kate revels in the fact that her children are royal but pays lip service to a vague idea of what constitutes a 'normal' childhood, as one former member of staff explained:

The younger generation have to insist they want a normal or ordinary upbringing for their children because that goes down well with the public, but this is just window dressing. They want the most expensive schools, and even at Adelaide Cottage [where Kate and William now live] the couple continue the royal tradition of farming out the main tasks of childrearing to paid staff. Kate is a lovely person, but she is far more ambitious for her children even than Meghan. She is the Anne Boleyn of our time!

This fits with what we know of the children's school, Lambrook, near Windsor. A prep school based in a palatial Victorian mansion, Lambrook has taught the children of the immensely wealthy since the mid-nineteenth century. According to one member of the palace staff, 'the appeal of the school is that it taught several of the grandsons of Queen Victoria. It was really a compromise school – grand enough for William and with royal connections, it pleased Kate because it meant the children would not be boarding.' So at last, early in the twenty-first century, there has been a shift – a generation of royals will not be sent to live away from home in order to ensure they become tough independent adults as early as possible.

In terms of its curriculum, Lambrook offers a curious mix of the ancient and the modern – the children are encouraged to look after a range of animals and there has been speculation that this may change the attitude of a new generation of royals to the old obsession with shooting. This is unlikely, however, as members of the royal family have always adored animals, whether horses or dogs, while seeing no contradiction in also enjoying shooting and hunting.

But however modern the curriculum at Lambrook, one thing is certain: it will not provide what most of us would think of as a normal childhood for children who know they are different.

And besides, a normal childhood does not fit or prepare children for life in the royal family and this is especially true for younger royals who cannot take ordinary jobs and lead ordinary lives yet have no real role beyond opening hospitals, attending charity lunches and allowing good causes to add their names to their letterheads.

Charlotte and Louis will always know that in the strange world in which they find themselves, George has a kind of glow they lack. Kate is a warm, maternal woman and the children will not suffer as William and Harry suffered as youngsters, but as in every generation of royals, the shackles of the past cannot entirely be removed. The terror in royal circles is that Louis will find himself a lost soul like his uncle Harry.

It is often suggested that Kate and William really do need the teams of nannies and maids and nursery staff they employ because they are incredibly busy, but as one former staffer explained, this idea is 'nonsense'.

They just have all that because it is what's expected and they have the money. It's a truism throughout life that our expenditure expands to fill the money available and money for the royal family in practical terms is almost limitless. It's like Mick Jagger having a house in London and a house in New York or Charlie Watts owning half a dozen classic cars when he can't even drive – when you have the money, you do stupid things. When Kate suggested they might not need quite so many staff, William was baffled.

He has never been alone and without paid staff in his life. He would be unable to function without staff. It would be like being abandoned on a desert island when you have no idea where food comes from or how to build a shelter.

Certainly, for Kate, the desire that her children should have a 'normal' childhood simply means that she is involved in their day-to-day lives. It does not mean they will not enjoy the luxuries and privileges of a royal upbringing. This has been an area of some conflict between Kate and William. She rarely tires of the daily grind of looking after three sometimes boisterous children. William, on the other hand, 'heaves a sigh of relief when the children are taken away by their nanny'.

One acid commentator writing in the *Guardian* newspaper asked if Kate and William needed round-the-clock childcare and teams of servants because they are busier than a single woman trying to bring up three small children on her own. The writer concluded that today's royal nannies are employed for exactly the same reason royal nannies have always been employed: 'It's just what they do.'

William and Kate's apartment at Kensington Palace is actually more like a four-storey house. It's the apartment formerly lived in by Princess Margaret, although like all royals they had to have the whole house refurbished before they were able to move in. The house has staff quarters, dressing rooms, a gym, numerous bedrooms and bathrooms, a night nursery and a day nursery. The joke among staff at Kensington is that the apartment has far more staff than it has residents. When they are bored with both Kensington and their main home at Adelaide Cottage, Kate, William and the children retreat to ten-bedroom Anmer Hall on the Sandringham estate, where there are even bigger staff quarters, a day nursery, a night nursery, dressing rooms and numerous reception rooms. The house was a wedding present from the Queen.

Kate is said to be a very hands-on mother, but what this means in practice is difficult to assess. No one says of an ordinary mother 'she is very hands-on' as if that were somehow astonishing. In Kate and William's case, what is really meant is that unlike previous generations and despite having numerous full-time staff looking after their children, they still found time to change their nappies, read them bedtime stories and so on. The traditional once-a-day meeting for which the children were dressed by their nanny and formally presented to their parents has gone and the children run in and out of their parents' rooms and offices as they please.

A key aspect, curiously, of the children's education is that they should learn how to manage staff. This would always have been an issue as the children, especially George, will always have staff, but the media headlines generated by Meghan Markle's relationship with palace professionals has made it very clear that in the modern world, where staff must be treated kindly and with respect, new skills are required. Few families still exist in England where children are taught how to behave to their staff, but it is seen as an essential part of growing up in the royal family. For Charles and Anne, Andrew and Edward, a key part of this was being taught not to be over-familiar with the staff and under no circumstances to treat them as friends; for William and Kate and their children, this is more difficult because of the sheer terror that any high-handed treatment of their staff should reach the newspapers.

A former member of the palace communications staff said, 'It's all so much more difficult now. Older royals dislike modern egalitarianism because, having lost all real political power, one of the few areas where they could still exert power was over what we used to call servants. Now they can't even lord it over their servants!'

And there are a lot of servants. Leaving aside the maids and kitchen staff, William and Kate's staff include a private secretary; two army orderlies, who clean shoes, carry notes around the royal residences, collect takeaway meals and walk the dog; a housekeeper; a house help, who doubles occasionally as a chauffeur; Kate's stylist Natasha Archer, who doubles as her PA; and hair stylist Amanda Cook Tucker.

Of course, when it comes to servants, nannies and governesses were always rather special, always one up from cooks and footmen. When Tony Armstrong-Jones, later Lord Snowdon, was a humble photographer prior to his marriage to Princess Margaret, he was made to use the servants' entrance when he visited Lord Glenconner. He was told in no uncertain terms that photographers did not even rank as high as nannies and governesses, a slight he never forgot.

The result is that so long as they behave as the royal family say they should behave, nannies and governesses can almost (but perhaps not quite) be treated as friends.

This is why William and Harry's old nanny Jessie Webb was invited not just to William's twenty-first birthday party but also to his wedding to Kate in 2011 and to Harry and Meghan's wedding in 2018. Jessie had devoted her life to the royals – she also looked after Viscount Linley's children. But is there not something odd, as we discovered with Marion Crawford, in deciding to spend your life looking after other people's children night and day?

Though Catherine Middleton really is hands-on when it comes to her three children, this is true only relative to earlier royal mothers. Much as she would like to be a normal mother who spends most of her time with her children, the huge pressure of royal tradition cannot be ignored and those day and night nurseries and the other children's rooms at Kensington Palace (and more recently Adelaide Cottage at Windsor Castle) did not resound to the sounds of Kate Middleton but rather to the sound of the remarkable bowler hat-wearing Maria Teresa Turrion Borrallo, a Spanish nanny employed in 2014 when Prince George was just eight months old. Nannies and nurserymaids for the royals are rather like houses and expensive cars for the ordinary rich – they just can't have enough of them. It's the same with midwives – Kate had three in the private Lindo Wing of St Mary's Hospital, Paddington, where all three of her children were born. No one is quite sure why three midwives were necessary. But when the royal family are involved, three midwives are just the beginning: as the *Sun* newspaper pointed out, 'Kate had a twenty-strong team of professionals in her childbirth team, including two obstetricians, three midwives, three anaesthetists, four surgical staff, two special care baby-unit staff, four paediatricians, one lab technician and three or four managers.'

One insider said of William and Kate's supernanny:

Maria is a Picasso among nannies. Highly intelligent and endlessly patient, she seems to have a deep instinct for childcare, although as with Diana and her nannies, there is a feeling that occasionally Kate worries that the children are actually closer to Maria than they are to either her or her husband.

Others are not so kind about the supernanny. One former member of staff said:

> She is super-efficient and very good with the children, but she is like something from a Victorian novel in the sense that she seems to relish the antiquarian nature of her life like one of those governesses in a Brontë novel who feels the need to have no real life of her own. It's very odd and very odd to be around and I think Kate feels the oddness of it but just has to deal with it. Just think of it – Maria trained at the Norland school in Bath (founded in Shepherd's Bush, which is no longer mentioned). She is occasionally seen wearing the terrible Norland uniform – a plain brown dress and brown hat that make the poor nanny look like a prisoner about to be transported to Australia.

Norland nannies are also trained in martial arts and how to drive a car like a police officer chasing a criminal. Even those sympathetic to the difficulties of being royal admit that employing a Norland nanny is more about status than real need. Norland is the favourite agency for Russian oligarchs and the super-rich, as one former Norland employee explained.

The Norland nanny just goes with the territory of being very, very rich; Americans with money who married into the English aristocracy early in the twentieth century always employed them.

They are a must-have like Eton and superyachts. It's just conspic-
uous consumption.

Kate was persuaded that Norland nannies and all the rest of
the staff were essential. When she demurred and suggested that
she would like to do a little more of the nitty-gritty part of the
childcare, it was made very clear to her that this was best left to
the professionals, and Kate is nothing if not obedient to the rules
of life in the royal family.

Like most so-called top-drawer nannies, Maria Teresa Turrion
Borrallo is a curious character. As one insider, widely quoted in the
newspapers, put it, 'She is not married and doesn't have a boyfriend,
as her life is totally dedicated to the family she is working with. She
is known for being totally professional – married to the job.'

It is striking that being professional here seems to be equated
with having no life of one's own, and it is only in the employment
of the royal family that such levels of selflessness are expected.
Would we say of a City banker that they are totally professional because they are not married? One remembers Queen Mary's
bafflement that Elizabeth and Margaret's nanny Marion Crawford
should have any sort of a life independent of the royal children.
The selflessness of royal employees is matched by the selfishness of
their employers. The Queen Mother delighted in the fact that her
servants were mostly gay men, as they were unlikely to get married and have children, so they would always be there to serve her.
As she said to a stuffy equerry who complained at the numbers of
gay men at Clarence House, 'Without them we would have to go
self-service, wouldn't we?'

As William Tallon, the Queen Mother's Page of the Backstairs, put it in an interview shortly before his death:

What you have to remember is that living in the royal family is like living in an insane asylum – many of the people are very nice, but they are all actually quite mad and I always included myself in that category. I did not have a family so I tried to make the royal family mine, which I think I did. I was always a servant, but the Queen Mother found me amusing and reliable and she could see I was utterly devoted to her. If you work for the royals, you are expected to work for them body and soul. You are not to have a life of your own and I don't think that will ever change.

The stresses of having children and being part of the royal family mean that Kate and William's carefree attitude to life as it was when they were at university together has long gone. Despite William's horror of confrontation, there are occasional rows, which all couples have but which are exacerbated in the case of William and Kate by William's circle of friends. Among his oldest friends are a number of young aristocratic women among whom there was at one time a competition to see who could get William into bed. One of William's friends from St Andrews University said:

It's almost a kind of joke but with a serious edge – the problem is that William is like a magnet for a certain kind of aristocratic idle young woman, and most of William and Kate's friends are either aristocratic idle young men or aristocratic idle young women.

William, through no fault of his own, becomes a sort of focus of sexual fantasy rather like a famous pop star might.

No one is suggesting Rose Hanbury, the Marchioness of Cholmondeley (pronounced Chumley), was part of this group, but unfounded rumours about a rift between her and Kate certainly led to speculation – again entirely false – that Hanbury had had an affair with William. With the disaster of his parents' own marriage and their affairs still very much in the public mind, William must always be seen to have a perfect or near perfect marriage, so any rumours about affairs are highly dangerous. Suddenly cold-shouldering a former friend about whom there is speculation of sexual impropriety becomes a risky issue in itself, as it may seem to confirm something that has never happened. The long and the short of this is that Kate and William's lives have to be managed down to the last detail.

And this also applies to their children. When they misbehave in public, every detail is noted by the press. This can bring both praise and blame and it is easy to imagine the difficulties involved in trying to live in the glare of this level of scrutiny. When Prince Louis misbehaved at the late Queen's Platinum Jubilee, for example, by sticking his tongue out at his mother and then putting his hand over her mouth, Kate's reaction was praised by teams of expert commentators. She apparently used a secret code to calm the children as she does on occasions – she simply says, 'Let's take a break.' But as a former staffer explained, the children know these few words carry far more weight than we might imagine.

It's been drummed into the children that when Mummy says, 'Let's take a break,' she actually means, 'This is very serious and if you don't stop mucking about and embarrassing me, there will be consequences when we get back to the palace.' That's why it works. If Kate says there will be consequences, then there really will be. She is good at boundaries and not nearly such a pushover as she might look.

Aware from their earliest years of this intense public interest, all three of Kate and William's children struggle to behave like adults at public events – and who can blame them? When Prince George and Princess Charlotte started squabbling at their great-grandmother's funeral – George apparently pinched Charlotte – the story spread across the world. But the real interest of the story was that Kate was apparently reprimanded by a senior, unnamed member of the royal family. According to a member of Kate's staff:

The royal who was rather snappy with Kate about her children was snapped at in turn, as the person involved – and I'm not going to identify the person involved – is famous for irritability and bad behaviour. This was just one in a series of mild and some-times not-so-mild criticisms of Kate and the truth is a lot of it is just jealousy – the older royals see Kate's children getting the sort of maternal attention and love they did not get themselves and they are bitter about it. They rationalise their criticisms by saying Kate is mollycoddling the children. It also infuriates the older royals that Kate, not a princess of royal blood, will one day surpass them all. I think this is something that especially infuriates Harry as his children will not be as important – ever.

Kate then is a moderniser but a moderniser who treads warily. Unlike Meghan Markle, she has a very precisely tuned sense of how far she can go and when it is best not to fight back against 'the Firm'. And just as Kate cannot entirely modernise royal childcare so William is struggling with the traditional pastimes of the royal family as they become ever more unpopular with the public. Fishing is not going to be a problem, as it can be carried out well away from prying eyes on the royal family's own beats of the Dee at Balmoral, but pheasant shooting at Sandringham is more difficult. William loves shooting – a love he shares with his father – but he is also conscious that the tide is now moving against what many people now refer to as blood sports (the royals prefer to refer to them as field sports). But are they suitable for George, Charlotte and Louis? In terms of fishing and shooting, the royals are still living in the Edwardian era when William's great-great-great-grandfather Edward VII would happily shoot thousands of pheasants in a single day. At Sandringham, shooting days in the twenty-first century involve what the royals refer to as small bags – around 200–300 birds in a day – but the Sandringham shoot is under increasing pressure because to guarantee 200–300 birds in a day, the Sandringham keepers feel the need to set traps for what they refer to as vermin, which means everything that might eat the pheasant chicks reared on the estate specifically to be shot. William was intensely embarrassed as patron of the British Trust for Ornithology, for example, when it was widely reported that a little owl, a protected species, had been caught in one of his keepers' traps.

Despite these difficulties, William is keen that his sons should learn to shoot, but few expect Catherine will allow any of her children to be blooded – their faces smeared with blood from their first kill – which, as we have seen, was an important rite of passage in all previous royal princes' and princesses' childhoods. An even bigger problem is stalking. Crawling across Scotland's deer forest with a professional stalker and shooting a stag has always been a royal tradition (even the late Queen enjoyed stalking) and William is hoping that the remoteness of the Scottish hills will make this something George and Louis may be able to get away with at some point, although it would be extremely controversial if publicly known.

Army visits will also loom large for George, Charlotte and Louis. That the royals should still be seen as closely linked to the military is a given and we will see pictures of George and Louis riding on tanks and armoured vehicles because always at the back of every royal prince's mind is this compulsion to appear to be ready to fight.

When the time comes, George and Louis will almost certainly be sent to Eton, Charlotte to Princess Anne's old school Benenden. Gordonstoun is out of the question. It is now too tainted and not just by Prince Charles's criticisms and its remote location. A number of other former pupils have made detailed claims about bullying and sexual abuse at the school, which were heard by the Scottish Child Abuse Inquiry. A private Facebook page was set up in 2013, where victims of abuse at the school were able to share their experiences. Eton, a stone's throw from Windsor Castle and

Adelaide Cottage, is a safer bet and ensures that royal children mix only with the children of the aristocracy and the very wealthy. A former Kensington Palace staffer said:

Most of what the royal family do so far as choosing schools is concerned is based on the fact that if you don't pay for it, it's not worth having and on the fact that whatever they say to the contrary, no member of the royal family wants their children to mix with the sort of people who may end up as their servants or, to use the more politically correct term, their staff. Sending George and Louis to Eton will ensure that this does not happen. Even Gordonstoun, though paid for, was an aberration based on Prince Philip's obsession with manliness. George and Louis mixing with people below a certain social level is seen bizarrely as a security risk – but this is nonsense when you remember the number of children at Eton who come from Russian and Chinese backgrounds. The truth is that Eton is far more of a security risk than an ordinary comprehensive.

This is a worry for the royals, but there are enough home-grown aristocrats at what they jokingly refer to as Slough Grammar School to make this the 'safest' option, and they are similarly unlikely to be deterred by what the author James Fox, himself an Old Etonian, refers to as Eton's 'reputation for homosexuality'. Best of all, Eton knows how to treat the children of the royal family: with children from some backgrounds, the entrance exam is more flexible and Eton has a happy tradition of not expecting too much of royal children when it comes to the academic side of things.

Royal children *are* different and if they are no longer taught at home – which is a departure from much of royal history – it is a small concession and one designed to avoid the very worst products of the old system: products such as James II, or the Prince Regent, or Edward VII, or Princess Margaret and any number of other damaged and, worse, damaging individuals.

According to one insider, William and Kate discussed the possibility of sending their children to state schools, at least at the primary level, but this caused panic among officials at Kensington Palace and Buckingham Palace.

The children began their school life at various nurseries – Westacre Montessori Nursery for George and Willcocks in Kensington, before moving to Thomas's in Battersea (£20,000 a year in 2017).

William has publicly stated, 'The materialism of the world I find quite tricky sometimes. I would like George and Charlotte to grow up being a little bit more simple in their approach and their outlook and just looking after those around them and treating others as they would like to be treated themselves.'

This is an updated version of the royal family's sense that they must emphasise their democratic credentials – it's a mantra that repeats the idea that royal parents want their children to have a 'normal' childhood, but of course it has to be couched in these vague terms because not many 'normal' people could afford £20,000 a year for each of their children to attend a junior school. In truth, the children will grow up next to wealthy foreigners (some of whom may have acquired their wealth illegally) and aristocrats. A journalist writing about the royal children at their first school pointed out that £20,000 a year is 'an awful lot to pay for what inevitably boils down to a bit of finger-painting'.

The children's teachers are understandably reluctant to talk about their royal charges, but the old pattern of royal princesses having more drive than their brothers may be about to repeat itself. A former teacher at Thomas's was only prepared to say, 'George has a slightly detached, vague air about him – delightful though he is, he is not a determined character. Charlotte is far more curious, far more definite!'

But as the children grow, the royal couple will be hoping that none of them inherit their uncle Harry's fraught relationship with his status as part of the monarchy – nor their male royal ancestors' more eccentric tendencies. Key to this will be efforts to prevent Charlotte and Louis growing up with a sense that they have no real role. George, by contrast, may find that as society changes ever more rapidly, and what remains of the crown's dominions continues to shrink, by the time he becomes king, he will be king of a far smaller country than that ruled by any of his ancestors.

CHAPTER ELEVEN

CHILDREN IN EXILE: THE CHILDREN OF MEGHAN AND HARRY

'Each generation imagines itself to be more intelligent than the one that went before it, and wiser than the one that comes after it.'

GEORGE ORWELL

It is very difficult to write about Harry (1984–) and Meghan (1981–), the Duke and Duchess of Sussex, and how their children are likely to cope in the goldfish bowl created by their parents without taking a long look at the strange lives of this oddly matched couple. Their personal histories and their role in the world as adults are likely to affect their children's development profoundly. But one thing is certain: damaged people – and both Meghan and Harry do seem damaged – tend to pass on some of this damage to their children. This is by no means inevitable, but as the poet Philip Larkin neatly and famously summed it up, 'They fuck you up, your mum and dad / They may not mean to but they do.'

Before we look at Harry and Meghan's own difficult childhoods, what can be said about them as adults?

Both Meghan and Harry, understandably, like to think of themselves as important players on the world stage and both believe themselves deeply misunderstood and unfairly treated by everyone except their friends – and even their friends occasionally come under suspicion. There is no doubt that Meghan has a sincere desire to emulate Harry's mother, the late Diana, Princess of Wales, and be a force for good, but the more she kicks and screams at the mere hint of criticism, the more people point at the kicking and screaming as evidence that she is entitled, overcontrolling and lacking in self-awareness.

Almost every article and book written about Meghan or about Meghan and Harry paints her as either a Lady Macbeth character or (less often) a woman wronged because she is biracial and an American. No one has yet produced a balanced account of Meghan – and this is partly Meghan's own fault.

If Meghan's biographer Tom Bower is correct, for example, she made every effort to stop her friends talking to him. In Bower's view, this spoke volumes about Meghan's controlling personality. It also produced a situation where almost all those prepared to be interviewed by Bower and other biographers are those who have either fallen out with Meghan or never liked her in the first place. Had Meghan been less worried about her friends speaking to Bower – less concerned to control the narrative, as she might have put it – she might have got some part of her side of the story across. As Bower himself claimed in a magazine interview, 'Meghan did everything she could to stop me from talking to her friends and people that worked with her. It was foolish of her to ignore me, because they would probably be happier with the book if they could tell their story.'

Meghan's childhood, her personality and her behaviour since marrying Prince Harry will inevitably be central to her role as a mother to Archie (born in 2019) and Lilibet (2021), as indeed will Harry's childhood and the history of his relationship with Meghan.

Meghan is, in some senses, a construct; she is someone who skilfully edits her public persona to create a character for herself that appears admirable and sympathetic, skirting around her flaws. She seems almost pathologically ambitious and the seeds of this ambition can be seen in many of her pronouncements about her own past. Having claimed she effectively grew up as an only child, she had to cope with the upset this caused her half-brother Tom Junior, not to mention a lawsuit from her half-sister Samantha. Meghan's claims that her family struggled financially when she was a child appeared to be contradicted by many people who reminded her that she had attended an expensive fee-paying school, paid for in part by her father's successful career as a Hollywood lighting director. She was disturbed certainly by her parents' divorce and by what she increasingly felt about her father's lack of loyalty to her. According to Tom Bower, who interviewed her father Thomas Markle at length, Meghan increasingly saw him as an embarrassment. One of her former college friends claimed that Meghan's growing sense of her own mission in the world made her increasingly identify with her black mother, Doria Ragland, rather than her white father.

In America, as in the UK, people in earlier periods rewrote their personal histories to try to emphasise their elevated status, but that has all changed – now successful people tend to emphasise their humble if not poverty-stricken origins to demonstrate how far they have travelled in life and to show that they have made it without the advantages of privilege. This is the category into which Meghan fits. Her parents' divorce did not lead to poverty, but it did mean, as it does with many children of divorced parents, that the young Meghan was shuttled back and forth between two different worlds. With her father, Meghan learned to love acting and the world of TV, and it is open to question whether she would have been the moderately successful actor she became without his influence. But she loved her mother too and admired her numerous attempts to set up and run various businesses, even when this led to bankruptcy, and her mother became a more central figure as Meghan increasingly identified with her black heritage.

Many people are embarrassed about or even ashamed of their parents – but in Meghan, this already fraught relationship with her father is complicated by the fact that she is a public figure who wants full control over her own image. She seems to see living life as equivalent to playing a part and Meghan's years acting and especially acting in the series *Suits* may have deepened her need to tell 'my truth' rather more than 'the truth' about her own past. Even her own lawyers, in defending Meghan against her half-sister's legal action, had to come up with the lame explanation that when Meghan said she grew up as an only child she was not describing objective reality but 'how it felt'. Nothing wrong with that, one might say, given that there is a seventeen-year age gap between Meghan and her sister and that Meghan may have felt Samantha was trying to cash in on her sister's fame. It might also be said that Thomas and Samantha Markle are, objectively speaking, an embarrassment, but that is merely to confirm the family's dysfunction. Whatever the objective truth, we are in the territory staked out in Meghan's interview with her friend Oprah Winfrey, where the phrase 'my truth', like the phrase 'alternative facts', can be used to legitimise any amount of factual inaccuracy. 'My truth' is just a way to make 'my opinion' sound less subjective and it is part of that general air of Californian 'therapy-speak' to which Meghan and Harry seem to have become addicted. No doubt this delights as many observers as it irritates others. And besides, leaving the past behind, whether family or friends, is not that unusual. As people move through life, they often feel the need to keep different groups of their friends apart – psychologists call it compartmentalising. Some, for instance, find that when they arrive at university, their old friends at home seem unsophisticated or embarrassing in some other way so they are unceremoniously dropped – in more recent parlance, they are ghosted or blanked.

Trying to stop one's friends finding out about one's past is difficult and stressful enough, but trying to do it when you are married to Prince Harry must be a nightmare from which the only escape is retreat into a gated compound as far from England as possible.

Time will tell whether this has any repercussions on their children, Archie and Lilibet, but, as we have seen, history sometimes repeats itself. We are very likely to be the sort of mother or father we have learned to be through watching our own parents. This doesn't mean we slavishly do as they did, but echoes of our own early biographies embed themselves deeply in our own parenting. The children of broken homes are more likely to end up creating broken homes; children with divorced parents get divorced more often than children whose parents did not divorce. And we have to remember that before she met Harry, Meghan had already been married and divorced.

Meghan's attempts to control access to her parents and her siblings really began in earnest in 2016. When she was a minor Hollywood actor, no one was especially interested in her past, but when she began to date Prince Harry, the British tabloid press turned its full attention to a woman who wanted any and all publicity to emphasise that she was a successful actor, an activist for the rights of the less privileged and for women and black people. She certainly did not want the press ferreting around in her own difficult personal history. And the harder Meghan tried to shut down her father and half-siblings Samantha and Tom Junior, the more the press felt they were on to a good story. The years during which Meghan was largely able to control what people said about her ended, and all she could do was turn increasingly to litigation, employing what a *Private Eye* journalist called the royal couple's legal 'attack dogs'. The magazine teasingly suggested that we might reach a situation where Harry and Meghan issued writs so frequently that they might end up threatening to sue anyone who suggested they were overly keen on suing!

What Meghan cannot seem to grasp is that it is much better to accept her own past with all its difficulties and to accept the rough ride the press will always give her. By attacking press criticisms and resorting to legal action when much that is said about her and her husband could be said to fall within the boundaries of fair comment, she merely draws more attention to any and every story to which she objects. She is encouraged in this by Harry, who seems to have conflated Meghan's treatment by the press with his mother's treatment by the press. He seems to have forgotten that his mother used the power of the press for her own ends, as he is now doing. 'The media are like children,' Diana once said, during a brief interview with the present author, and we know how much she loved children. Journalists were brilliantly manipulated by Diana, and journalists helped create Diana as a global icon. The truth, which Harry insists on trying to rewrite, is that the press made Diana, and a drunk driver killed her. Diana, unlike her son and his wife, was intelligent enough to know that with the press, you have to be creative rather than scream and shout that everything they say about you is unfair.

A former Kensington Palace aide who worked closely with Meghan said:

Meghan completely buys into the idea that Princess Diana was unfairly treated by the press and then hounded to death by them – she sees herself as being treated in the same way and for similar reasons. This is the glue or a large part of it that keeps Meghan and Harry together. They feel it's the two of them against a cruel world and that their battle isn't just for them – it's for everyone who has been badly treated by the press. They can't do anything without feeling it has global significance. Harry was never like this before he met Meghan. He had no ideas of his own. He rarely, if ever, spoke about global warming. He was a sort of

Tim-Nice-but-Dim character who liked getting pissed with his army and Eton friends, did a bit of shooting and fishing and was otherwise undistinguished.

Harry, perhaps unfairly, has always been seen as the weaker partner, dazzled not just by his wife's beauty but also by her ferocious determination to reshape the world into something she finds acceptable.

Unsure about himself and his life, Harry is in some sense a creation of his wife's certainties; in a newspaper article, his father's friend Jonathan Dimbleby described Harry being 'led by the nose' by Meghan. A friend from Harry's time at Eton said, 'Harry was always looking for a woman to whip him into shape; nice chap but no idea where he was going or what he should do – at least until Meghan came along.'

Harry had been a key figure in a group of friends formed during his late teens, a period of his life when he once dressed up as a Nazi, when he was seen throwing up outside clubs and making sexist and racist jokes. One Eton contemporary said:

Harry hated all that politically correct stuff – all that woke nonsense. He was funny, a bit cynical and great company because like the rest of us he made jokes that we are no longer allowed to make. After Meghan came along, he changed completely into what he would once have been the first to mock: a sort of a *Guardian*-reading tree hugger. It was all Meghan's influence. We used to joke that she must be very good in bed to have turned his head that far.

One staffer at Kensington Palace who remembered Meghan well
said:

She is basically a very nice, smiley, super-positive person, but
having always felt in control of her own destiny and with the
sort of personality that strives to be the best, she suddenly found
herself in an institution she found she couldn't influence and that
assigns roles to people that do not change. She was dazzled by the
worldwide fame that being a princess would bring, but she was
shocked by the palace protocol and by the fact that she was not
and never could be first in the pecking order. She hated the constraints and the rules; she hated being a second-rate princess –
second to Catherine Middleton, I mean. She thought she would
be living in Windsor Castle, for example, and just couldn't believe
it when she and Harry were given Nottingham Cottage in the
grounds of Kensington Palace. Most of all she hated the fact that
she had to do what she was told and go where she was told in the
endless and to a large extent pointless royal round. I don't think
in the whole of history there was ever a greater divide between
what someone expected when they became a member of the royal
family and what they discovered it was really like. She was hugely
disappointed. She was a global superstar but was being told what
she could and could not do, what she could and could not say. She
hated it. The other side of this is that she quickly realised that she
was treated by the royal establishment and the aristocratic advisers in a slightly condescending way because she was not a blood
royal. Kate had to put up with the same thing, but she was better
at dealing with it because she does not have Meghan's messianic

tendencies and she used charm and patience to get people on her side rather than trying to hector them into being nice to her. The thing to remember is that there is no limit to Meghan's ambition, and like most fiercely ambitious people, she never thinks, 'Have I got this wrong? Am I overreacting?' But it remains true that she is a lovely person so long as she is never crossed. For a weak boy unsure of himself like Harry, she is perfect because her absolute certainty makes him feel safe.

The weak boy theory is backed up by Tom Bower's unauthorised biography of Meghan. He details a pheasant shoot arranged by Harry early on in his relationship with Meghan. Not knowing yet quite what Meghan was like, he invited her along with a dozen or so of his old friends from Eton and the army. They hated anything that smacked of tree-hugging 'wokery' – they drank heavily, made politically incorrect jokes about people and were all the sons and daughters of very reactionary aristocratic landowners. Harry felt comfortable with them and was enjoying his shooting day with all the usual banter. No doubt he felt Meghan would be impressed. In fact, he was astonished at how Meghan reacted to them, as Bower explains.

According to Harry's friends, again and again she reprimanded them … Nobody was exempt … Meghan was a dampener on the party [Harry's friends] concluded. She lacked any sense of humour. Driving home after Sunday lunch, the texts pinged between the cars: 'OMG what about HER?' said one; 'Harry must be fucking nuts.'

Meghan may have been in the right – braying racist aristocrats are not to everyone's taste – but they had been Harry's world and they were about to be dropped on Meghan's orders. Meghan had always dropped unsuitable people from her past and now Harry was encouraged to do the same thing.

Reasonable enough, one might say, to drop unpleasant sexist and racist friends, but the arrival of Meghan also led eventually to the well-publicised fallout between Harry and his brother and sister-in-law. The seeds of this were always there because, like his great-aunt Margaret, Harry always knew his brother had a real role while he had none. This may be why he seems always to have something of a lost soul about him and why he was always vulnerable to someone strong willed coming along and giving him a role and a cause.

Certainly, the difficulties between William and Harry were exacerbated after the brothers married and especially after Harry married Meghan. Even Harry admitted at one point that he and his brother were on 'different paths' and although he also said that he would always be there for his brother, he pointedly avoided answering with a simple yes when a journalist asked him if things were OK between him and Meghan and William and Kate.

Harry's lack of nous can be judged by, for example, his claim – made to the US television network NBC – that he had called in on his grandmother Queen Elizabeth on his way to the Invictus Games in 2022 to make sure she was 'protected and has the right people around her'. He was widely mocked for this, the journalist Giles Coren writing in *The Times*, 'If he doesn't keep his grandmother on the straight and narrow, who knows what could happen?

She could, say, marry someone unsuitable, or fall out with her entire family.' Harry's lack of self-awareness is matched only by that of his wife; in the now notorious Oprah interview, he lamented the lack of financial support from his father, despite the fact that he must have known it was common knowledge that he inherited a fortune from his mother. His legal action against the Home Office over his family's security arrangements when they visited the UK cost the British taxpayer more than £100,000. Harry's London lawyers were even criticised for their 'manifestly disproportionate' costs by Mr Justice Nicklin during another action brought by Harry.

Other gaffes based on a kind of breathtaking naivety include the couple's complete failure to realise that you cannot make speeches about the world needing to do something about global warming and then fly by private jet, as Meghan did when she flew from Toronto to Jamaica for the wedding of one of Harry's Old Etonian chums. Even sixteen-year-old environmental campaigner Greta Thunberg, more than twenty years Meghan's junior, had the sense to realise she would be pilloried if she attended a conference on global warming and took a jet to New York to attend. Instead, she went by solar-powered ship.

So, these are the parents of Archie and Lilibet. Both are in many ways like children who have never grown up. What will it be like having these naive but also wealthy and famous parents?

Archie, their firstborn, arrived in the world on 6 May 2019 at the Portland Hospital in London. According to press reports at the time, the Portland's charges per night came in at a cool £15,000. Harry was with Meghan at the time of the birth, which was announced on Instagram.

For a short time, this new arrival produced the sort of newspaper headlines for which Meghan and Harry continually thirst, but the period of positivity and celebration was never going to last. Less than a year later and having spent millions on their new home Frogmore Cottage in the grounds of Windsor Castle, the couple moved to America permanently. Soon after that, they set up their charitable foundation, Archewell. Then they launched a podcast called *Archetypes*. They had hoped to use their royal status as a brand and although this idea was rejected by Harry's grandmother, the couple's status and numerous commercial enterprises exist at their current level solely because the couple are in a sense still royalty.

What will Archie think of the fact that an organisation and a podcast were set up in his name so soon after his birth? Is this a good thing or is it the couple making use of every asset – including Archie – to promote brand Sussex?

Perhaps the downside for the couple's future relations with their growing children and indeed with the public was best summed up by the *Washington Post* columnist Alyssa Rosenberg when she wrote, 'The only way for the Sussexes to build a truly new life, and have a wider impact on the causes they care about, is to stop making themselves the center of the story.'

A friend of Harry from his clubbing days said:

[Meghan] will be great when her children are very young because she will show them an example of someone who goes out and tries to grab the world by the scruff of the neck – she has such a level of certainty about herself and the world that Archie and Lilibet will feel safe – very safe, perhaps too safe! We know she has been very hands-on with the children. But she could end up dominating their every move when they are older. She is a very dominating not to say domineering character and it will be hard to keep that out of her parenting. It might all be OK or it might lead to problems – we have all seen how the children of celebrities struggle in the shadow of their famous parents when they grow up, and Meghan likes to mix exclusively with celebrities. That was a major part of her problem in the UK – American culture is so different from UK culture. Celebrities all suck up to each other. When you are an American celebrity and you mix with celebrities in the US, you just get used to everyone around you saying how marvellous you are. Meghan hated the UK because as a member of the royal family she realised she was going to be treated not as a celebrity but as a servant of the people. That was unbearable for her.

And how will the children be influenced by their parents' increasing sense that the outside world, at least in England, cannot be trusted? At Frogmore Cottage, the couple reacted to their staff in a manner entirely out of keeping with royal tradition, which stipulates that you trust your staff unless there are very good reasons not to trust them.

For the short while that they lived at Windsor, they had become so concerned – according to some reports – about people talking to the press about them that they retained only two live-in staff to help with the baby and with housekeeping. But it may be that Meghan and Harry were simply trying as much as possible to be different from William and Kate, who rely on large numbers of staff. It's easy to imagine that Harry would initially have been excited by the novelty of *not* having the sort of teams of people around him that he had had for most of his life, but that excitement was short-lived as the dull routine of day-to-day life kicked in.

A former member of the couple's staff from Kensington Palace said, 'Moving to Frogmore was the shortest honeymoon in history – they expected it to be so much more enjoyable than the claustrophobic atmosphere at Kensington, but they quickly realised it was like being banished to the dull depths of the countryside without even sunshine to compensate!'

The couple's eventual move to the US was blamed on press intrusion rather than the fact that Meghan was always bound to feel more comfortable in her home country. But already deep contradictions have emerged. In an interview with American magazine *The Cut*, Meghan explained that she had refused to give photographs of her children to the British media because they were 'the very people that are calling my children the N-word'. It is unclear which British magazine or newspaper she was accusing of having used the N-word about her children.

Meghan went on to say that if Archie had gone to school in England, she would 'never be able to do school pickup and drop-off without it being a royal photocall with a press pen of forty people snapping pictures'.

In fact, since the mid-1990s, the Editors' Code followed by all the UK's media states that the press cannot photograph royal children leaving or arriving at school or anywhere else when they are very young. Photographs of royal children can only be taken at official photocalls organised by and agreed with the royal household. This rule has been observed for decades.

In California, by contrast, there are no restrictions on press coverage of Meghan's children – which is why the *New York Post* (followed by numerous other US papers) was able to print paparazzi shots of Archie (plus his lunchbox) being carried by his mother. And Meghan, though she hates the press, invited the *Cut* journalist to accompany her to Archie's nursery (a nursery which makes a point of teaching toddlers 'emotional literacy') when she picked him up. The *Cut* journalist's report was predictably gushing.

So, the press are terrible unless they are American and unless they agree to play nice.

The *Cut* journalist emphasises Archie's red curly hair – just like his father's – and his kindness. Meghan is quoted as saying that Archie regularly takes a week's supply of fruit into his nursery for his friends and we hear a good deal about how Meghan is determined he should have good manners and eat his vegetables.

The underlying message of the interview is that Meghan is just trying to be an ordinary mum, which is reasonable enough, but it seems unlikely that she will disappear into quiet maternal domesticity. According to a former friend, Meghan is on a mission: she believes she can change the world for the better, and her children will no doubt be a part of that – hence the use of the couple's son's name in their charitable foundation. Meghan's acting career may have been flagging before she met Harry, but it was given a huge boost by her elevation to the British royal family and the battles that followed with that institution and the press.

Like the children's grandmother Diana, Meghan is concerned her children should know about the less well off, although as with her attitude to climate change, this can lead to accusations of inconsistency. When we hear that she wants her children to understand homelessness, we inevitably remember how rough-sleepers were unceremoniously removed from the streets of Windsor on the day of Harry and Meghan's wedding.

But in at least one area Meghan and Harry are likely to be very different from other royals when it comes to parenting: Meghan's fierce belief that women, even princesses, should be well educated and have challenging, rewarding careers will undoubtedly mould Lilibet's character.

But there is a tension here that Lilibet will also absorb: her mother's belief that women should progress on their own merits, through education and hard work, sits uncomfortably with the idea of using royal status as a tool. As with all royal children, as we have seen, the consciousness of status starts early.

*　*　*

If a small staff was able to run Harry and Meghan's former home, Frogmore Cottage, the same is certainly not true of their palatial estate in Montecito. Perhaps partly because their American staff can be trusted in a way that British staff could not, Meghan and Harry employ a big team to look after the house, the cooking and cleaning and the extensive grounds. Much of the childcare is also shared with Meghan's mother Doria. Thomas Markle is unlikely to be involved in the lives of his grandchildren.

Whatever sort of parents Meghan and Harry turn out to be in the long run, there is always a risk – since we all turn into our parents to a greater or lesser extent – that their children might inherit

their parents' sense of permanent grievance against the world combined with an almost instinctive feeling that they are uniquely
special; they may be exiles, but they are still, after all, in some sense
members of the British royal family and they will not be allowed
to forget it.

Meghan and Harry's second child, a daughter, was born in Santa
Barbara, California, on 4 June 2021. Even naming this child sparked
a diplomatic scuffle. Hating even to think about the admittedly
labyrinthine rules of protocol that surround the British royal family,
Meghan and Harry called her Lilibet, apparently in the belief that
it would be a wonderful surprise for her great-grandmother, Queen
Elizabeth.

That Harry did not have the sense to predict that this would
cause trouble is beyond belief. He surely would have known that
appropriating the monarch's beloved childhood nickname would
be perceived by many as disrespectful and intrusive in a way that
naming their daughter Elizabeth would not have been. Some commentators speculated that it could be a 'cynical' effort to enhance
their 'royal currency' at a time when they were still navigating life
outside the royal family.

The Queen may well have been upset that her grandson and his
family laid claim to the intimate nickname that had always been
very much part of the Queen's private life, but it is perhaps more
likely that the flunkeys who surround the monarch and some of the
starchier older royals were irritated by what they saw as a presump-
tion. The late Queen may even have been touched by the gesture – a
claim made by royal biographer Gyles Brandreth.

But this points to a fundamental misunderstanding based on

differences between American and UK culture. Meghan would never have thought naming her daughter Lilibet was anything other than a huge compliment; in the UK, it looks like an impertinence, and this is emblematic of many of Meghan's difficulties. Her reputation from her years with Harry in the UK is in tatters because the conservative, slow-moving royal system and its slow-moving staff disliked Meghan's energy, her desire for change, her disregard for what she saw as pointless rigamarole, as one of her former advisers explained:

Meghan hated being controlled by royal protocol – the fact, for example, that at Kensington Palace royals have to announce in advance when they are leaving the palace and where they are going. This is partly for security but partly also to avoid a situation where a senior royal is upstaged by a more junior royal leaving just when the more important person leaves. To an outsider like Meghan, this just looked silly, but to the palace it is absolutely essential. I think Charles agreed with Meghan on many points – he thought much of the protocol was silly, but it is hard to change. William has bought into it, which is why George and Louis and Charlotte are so conventional and look like something out of the 1950s. Meghan wants something different from this for her children – she wants American freedom to do and say what you like and go where you like.

Both Archie and Lilibet have this freedom but within a different set of constraints. They will grow up in their huge house surrounded by beautifully tended grounds and numerous servants, but they will always be aware that security issues mean they have to be accompanied everywhere until and perhaps even after they become adults. They have exchanged a gilded cage with its dull protocol in England for a gilded cage in America with all its risk of gun violence and kidnap.

Archie and Lilibet's difficulties will be comparable to the difficulties faced by the children of rock stars and film stars across the world. The list of troubled offspring is a long one. But Archie and Lilibet may find life even more difficult, as their parents are famous for who they are, not for what they do. Archie and Lilibet cannot follow their parents into music or films or modelling as so many Hollywood offspring do – but, equally, a life as working royals seems unlikely, particularly in the wake of their parents' high-profile revelations about the monarchy.

According to the rules laid down by George V in 1917, all grandchildren of the monarch are entitled to be styled HRH. So, when their grandfather Charles became king, in theory Archie and Lilibet automatically received HRH titles, though four months later, Buckingham Palace had yet to confirm this styling. If they do receive honorifics, we will have a bizarre situation where Archie and Lilibet are entitled to use the HRH title while their parents are not. Is this the first sign that Archie and Lilibet will grow up feeling curiously lost between two entirely different worlds?

The other difficulty before the children's eyes will be that their father, a man who hasn't had a real job since he retired from the army in 2015, is very much a round peg in a square hole in America. What kind of a role model will this make him? They will grow up with a father who takes the Labrador for a walk and a mother who believes that from her ivory tower she can save the world and the planet.

An old friend who visited the couple at Montecito said:

Meghan and to a lesser extent Harry will focus all their energies on the next generation – their lives are now fixed. They are the royal couple who gradually fade out of the public's consciousness, but Meghan will send both children to the best schools money can buy and she will be determined that they achieve a great deal in adult life despite the huge difficulties of being the children of royals in exile.

Harry will perhaps have few regrets that Archie does not follow him to Eton, whose elitist, sexist and often racist alumni were the very people from whom Meghan was determined to extricate him.

Harry may also have few regrets that Archie will not don his breeks and his tweed coat to shoot pheasants, that he will not ride to hounds and be blooded at his first kill; perhaps his only regret will be that Archie will not follow his father and uncle into one of the 'best regiments' to prepare him to lead his country into battle as his medieval ancestors once did.

On a more positive note, time and parenthood may mellow the royal couple; perhaps, having got their side of the story across, they will begin to emulate Harry's much-admired grandmother, the late Queen Elizabeth, in her refusal to respond to press criticism. Even better, they may quietly work behind the scenes to genuinely improve the lives of the less fortunate, away from the glare of public attention.

As the journalist Clare Foges astutely put it about Meghan and Harry when they were still working royals, they should 'pick gritty, unfashionable causes, not just the latest woke obsession'. They are 'servants of the nation, not celebrities'.

That Meghan never saw herself as a servant of the nation can be judged by the extraordinary revelations in Valentine Low's book *Courtiers: The Hidden Power Behind the Crown*. During a tour of Australia in 2018, for example, Meghan is said to have complained, 'I can't believe I'm not getting paid for this.'

Perhaps Meghan and Harry should remember that royal exiles often become bitter and twisted as time wears away at their glitter. Like Harry's great-uncle Edward VIII, Harry will no doubt think he and Meghan will always be important, but he may discover – as Edward and Mrs Simpson discovered long ago – that outside the royal family, they are mere shadows, creatures of ever-decreasing relevance.

It is even perhaps possible that some time in the future Harry, Meghan and their children will long for the newspapers to write about them again. For, as Oscar Wilde might have said, there is only one thing worse than the newspapers saying unkind things about you, and that is them saying nothing at all about you.

EPILOGUE

The broad sweep of royal history is one of slow change. Some would say glacially slow change and nowhere is this more true than when it comes to the early lives of princes and princesses. Certainly, over the long centuries there have been changes: sending royal princes to live away from home at the age of seven, a prerequisite of medieval royal childhood, has been replaced by the practice of sending royal children to elite boarding schools where a similar process of forced early maturity takes place, and if this all happens among the children of some of the world's most unsavoury characters (among whom we must number the children of oligarchs and dictators), it is a small price to pay.

King Charles III's desire to modernise the British royal family echoes the desire of his ancestor George V to be as dutiful and unobtrusive as possible – in both cases the motive is to ensure the survival of an institution unsure of its role in the modern world, a world in which royalty is no longer above criticism.

Part of this modernising process is to make sure royal children are seen to be sensitive to the plight of the less well off, to avoid flaunting their wealth and status, to see themselves as servants of the people rather than, as in the past, rulers of the people. But these are barely meant survival strategies and they do not imply that King Charles III will dispense with his valet and his palaces, nor indeed that royal princes and princesses will be found attending the village school.

A new generation of royal children will grow up increasingly aware of the need to combine extraordinary privilege with extraordinary responsibility. Those who find it difficult or impossible to find happiness and fulfilment within the archaic institution they are born into now have far more freedom to leave – to divorce and to marry the divorced, to live in exile, to work in the real world in ways that would once have been impossible. But for royal children, whether they are heirs or spares, whether they live at home or abroad, the long shadow of their gilded heritage can never be completely left behind.

ACKNOWLEDGEMENTS

I would like to thank all those who agreed to talk to me for this book and for my three previous books about the royal family. My interest in the royal family goes back to those less-guarded days in the 1980s when I was able to interview everyone from the late Queen's gillies at Balmoral to retired domestic staff who had worked at Sandringham, Buckingham Palace, Kensington Palace and Windsor Castle. Many of my contacts from that time are now dead, but I would like to record my grateful thanks to them and, of course, to those who, happily, are still with us.

Thanks also to the myriad authors both still alive and long gone whose books I have trawled through for insights into the curious history of a very curious institution. My trawling was greatly assisted by the ever-helpful staff of the British Library and the Public Record Office at Kew.

But the real unsung heroes of a book like this, indeed of all books, are the publishers. I particularly wish to thank my editor at Biteback, Ella Boardman, editorial director Olivia Beattie, publisher James Stephens and publicity director Suzanne Sangster.

On the domestic front, I owe a huge debt of gratitude to my eagle-eyed children (and most perceptive critics) Katy, Alex, James and Joe, as well as to my wife, Charlotte, who, more than anyone, knows a hawk from a handsaw.

BIBLIOGRAPHY

Alexandra, Queen of Yugoslavia, *Prince Philip: A Family Portrait*, Hodder & Stoughton, 1960

Alice, Princess, Duchess of Gloucester, *Memories of Ninety Years*, Collins & Brown, 1991

Alice, Princess, *For My Grandchildren*, Evans Brothers, 1966

Appleyard, John, *William of Orange and the English Revolution*, Dent, 1908

Aronson, Theo, *Prince Eddy and the Homosexual Underworld*, Lume Publishing, 2020

Ascham, Roger, *The Schoolmaster*, Cassell, 1909

Ashdown, Dulcie M., *Royal Children*, Hale, 1979

Asquith, Lady Cynthia, *Haply I may remember*, James Barrie, 1950

Asquith, Lady Cynthia, *The King's Daughters*, Hutchinson, 1937

Aston, Sir George, *The Duke of Connaught and Strathearn: A Life*, Harrap, 1929

Bagehot, Walter, *The British Constitution*, ed. Paul Smith, Cambridge University Press, 2001

Bain, Joseph, ed., *The Border Papers: Calendar of Letters and Papers*

Relating to the Affairs of the Borders of England and Scotland, 2 vols, Edinburgh, 1894–95

Baker, Richard, *A Chronicle of the Kings of England*, London, 1653

Baldry, A. L., *Royal Palaces*, The Studio, 1935

Basford, Elizabeth, *Princess Mary: The First Modern Princess*, The History Press, 2021

Bathurst, Benjamin, ed., *Letters of Two Queens*, Holden & Co., 1925

Battiscombe, Georgina, *Queen Alexandra*, Constable, 1969

Baxter, Stephen, *William III*, Longmans, 1966

Baxter, Stephen, *William III and the Defense of European Liberty, 1650–1702*, Harcourt, 1966

Bayne-Powell, Rosamond, *The English Child in the Eighteenth Century*, John Murray, 1939

Beamish, Noel de Vic, *A Royal Scandal: The Story of Sophie Dorothea of Celle, Wife of George I of England*, Hale, 1966

Beaton, Cecil, *The Royal Portraits*, ed. Roy Strong, Thames & Hudson, 1988

Bennett, Daphne, *Queen Victoria's Children*, Gollancz, 1980

Bennett, Daphne, *Vicky: Princess Royal of England and German Empress*, Collins, 1971

Benson, Arthur Christopher and Viscount Esher, *The Letters of Queen Victoria: A Selection from Her Majesty's Correspondence*, John Murray, 1907

Berg, Maxine, *Luxury and Pleasure in Eighteenth-Century Britain*, Oxford University Press, 2005

Bergeron, David, *King James and Letters of Homoerotic Desire*, University of Iowa Press, 1999

Bloch, Michael, *The Duchess of Windsor*, Weidenfeld & Nicolson, 1996

Bolitho, Hector, ed., *The Prince Consort and his Brother, Two Hundred New Letters*, Cobden-Sanderson, 1933

Bower, Tom, *Revenge: Meghan, Harry and the War Between the Windsors*, Blink Publishing, 2022

Boyd, William K., ed., *Calendar of the State Papers Relating to Scotland and Mary, Queen of Scots, 1547–1603*, Edinburgh, 1898–1969

Broadley, A. M., *The Boyhood of a Great King 1841–58*, Harper, 1906

Brown, Craig and Cunliffe, Lesley, *The Book of Royal Trivia*, Bounty Books, 1990

Brown, Craig, *Ma'am Darling: 99 Glimpses of Princess Margaret*, Fourth Estate, 2017

Bruce, Marie Louise, *The Making of Henry VIII*, Collins, 1977

Bryant, Arthur, *King Charles II*, Longmans, 1931

Bryant, Chris, *Entitled: A Critical History of the British Aristocracy*, Doubleday, 2017

Burn, Richard, *The Justice of the Peace and Parish Officer*, A. Millar, 1755

Burnet, Bishop Gilbert, *History of His Own Time*, vol. 1, William Smith, 1838

Burnet, Bishop Gilbert, *History of His Own Time*, vol. 2, Clarendon, 1823

Campbell, James et al., *The Anglo-Saxons*, Penguin, 1991

Campbell, Judith, *Anne, Portrait of a Princess*, Cassell, 1970

Carey, Mabel C., *Princess Mary: A Biography*, Nisbet & Co., 1922

Carter, Miranda, *Anthony Blunt: His Lives*, Pan, 2002

Castiglione, Baldassare, *The Book of the Courtier*, trans. Thomas Hoby, Dent, 1970

Chance, Michael, *Our Princesses and their Dogs*, John Murray, 1936

Chandler, Glenn, *The Sins of Jack Saul*, Grosvenor House, 2016

Channon, Sir Henry, *Chips: The Diaries of Sir Henry Channon*, Weidenfeld & Nicolson, 1993

Chapman, Hester W., *Mary II, Queen of England*, Jonathan Cape, 1953

Chapman, Hester W., *The Tragedy of Charles II in the Years 1630–1660*, Jonathan Cape, 1964

Chenevix Trench, C., *George II*, Allen Lane, 1973

Claydon, Tony and Speck, M. A., *William and Mary*, Oxford University Press, 2007

Clayton, Michael, *Prince Charles: Horseman*, Stanley Paul, 1987

Cook, Andrew, *Prince Eddy: The King Britain Never Had*, The History Press, 2011

Courtney, Nicholas, *Royal Children*, Dent, 1982

Crawford, Marion, *The Little Princesses*, Cassell, 1950

Curzon, Catherine, *Life in the Georgian Court*, Pen & Sword Books, 2016

Daiken, Leslie, *Children's Games Throughout the Year*, Batsford, 1949

Dalton, John N., ed., *The Cruise of HMS Bacchante 1879–82*, 2 vols, Macmillan, 1886

Darton, Frederick J. H., *Children's Books in England: Five Centuries of Social Life*, Cambridge University Press, 1960

Davies, Philip, *Lost London, 1870–1945*, Transatlantic Press, 2009

Dempster, Nigel and Evans, Peter, *Behind Palace Doors*, Orion, 1993

Dempster, Nigel, *HRH The Princess Margaret: A Life Unfulfilled*, Chivers, 1982

Dennison, Matthew, *Queen Victoria: A Life of Contradictions*, William Collins, 2013

Dobson, Austin, *Old Kensington Palace and Other Papers*, Humphrey Milford, 1926

Donaldson, Frances, *Edward VIII*, Weidenfeld & Nicolson, 1974

Duff, David, *The Shy Princess*, Evans Brothers, 1958

Dunlop, Olive, *English Apprenticeship and Child Labour*, Fisher Unwin, 1912

Edgar, Donald, *Prince Andrew*, A. Barker, 1980

Epton, Nina, *Queen Victoria and her Daughters*, Weidenfeld & Nicolson, 1971

Faulkner, Thomas, *History and Antiquities of Kensington*, T. Egerton, 1820

Field, Ophelia, *The Favourite: Sarah, Duchess of Marlborough*, Hodder & Stoughton, 2002

Finch, Barbara Clay, *Lives of the Princesses of Wales*, Remington & Co., 1883

Fisher, Graham and Heather, *Monarchy and the Royal Family*, Hale, 1979

Fisher, Graham and Heather, *Prince Andrew*, W. H. Allen, 1981

Flanders, Judith, *Consuming Passions: Leisure and Pleasure in Victorian Britain*, Harper, 2006

Foot, Percy W. R., *The Child in the Twentieth Century*, Cassell, 1968

Fox, James, *Five Sisters: the Langhornes of Virginia*, Simon & Schuster, 2000

Frankland, Noble, *Prince Henry, Duke of Gloucester*, Weidenfeld & Nicolson, 1980

French, George Russell, *The Ancestry of Her Majesty Queen Victoria and His Royal Highness Prince Albert*, William Pickering, 1841

Fryman, Olivia, ed., *Kensington Palace: Art, Architecture and Society*, Yale University Press, 2018

Fulford, Roger, ed., *Dearest Child: Letters between Queen Victoria and the Princess Royal, 1858–61*, Evans Brothers, 1964

Fulford, Roger, ed., *Dearest Mama: Letters between Queen Victoria and the Crown Princess of Prussia, 1861–64*, Evans Brothers, 1968

Fulford, Roger, *The Prince Consort*, Macmillan, 1949

Fulford, Roger, *Royal Dukes: The Father and Uncles of Queen Victoria*, Duckworth, 1933

Fulford, Roger, *The Wicked Uncles: The Father of Queen Victoria and His Brothers*, Arno, 1968

Gathorne-Hardy, Jonathan, *The Rise and Fall of the British Nanny*, Hodder & Stoughton, 1972

Glasheen, Joan, *The Secret People of the Palaces*, Batsford, 1998

Glenconner, Anne, *Lady in Waiting: My Extraordinary Life in the Shadow of the Crown*, Hodder & Stoughton, 2019

Godfrey, Elizabeth, *English Children in the Olden Time*, Methuen, 1907

Gore, John, *King George V: A Personal Memoir*, John Murray, 1941

Graham, Eleanor, *The Making of a Queen: Victoria at Kensington Palace*, Jonathan Cape, 1940

Greig, Hannah, *The Beau Monde: Fashionable Society in Georgian London*, Oxford University Press, 2013

Hadlow, Janice, *The Strangest Family: The Private Lives of George III, Queen Charlotte and the Hanoverians*, William Collins, 2014

Haley, K. H. D., *William of Orange and the English Opposition, 1672–4*, Clarendon, 1953

Hamilton, Anthony, *Memoirs of the Count de Grammont*, The Bodley Head, 1928

Hartmann Cyril H., *The King My Brother*, Heinemann, 1954

Hatton, Ragnhild, *George I*, Yale University Press, 1978

Hecht, J. Jean, *The Domestic Servant Class in Eighteenth-Century England*, Routledge & Kegan Paul, 1956

Hervey, John, *Lord Hervey's Memoirs*, ed. Romney Sedgwick, Penguin, 1984

Hervey, Mary, *Letters of Mary Lepel, Lady Hervey*, ed. John Wilson, BiblioBazaar, 2009

Hibbert Christopher, *Charles I*, Weidenfeld & Nicolson, 1968

Hibbert, Christopher, *Edward VII: The Last Victorian King*, Griffin, 2007

Hoare, Philip, *England's Lost Eden: Adventures in a Victorian Utopia*, Harper, 2010

Hoey, Brian, *Anne: The Princess Royal*, Grafton, 1989

Holden, Anthony, *Charles, Prince of Wales*, Pan, 1980

Hole, Christina, *English Home Life, 1500 to 1800*, Batsford, 1947

Honeycombe, Gordon, *Royal Wedding*, Michael Joseph, 1981

Hoskins, W. G., *The Making of the English Landscape*, Penguin, 1970

Impey, Edward, *Kensington Palace: The Official Illustrated History*, Merrell, 2003

Jackman, Nancy and Quinn, Tom, *The Cook's Tale*, Coronet, 2012

Jesse, John Heneage, *Memoirs of the Court of England*, Bohn, 1857

Jordan, Don and Walsh, Michael, *The King's Bed: Ambition and Intimacy in the Court of Charles II*, Pegasus, 2017

Judd, Denis, *Prince Philip: A Biography*, Michael Joseph, 1980

Junor, Penny, *Charles*, Sidgwick & Jackson, 1987

Keay, Douglas, *Elizabeth II: Portrait of a Monarch*, Century, 1991

Kennedy, David, *Children*, Batsford, 1971

King-Hall, Magdalen, *The Story of the Nursery*, Routledge & Kegan Paul, 1958

Kroll, Maria, *Sophie, Electress of Hanover: A Personal Portrait*, Gollancz, 1973

Lacey, Robert, *Majesty: Elizabeth II and the House of Windsor*, Hutchinson, 1977

Lane, Peter, *Prince Philip*, Robert Hale, 1980

Langford, Paul, *Eighteenth-Century Britain: A Very Short Introduction*, Oxford University Press, 2000

Lascelles, Alan, *King's Counsellor: Abdication and War: The Diaries of Sir Alan Lascelles*, ed. Duff Hart-Davies, Weidenfeld & Nicolson, 2020

Latham, Jean, *Happy Families: Growing Up in the Eighteenth and Nineteenth Centuries*, Adam & Charles Black, 1974

Law, Ernest, *Kensington Palace: The Birthplace of Queen Victoria*, G. Bell & Sons, 1899

Leslie, Anita, *Edwardians in Love*, Arrow Books, 1974

Liversidge, Douglas, *Prince Charles: Monarch in the Making*, Panther, 1979

Loftie, William John, *Kensington Palace and Gardens*, Farmer & Sons, 1900

Longford, Elizabeth, *The Royal House of Windsor*, Weidenfeld & Nicolson, 1974

Longford, Elizabeth, *Victoria R. I.*, Weidenfeld & Nicolson, 1964

Low, Valentine, *Courtiers: The Hidden Power Behind the Crown*, Headline, 2022

Lownie, Andrew, *The Mountbattens: Their Lives and Loves*, Blink Publishing, 2020

Lynd, Sylvia, *English Children*, William Collins, 1942

Lyttelton, Lady Sarah, *Correspondence of Sarah Spencer, Lady Lyttelton, 1787–1870*, ed. Hon. Mrs Hugh Wyndham, John Murray, 1912

Machiavelli, Niccolò, *The Prince*, Oxford World's Classics, 2008

Mackenzie, Compton, *The Windsor Tapestry*, Rich & Cowan, 1938

Magnus, Philip, *King Edward the Seventh*, John Murray, 1964

Malcolm, James Peller, *Anecdotes of the Manners and Customs of London during the Eighteenth Century*, Longmans, 1810

Marie Louise, Princess, *My Memories of Six Reigns*, Evans Brothers, 1956

Marot, Christopher, 'Victoria's Other Self', unpublished PhD

Melville, Lewis, *Lady Suffolk and Her Circle*, Hutchinson, 1924

Micheletto, Beatrice Zucca, 'Margaret Hunt, *Women in Eighteenth-Century Europe*', *European History Quarterly*, vol. 45, no. 1, 2015

Mitford, Nancy, 'The English Aristocracy', *Encounter*, September 1955

Montgomery Hyde, H., *The Cleveland Street Scandal*, W. H. Allen, 1976

Mortimer, Ian, *The Time Traveller's Guide to Restoration Britain*, Vintage, 2018

Morton, Andrew, *17 Carnations: The Windsors, the Nazis and the Cover-Up*, Michael O'Mara Books, 2015

Morton, Andrew, *Diana: Her True Story*, Michael O'Mara Books, 1992

Morton, Andrew, *Inside Kensington Palace*, Michael O'Mara Books, 1987

Mosley, Nicholas, *Beyond the Pale*, Secker, 1983

Murphy, N. T. P., *One Man's London*, Hutchinson, 1989

Newsome, David, *The Victorian World Picture*, John Murray, 1997

Nicolson, Harold, *King George V: His Life and Reign*, Constable, 1952

Ogilvy, Mabell, *Thatched with Gold: the Memoirs of Mabell, Countess of Airlie*, ed. Jennifer Ellis, Cedric Chivers, 1972

Orme, Nicholas, *Medieval Children*, Yale University Press, 2001

Pain, Nesta, *George III at Home*, Eyre Methuen, 1975

Pakula, Hannah, *An Uncommon Woman: The Life of Princess Vicky*, Weidenfeld & Nicolson, 2006

Pasternak, Anna, *Untitled: The Real Wallis Simpson, Duchess of Windsor*, William Collins, 2019

Pepys, Samuel, *The Diary of Samuel Pepys*, eds Robert Latham and William Matthews, Bell & Hyman, 1985

Picard, Liza, *Restoration London: Everyday Life in the 1660s*, Weidenfeld & Nicolson, 2004

Picard, Liza, *Victorian London: The Life of a City 1840–1870*, Weidenfeld & Nicolson, 2006

Pinchbeck, Ivy and Hewitt, Margaret, *Children in English Society*, Routledge & Kegan Paul, 1969

Plowden, Alison, *The Young Elizabeth*, Macmillan, 1971

Plowden, Alison, *The Young Victoria*, Weidenfeld & Nicolson, 1981

Pope-Hennessy, James, *Queen Mary*, Allen & Unwin, 1959

Pope-Hennessy, James and Vickers, Hugo, *The Quest for Queen Mary*, Hodder & Stoughton, 2019

Prescott, H. F. M., *Mary Tudor*, Eyre & Spottiswoode, 1952

Pyne, W. H., *The History of the Royal Residences*, A. Dry, 1819

Queen Victoria, *Leaves from the Journal of Our Life in the Highlands, from 1841 to 1861*, Smith, Elder & Co., 1868

Queen Victoria, *The Letters of Queen Victoria*, eds Arthur Christopher Benson and Viscount Esher, John Murray, 1907

Queen Victoria, *More Leaves from the Journal of a Life in the Highlands, from 1862 to 1882*, Smith, Elder & Co., 1884

Quinn, Tom, *Backstairs Billy: The Life of William Tallon*, Biteback Publishing, 2015

Quinn Tom, *The Butler's Tale*, Coronet, 2012

Quinn, Tom, *The Maid's Tale*, Coronet, 2011

Quinn, Tom, *Mrs Keppel: Mistress to the King*, Biteback Publishing, 2016

Ridley, Jane, *Bertie: A Life of Edward VII*, Chatto & Windus, 2012

Ring, Anne, *The Story of Princess Elizabeth*, John Murray, 1930

Robertson-Scott, J. W., *The Story of the Pall Mall Gazette*, Oxford University Press, 1950

Roe, Frederic G., *The Georgian Child*, Phoenix House, 1961

Rose, Kenneth, *King George V*, Weidenfeld & Nicolson, 1983

Rousseau, Jean-Jacques, *Émile, or On Education*, Penguin, 1991

Rubin, Miri, *The Hollow Crown: A History of Britain in the Late Middle Ages*, Penguin, 2005

Russell, Bertrand, *The Autobiography of Bertrand Russell, 1872–1914*, Allen & Unwin, 1967

St Aubyn, Giles, *Edward VII: Prince and King*, HarperCollins, 1979

de Saussure, César-François, *A Foreign View of England in the Reigns of George I and George II*, trans. M. van Muyden, John Murray, 1902

Scobie, Omid and Durand, Carolyn, *Finding Freedom*, HQ, 2021

Sebba, Anne, *That Woman: The Life of Wallis Simpson, Duchess of Windsor*, Phoenix, 2012

Seward, Ingrid, *Diana*, Weidenfeld & Nicolson, 1988

Seward, Ingrid, *Royal Children of the Twentieth Century*, Harper-Collins, 1993

Seward, Ingrid, *Sarah: HRH the Duchess of York*, HarperCollins, 1991

Shaw, Karl, *The Mammoth Book of Eccentrics and Oddballs*, Robinson, 2000

Simms, R. S., *Kensington Palace*, HMSO, 1936

Sinclair, David, *Queen and Country: the Life of Queen Elizabeth the Queen Mother*, Dent, 1979

Somerset, Anne, *Queen Anne: The Politics of Passion*, HarperPress, 2012

de Sorbière, Samuel, *A Voyage to England*, J. Woodward, 1709

Spinks, Stephen, *Edward II the Man*, Amberley Publishing, 2019

Stanley, Lady Augusta, *Letters of Lady Augusta Stanley*, ed. A. V. Baillie and H. Bolitho, Gerald Howe, 1927

Stockmar, Ernst, *Memoirs of Baron Stockmar*, trans. G. A. Müller, ed. F. M. Müller, Longmans, 1872

Strachey, Lytton, *Eminent Victorians*, Chatto & Windus, 1918

Strachey, Lytton, *Queen Victoria*, Chatto & Windus, 1921

Stuart, Dorothy M., *The Daughters of George II*, Macmillan, 1939

Sundon, Viscountess, *Memoirs of Viscountess Sundon*, ed. Katherine Thomson, 2 vols, Henry Colburn, 1847

Synge, V. M., *Royal Guides*, Girl Guides Association, 1948

Thackeray, William Makepeace, *The Four Georges and the English Humourists*, Alan Sutton, 1995

Thomas, Keith, *The Ends of Life: Roads to Fulfilment in Early Modern England*, Oxford University Press, 2009

Thornbury, Walter, *Old and New London*, Cassell, 1878

Thorold, Peter, *The London Rich*, Viking, 1999

Tinniswood, Adrian, *Behind the Throne: A Domestic History of the Royal Household*, Vintage, 2018

Tinniswood, Adrian, *His Invention So Fertile: A Life of Sir Christopher Wren*, Jonathan Cape, 2001

Trethewey, Rachel, *Before Wallis: Edward VIII's Other Women*, The History Press, 2020

Trevelyan, George Macaulay, *The England of Queen Anne*, Longmans, 1932

Trevisano, Andrea, *A Relation, or Rather a True Account of the Island of England*, trans. Charlotte Sneyd, London, 1847

Troost, Wout, *William III, the Stadholder-King: A Political Biography*, Routledge, 2005

Tschumi, Gabriel, *Royal Chef: Recollections of Life in Royal Households from Queen Victoria to Queen Mary*, William Kimber, 1954

Van der Kiste, John, *George V's Children*, Alan Sutton, 1991

Van der Kiste, John, *Queen Victoria's Children*, The History Press, 2009

Van der Kiste, John, *William and Mary: Heroes of the Glorious Revolution*, The History Press, 2008

Vansittart, Peter, *London: A Literary Companion*, John Murray, 1992

Vergil, Polydore, *The Anglica Historia of Polydore Vergil*, trans. and ed. Denys Hays, Office of the Royal Historical Society, 1950

Vickers, Hugo, *Elizabeth, the Queen Mother*, Arrow Books, 2006

Vickery, Amanda, *Behind Closed Doors: At Home in Georgian England*, Yale University Press, 2009

Vickery, Amanda, *The Gentleman's Daughter: Women's Lives in Georgian England*, Yale University Press, 1998

Vincent, James E., *HRH The Duke of Clarence and Avondale*, John Murray, 1893

Wakeford, Geoffrey, *The Princesses Royal*, Hale, 1973

Walpole, Horace, *Reminiscences*, Oxford University Press, 1924

Warner, Kathryn, *Edward II: The Unconventional King*, Amberley Publishing, 2014

Warner, Marina, *Queen Victoria's Sketchbook*, Macmillan, 1979

Warwick, Frances Countess of, *Life's Ebb and Flow*, Hutchinson, 1929

Weinreb, Ben and Hibbert, Christopher, *The London Encyclopaedia*, Macmillan, 1983

Weintraub, Stanley, *Albert: Uncrowned King*, John Murray, 1997

Weintraub, Stanley, *Victoria: Biography of a Queen*, HarperCollins, 1987

Weir, Alison, *Elizabeth, the Queen*, Vintage, 2009

Weldon, Sir Anthony, *A Brief History of the Kings of England*, J. Williams, 1766

Weldon, Sir Anthony, *The Court and Character of Kings James*, Smeeton's Historical and Biographical Tracts, 1817

Wheeler-Bennett, Sir John, *King George VI: His Life and Reign*, Macmillan, 1958

Wheen, Francis, *The Soul of Indiscretion: Tom Driberg*, Fourth Estate, 2001

Williams-Wynn, Frances, *Diaries of a Lady of Quality, from 1797 to 1844*, ed. A. Hayward, Longmans, 1864

Wilmot, John, *The Complete Poems of John Wilmot, Earl of Rochester*, ed. David Vieth, Yale University Press, 1968

Wilson, A. N., *After the Victorians*, Picador, 2006

Wilson, A. N., *Victoria: A Life*, Atlantic Books, 2014

Wilson, John, ed., *The Rochester–Savile Letters 1671–1680*, Ohio State University Press, 1941

Windsor, Duke of, *A Family Album*, Cassell, 1960

Windsor, Duke of, *A King's Story: The Memoirs of HRH the Duke of Windsor*, Cassell, 1951

Wormald, Patrick, *The Making of English Law: King Alfred to the Twelfth Century*, Blackwell Publishers, 1999

Wormald, Patrick, 'The Uses of Literacy in Anglo-Saxon England and Its Neighbours', *Transactions of the Royal Historical Society*, vol. 27, 1977

Worsley, Lucy, *Courtiers: The Secret History of Kensington Palace*, Faber & Faber, 2010

York, Rosemary, *Charles in His Own Words*, W. H. Allen, 1981

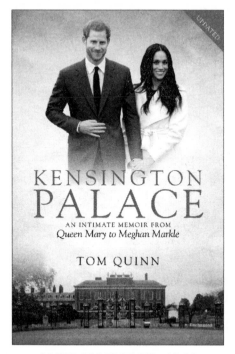

304PP PAPERBACK, £9.99

For more than 300 years, Kensington Palace has played host to a colourful cast of kings, queens and assorted aristocratic hangers-on. A stone's throw from the bustling streets of central London, this grand building has served as the stage for some of the most dramatic and bizarre events in the history of the royal family.

It was here that the young Queen Victoria was held a virtual prisoner for eighteen years; and it was here that George II installed both his wife and his mistress, giving the latter rooms so damp that there were said to be mushrooms growing on the walls. More recently, the palace has witnessed an extraordinary series of scandals, from Princess Diana's bombshell TV interview with a journalist smuggled into the palace disguised as a salesman, to Prince Harry and Meghan Markle's shock departure – first for Frogmore Cottage, and then for America – amid rumours of a rift with William and Kate.

With exclusive interviews with palace staff past and present, fascinating historical details and a fully updated postscript considering what life after Kensington holds for Harry and Meghan, *Kensington Palace: An Intimate Memoir from Queen Mary to Meghan Markle* offers a rare behind-the-scenes insight into one of Britain's most iconic residences.